I found Dr. Strawsburg's new book on apologetics. He takes on the thoroughly and cogently, but does so in a way everybody can understand. I predict that this will be a big hit in Bible study groups across North America. It's very well done.

Craig J. Hazen, Ph.D.
Founder and Director of the Christian Apologetics Program
Biola University
Author of the novel, *Five Sacred Crossings*

God calls us as Christians to be ready to make a defense for the hope we have in Christ. That doesn't happen automatically. It takes time, thought, and wise instruction. Thankfully, insightful books like *Footprints of Faith* provide just the guidance we need. Dr. Strawsburg addresses a number of foundational issues we must all carefully consider—and he has done so in an easy-to-grasp and succinct manner. I trust *Footprints of Faith* will strengthen your confidence in the truthfulness of the Christian message and prepare you to make an effective and reasonable defense of your faith in Christ.

Dr. Mike Fabarez
Senior Pastor, Compass Bible Church
Author of *Lifeline for Tough Times*

It is the responsibility of every Christian leader in every generation to equip believers to defend the truth claims of Christianity. With the heart of a pastor and the mind of a scholar, Dr. Brent Strawsburg has given a fantastic defense in an engaging, personal, and thought-provoking way. Dr. Strawsburg has taken from a wide array of voices within the Christian tradition and presented these timeless truths in a very timely way. I'm sure you will enjoy reading *Footprints of Faith*.

Jon Morrison
Associate Director of Apologetics Canada
Teaching Pastor at Maple Ridge Baptist Church
Author of *Clear Minds & Dirty Feet*

One rarely encounters a solid apologetic work that also has a strong pastoral perspective, but that's what Brent Strawsburg has accomplished in *Footprints of Faith*. The layman will find his writing approachable without sacrificing quality apologetic reasoning and evidence. Because it is warm, engaging, and full of clear-headed thinking, *Footprints of Faith* will help many people love the Lord with all their minds.

Dr. Clay Jones
Associate Professor of Christian Apologetics
Biola University

Footprints of Faith tackles some of the toughest questions people have today about God, faith, and other religions. What I appreciate most is that Brent provides solid biblical responses, but he does so with a pastoral heart.

Sean McDowell, Ph.D.
Biola University Professor, Speaker, Author

I am delighted to recommend Brent Strawsburg's work, *Footprints of Faith*. It's a wonderful resource that will benefit the next generation of seekers and followers of Jesus. It provides solid answers to some of the toughest questions and will be a great encouragement to its readers. I commend Brent and his book heartily!

Scott B. Rae, Ph.D.
Dean of Faculty and Professor of Christian Ethics
Talbot School of Theology, Biola University

Whether you are looking to believe, explain, or defend Christianity, this book—*Footprints of Faith*—can definitely help! Dr. Brent Strawsburg makes a difficult topic practical, easily grasped, and personal as only a pastor, whose own life and faith have repeatedly been rocked by adversity, can. As a friend for years, I wholeheartedly endorse this book because I have witnessed Brent and his family steadily walking forward, upward, and through life's challenges with grace, courage, and resiliency. Isn't that the purpose of real faith after all?

Bill MacLeod
Founder, CEO, Mission ConneXion

Footprints of Faith is a powerful and practical guide for those of us who simply want to stay on mission and be ambassadors for Christ. I've known Brent for over a decade—his gift for training others to think clearly, speak persuasively, and above all serve humbly is a gift to us all. Buy ten more copies of this book today and gather your friends to talk through it!

Dr. John Dix
Lead Pastor, Grace Church of Glendora

Footprints of Faith speaks to one of the biggest challenges of our time: How do we help a drifting irreligious culture to see the viability of the Christian faith. Strawsburg brings clarity to understanding and answering common questions or positions. This book is particularly unique in how he leans chapters in a pastoral direction, in order to help Christians know how to communicate with others, and often to help them see the richness of truth for their own lives.

Dr. Gary Comer
Author of *Soul Whisperer*, Soul Whisperer Ministries

Dr. Strawsburg has written an excellent single volume—it's a one-stop-shop for apologetics. *Footprints of Faith* is organized in a fashion that could tremendously benefit a small group. It is easy to read and the chapters are short enough to convey key thoughts but not too long to lose the average reader. I found *Footprints of Faith* to be a good mix between the head and the heart as well as faith and reason.

Dr. Brian Harris
Lead Pastor, Pine Acres Church
Weatherford, OK

Along with his own easy to understand thoughts on complex issues, Brent has brought together many scripture references and quotes from theologians to answer some tough questions of the Christian faith in this very helpful and practical book.

Dr. Jim Smith
Executive Director, Pacific Church Network

In its day, *More than a Carpenter* was the most accessible apologetics book you could read and share with others. Today, *Footprints of Faith* fills that same need. With a winsome conversational style and contemporary talking points, Brent has crafted what easily is my new #1 favorite apologetics book. Whatever you do, don't put this on a bookshelf. Read it! Enjoy it! Share it!

David Sanford
Corban University, www.corban.edu

Since our days at Biola together, I've felt that Dr. Strawsburg would one day make a useful contribution to Apologetic literature. *Footprints of Faith* more than fulfills that expectation. The book makes an impression upon the mind that, unlike other books of its genre, will not soon be washed away the by the ebb and flow of popular tides. Brent has left us with a clear path, lovingly marking out each step with its own lasting and visible footprint of faith.

Ben LeCorte
Founder & President of WordTrax.com

How many Christians have confidence in their ability to share their faith? Scripture tells us to "always be ready to give a defense to everyone who asks us to give an account for the hope that is in us." I have witnessed the passion that Dr. Strawsburg has for equipping believers to effectively share their faith. Our church has repeatedly invited Dr. Brent to address the topics within his book—the response has been awesome. *Footprints of Faith* is so well written, I can promise it will make a difference in your ability to be an effective witness for Christ.

Steve Soderstrom
Los Angeles County Sheriff's Dept.
Detective–Retired
Elder Board Chairman–First Baptist Church, Canoga Park

Footprints of Faith

Defending the Christian Faith in a Skeptical Age

Dr. Brent Strawsburg

Footprints of Faith: Defending the Christian Faith in a Skeptical Age

Published By: Apologetics Canada Publishing
Abbotsford, BC
Canada

©2015 by Dr. Brent Strawsburg

ISBN-13: 978-1512316551

Dedication

This book is dedicated to my wife, Cheri who has always believed in me. To our children, Michael and Janelle, our son-in-law Brad, and our daughter-in-law Bethany— you've always encouraged and supported me. And our three wonderful grandchildren who bring us great joy.

With all my love.

ACKNOWLEDGMENTS

Whenever a lifetime goal is achieved there are always many people to thank. The thanks I feel for people's encouragement in writing *Footprints of Faith* is no different.

I would like to thank my family for being very encouraging throughout the arduous process of writing a book from start to finish. I will always be grateful for the many times that my family expressed pride in my second career and for writing my book. Their comments brought joy to my heart and a smile to my face. Thanks!

I would like to thank my small group that has met in our house for 14 years. During the most difficult season in our life, Cheri and I found unbelievable strength, love, and support from an amazing group of friends. When I launched our non-profit, Brent Strawsburg Apologetics, the first group of people that stood by our side was our amazing small group. They will always hold a special place in our hearts—always!

I would like to thank a special friend, Jon Morrison who first inspired me to write a book. Jon was a fellow student in the Apologetics program at Biola University. From the very beginning Jon never wavered in his support of me writing *Footprints of Faith*. He gave me every tool necessary to believe I could write a book and get it published. I also want to thank Dan Bugarin and Ken Thomas for designing the cover. Their attention to detail and excellence was a blessing.

I would like to thank a handful of dedicated family members and friends who assisted me in refining the content of several chapters in *Footprints of Faith*. Their insight on certain topics was helpful and inspiring. Their attention to detail was everything I had hoped to see. Their loyalty and commitment to my desire to write the best book that I was capable of writing was a blessing beyond description. This special thanks goes to Jeff Boetto, Tim Erickson, Emily Frey, Ben LaCorte, Gene and Carol Pond, Nate Pond, and Michael Strawsburg.

TABLE OF CONTENTS

FOREWORD

Footprints of Faith is not just another apologetics book. Oh, yes, it covers most of the questions that a good apologetics book should address. But Dr. Strawsburg has done something different here, and that difference makes this a unique book, indeed.

He writes as a pastor to and for the church. This is evident in the pastoral tone of the writing, the number of chapters that deal with suffering and God's fairness (ten counting some appendices)—topics that come up regularly in church life—and it provides guidance for the book to be incorporated into the educational life of the local church.

Dr. Strawsburg is a Tim Keller type—a pastor and churchman who is intelligent and clear headed. This is an extraordinary book for ordinary people.

Dr. J.P. Moreland
Distinguished Professor of Philosophy
Talbot School of Theology, Biola University
Author of *The Soul: How We Know It's Real and Why It Matters*

INTRODUCTION

A person's footprint is a permanent record that his or her presence has been felt. It's a wonderful record when you can look back at your past travels and tangibly point to your progress. It is a tangible sign of where you started and a guide to where you must travel.

Will we leave a tangible reminder of our faith? Will we be able to transfer a vibrant picture of the Christian faith to the next generation? Will our children and grandchildren treasure our faith? Will they have the tools to defend the truthfulness of Christianity?

There has never been a more important time for the church—and individual Christians—to intentionally leave a legacy of faith. Christians are facing a unique challenge in the 21st century. Think for a moment about the perfect storm that surrounds the Christian faith and threatens to weaken the very fabric of Christianity. This perfect storm has three elements:

- **The church is Biblically illiterate** - A growing majority of Christians don't know the Bible or the significance of the Christian faith. Unfortunately, we have ignored the warning of Ephesians 4:14, which says, "Then we will no longer be infants, tossed back and forth by the waves, and blown here and there by every wind of teaching and by the cunning and craftiness of men in their deceitful scheming." The more illiterate we become, the weaker we become in understanding and defending the faith. In other words, we can't defend what we don't know.
- **The church is intellectually weak** - The vast majority of churches don't prepare their members to think through issues of faith and apologetics. We don't address apologetic topics and we don't value the cultivation of the mind. Most churches simply don't have doctrine and apologetics on the agenda.
- **Our culture minimizes and discourages religious discussion** - It is now politically incorrect to discuss religious differences because our society asserts there is no such thing as absolute truth or absolute morality. In this climate we are no longer encouraged to have religious conversations, to talk about the importance of differences, or to defend our Christian faith as the truth.

Dr. William Lane Craig, who is one of this generation's most well-known Christian apologists and philosophers, makes this observation about the challenge facing the Christian faith,

> One of the most dangerous threats to young Christians is an honest question left unanswered. . . . I've had multiple friends tell me that their beliefs began to crumble when they voiced sincere questions to a pastor or family member and were essentially told, 'You just need to have more faith.' . . . It's not enough anymore to just read Bible stories to our kids. They need doctrine, and they need apologetics.[1]

If Christians are going to leave footprints of faith that can withstand the challenges of our time, we must evaluate our faith through the lens of the skeptical questions of our secular culture. In other words, we Christians cannot leave a clear footprint of our faith without giving answers to the challenging issues of our day. Our children, our family, friends, and our neighbors will increasingly be unable to embrace their faith unless they are given practical and relevant tools to answer key questions.

Every generation must embrace the calling of Christian Apologetics. Apologetics is the process of defending the Christian faith through sound logic, evidence, and winsome conversation. This book is designed to help you defend your Christian faith and in the process leave a footprint for generations to admire and follow. This book is not an exhaustive guide to every issue facing the Christian faith. The topics addressed in this book are not confusing or over your head. This book looks at ten vital footprints or steps in leaving a legacy of faith. Each of these topics has been shared with churches throughout the United States—all of them with a favorable response by the ordinary people in the pew.

Footprints of Faith will accomplish the following things:

1) It identifies ten critical topics that address the heart of understanding and defending the Christian faith. During my thirty years of pastoral

---

[1] William Lane Craig, *A Reasonable Response: Answers to Tough Questions on God, Christianity, and the Bible* (Chicago: Moody Publisher, 2013), 19.

ministry I have honed an approach to each of these topics that resonates with ordinary folks and easily translates into conversations with the unchurched and unsaved. Our defense of the faith must make sense to the world. This book doesn't simply quote Bible verses. I make clear and compelling arguments that make sense to our unbelieving friends and family.

2) It includes eight appendices that provide additional answers that Christians can use in dialoguing with doubting Christians or skeptical non-believers. Each of these appendices is written in a language that makes sense to our secular family and friends.

3) Every issue addressed in *Footprints of Faith* is relevant and practical. All too often, apologetics is over the head of the garden-variety Christian. My goal is to make apologetics relevant for every single person.

4) It provides an intentional game plan for individual churches to address apologetics within the overall teaching and equipping ministry of their church. It provides suggestions, resources, and approaches for pastors, leaders, small group leaders, and staff who can translate this book into the life-blood of the church.

5) Finally, *Footprints of Faith* is formatted in a way that is easy to read and understand. Each chapter features big ideas, important quotations, bullet points, and necessary footnotes to give the reader immediate access to helpful resources.

Here's one of the appealing features of *Footprints of Faith*. A person can use this book as a resource by looking at one chapter at a time to help address any one of the ten apologetic topics discussed in the book. You can do the same with the appendices. Use *Footprints of Faith* as a short, concise apologetic resource guide by looking for answers to questions with which you struggle.

Footprints of Faith was also written so that one topic is logically connected to the next topic. Each chapter helps build a comprehensive foundation to help a Christian develop a spiritual legacy of faith. The following overview of each chapter demonstrates the connectedness of the chapters in *Footprints of Faith*.

Footprint #1: Defining Faith in a Skeptical Age Before we can begin to address specific Christian topics or doctrines we must defend the very concept of faith. Far too many of our skeptical friends dismiss everything we say about Christianity because they have already dismissed the very notion of faith. Many skeptics believe that practicing faith is simply sticking one's head in the sand. This footprint gives us specific talking points that address the all-too-common myths about faith.

Footprint #2: How Can Faith Survive a Relativistic Culture? It's vital that Christians are able to defend our faith in the presence of a thoroughly relativistic culture. Remember, our culture believes in relative morality and relative truth. If we can't defend the Christian faith in the face of those two challenges, we have nothing more to say. We have lost all credibility.

Footprint #3: How Can You Disarm Your Doubts? The topic of doubt is one of the biggest reasons why we look to the subject of apologetics. We need answers to the doubts that come into our lives. This footprint gives us three tangible tools to disarm our doubts.

Footprint #4: Where is God When It Hurts? If we don't have the tools to process our own grief, hurt, and pain it's unlikely that we will be in an emotionally and spiritually healthy position to defend our faith. This chapter provides the tools for Christians to better process the difficulties and trials that God allows into our lives.

Footprint #5: Why Does God Allow Evil & Suffering? This footprint provides a clear defense for those skeptical friends who doubt the existence of an all-powerful and all-loving God because of the evil and suffering in the world. It is not sufficient to merely process our own grief and pain. We must answer the accusations of skeptics who refuse to believe God exists because of evil and suffering.

Footprint #6: Is Belief in God Reasonable? This footprint lays a foundation for addressing the question of whether or not belief in God is something that an educated and reasonable person might consider. This chapter provides five specific reasons why a reasonable person can make a claim for belief in God.

Footprint #7: Can You Trust the Bible? This footprint addresses the crucial challenge that faces the Christian who believes in the truthfulness of the Bible. Our skeptical friends doubt whether they can trust the Bible due to its alleged errors, inconsistencies, and mythical stories. The Christian who is eager to pass his or her faith to the next generation must possess the tools to defend belief in the integrity of the Bible.

Footprint #8: Resurrection of Jesus Christ: Myth or Miracle? This footprint appears for the simple and compelling reason that without the resurrection Christianity is dead. However, the notion of the supernatural (Jesus coming back from the dead) is scoffed at in our skeptical age. Therefore, this chapter provides the modern believer with a compelling case to defend the Christian understanding of the resurrection.

Footprint #9: Is Mormonism Christian? Mormonism claims to be the only true Christian Church. In our day and age of politically correct speech it is hard to criticize other religious groups. However, this chapter will provide the tools to answer two specific questions: Is Mormonism uniquely Christian? Is Mormonism uniquely true?

Footprint #10: Is Islam or Christianity True? Islam and Christianity are the two biggest religions in the world. In the pursuit of truth a seeker must eventually come to the realization that Islam and Christianity can't both be true. This chapter will clarify how to make sense of these very different truth claims. It will also demonstrate the importance of gracious interaction with our Islamic friends and neighbors.

Warmly,

Brent

Dr. Brent Strawsburg
Apologetics Consultant, Pacific Church Network
Founder and President of Brent Strawsburg Apologetics

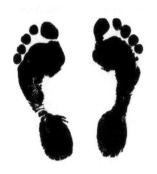

FOOTPRINT ONE:
DEFINING FAITH IN A SKEPTICAL AGE

Far too many people believe Christianity is a by-product of the intellectual dark ages. Anthropologist Max Muller expressed the sentiment this way,

> Every day, every week, every month, every quarter, the most widely read journals seem . . . to vie with each other in telling us that the time for religion is past, that faith is a hallucination or an infantile disease, that the gods have at last been found out and exploded.[2]

Unfortunately, our culture is not only tilted against the Christian faith, it is tilted against the very notion of faith. All too often, faith is placed in opposition to fact. Faith is viewed by skeptics as the option for the weak-minded or ill-informed.

As we attempt to leave a lasting footprint of our Christian faith, it is essential that we help the next generation to better define and defend the concept of faith. If we are going to be successful in cultivating a spiritual dialogue about the truthfulness of God, we must build conversation skills that utilize four very strategic talking points that help redefine the very concept of faith.

TALKING POINT #1: FAITH IS NOT IRRATIONAL

Unfortunately, we live in a culture where rhetoric about religion is increasingly hostile and negative toward Christianity. People of faith are

---

[2] Max Müller, quoted in Alister E. McGrath, *Intellectuals Don't Need God and Other Modern Myths: Building Bridges to Faith Through Apologetics* (Grand Rapids: Zondervan Publishing House, 1993), 65.

routinely ridiculed for their beliefs. In fact, Mark Twain is infamous for saying, "Faith is believing what you know ain't true."

One of the familiar secular talking points seems to be, "Faith in God is irrational." Alister McGrath describes the militant view of atheist Richard Dawkins like so: "Faith is about running away from evidence, burying your head in the sand, and refusing to think."[3] In his response to a debate between William Lane Craig and Alex Rosenberg, Victor Stenger began with the following comment:

Not only is faith in God unreasonable, faith in anything is unreasonable. Faith is belief in the absence of supportive evidence and even in the light of contrary evidence. No one disputes that religion is based on faith.[4]

Typically, skeptics quote Hebrews 11:1—"Now faith is being sure of what we hope for and certain of what we do not see"—as evidence that faith is merely a crutch for certain truths that religious people can't observe or explain. However, it is important to realize that, by definition, "faith has to do with substance and with evidence. . . . It is not mere whimsy . . . . Faith in God is not equivalent to belief in the Easter Bunny."[5]

Sometimes it is helpful to glean from the insights of great thinkers in history who were not limited by a purely naturalistic worldview. The great French Christian philosopher Pascal understood that although Christianity has a supernatural element, it is not itself irrational:

---

[3] Alister McGrath, *Mere Apologetics: How to Help Seekers & Skeptics Find Faith* (Grand Rapids: Baker Books, 2012), 73.

[4] Victor J. Stenger, "Faith in Anything is Unreasonable," quoted in William Lane Craig and Alex Rosenberg, "Existence of God" (class lecture, Biola University, La Mirada, CA, 2014), 1.

[5] Martin J. Medhurst, "Rhetoric as Hermeneutic Key: The Reasonableness of Faith in God," quoted in William Lane Craig and Alex Rosenberg, "Existence of God" (class lecture, Biola University, La Mirada, CA, 2014), 1.

If we submit everything to reason, our religion will contain nothing mysterious or supernatural. If we shock the principles of reason, our religion will be absurd and ridiculous.[6]

It is important to remind our skeptical friends and family that although we hold faith in the highest regard this doesn't necessarily mean that there are not solid reasons to buttress our beliefs. Faith in Christianity is not the

> We must win the battle against the idea that religious faith is opposed to reason. This is wrong.

same as faith in the Easter Bunny or Santa Claus. Great Protestant thinker and philosopher Alvin Plantinga states it this way:

> Christian faith is not at all like a leap in the dark. It is not a matter of believing something on the basis of scanty evidence. Faith is not to be contrasted with knowledge. . . . It just is a certain kind of knowledge, and knowledge of truths of the greatest importance.[7]

It is vital that we rescue the Christian concept of faith from the many caricatures expressed publically by skeptics. We have reasons for believing the truths that comprise the Christian faith. In fact, we have been persuaded by the sound judgment of reasonable evidence.

> We must present a convincing case for the notion that faith is not irrational. If we don't, then it will be increasingly difficult to create a climate in which our Christian faith can flourish.

This is very important because we must win the battle against the notion that religious faith is opposed to reason. This is wrong. Religious faith is not at odds with reason. Gifted British apologist Alister McGrath expresses

---

[6] Blaise Pascal, *Pensées and Other Writings* (New York: University Press, 2008), 60.
[7] Alvin Plantinga and Michael Tooley, *Knowledge of God* (Malden: Blackwell Publishing, 2008), 9.

the concept this way, "Human logic may be rationally adequate, but it is also existentially deficient. Faith declares that there is more than this— not contradicting, but transcending reason."[8]

We must present a convincing case for the notion that faith is not irrational. If we don't, then it will be increasingly difficult to create a climate in which our Christian faith can flourish. C.S. Lewis did more than anyone to dispel the notion that Biblical faith was irrational. Austin Farrer applauds the work of Lewis with this observation:

> Though argument does not create conviction, the lack of it destroys belief. What seems to be proved may not be embraced; but what no one shows the ability to defend is quickly abandoned. Rational argument does not create belief, but it maintains a climate in which belief may flourish.[9]

TALKING POINT #2: THE GOAL IS PLAUSIBILITY NOT CERTAINTY

After debunking the notion that faith is irrational, it is essential that the devout Christian clarify that evidence was never designed by God to create certitude. The Christian faith does not rise or fall upon absolute evidence; it rises or falls on reasonable evidence. In a world where God has granted humanity the dignity of free will, we must allow enough room for people to express faith in God. Certitude would remove the need for the expression of free will. Scientists seek certainty as it relates to their discoveries, experiences, and explorations of life. We can't limit our discussion solely to topics that we can scientifically prove. We have been so influenced by our skeptical culture that we

> In a world where God has granted humanity the dignity of free will, we must allow enough room for people to express faith in God. Certitude would remove the need for the expression of free will.

[8] Alister McGrath, *Mere Apologetics: How to Help Seekers & Skeptics Find Faith* (Grand Rapids: Baker Books, 2012), 81.
[9] Austin Farrer, "The Christian Apologist," *Light on C.S. Lewis* (London: Geoffrey Bles, 1965), 26.

routinely doubt anything that cannot be scientifically proved with absolute certainty.

We frequently depend upon information that lacks mathematical certainty—that's okay! Mathematics uses a unique style of thinking called deductive reasoning. When used correctly, this reasoning gives you a conclusion that has one hundred percent certainty—like 2 + 2 = 4. However, most areas of life can't be analyzed with the rigid structures of mathematical certainty. We have to use other ways of thinking, but we still end up with knowledge and information that is highly certain and reliable. Consider the following examples:

- **Moral Truths** - We know that it is wrong to murder someone, torture a baby, or rape someone. Our culture is based upon common moral truths. In fact, society breaks down when moral truth is ignored.

- **Human Rights** - We know that human beings have fundamental human rights. Our moral intuition is challenged when people are not shown basic human kindness, such as when people fail to extend human dignity to the unborn or the aged at the end of life.

> We depend upon information all the time that lacks mathematical or scientific certainty. Fortunately, this kind of information can be known with sufficient evidence.

- **Historical Events** - We know that certain events in history actually happened. For example, we know that a person by the name of Jesus lived and died. We also know that the Bible is the most attested book of antiquity.

- **Existence of God** - Science provides us many reasons for our belief in a Divine Creator:
  o The Big Bang theory tells us that the universe had a beginning.
  o The fine-tuning of the universe tells us that there is a designer.
  o The complexity of life itself and the presence of morality are used to argue against chance and for a Creator.

Faith is not the same as scientific fact. However, faith does have a thinking and intellectual component as its foundation. We cannot and should not look for certainty, but our faith can be held with a high degree of probability. The reality is that whenever we investigate the reality about the God of Christianity, we cannot find absolute certainty.

TALKING POINT #3: GOD IS NOT OBLIGATED TO PROVIDE ABSOLUTE PROOF

Famous atheistic skeptic Bertrand Russell was once asked why he didn't believe in God. His response was very simple: "Not enough evidence." All too often, our skeptical friends sound like Bertrand Russell as they claim that God hasn't given them enough evidence. Sometimes they ask why God doesn't simply demonstrate His presence in a more undeniable fashion.

It's very important that we constantly remind ourselves and our friends that God is committed to honor the dignity of free will. He is not obligated to reveal Himself with every single shred of evidence or by His supreme glory. God desires human beings who freely choose to pursue Him.

> We would all like greater certainty. If God regularly provided miracles or if He showed up to prove Himself with certainty He would violate the very concept of the dignity of free will.

As the mainstay of his ministry, Paul always presented Christianity in the public square of opinion (Acts 17). However, he was also keenly aware that the path to God was not always lit with unquestioned proof, clarity, and evidences. Listen to his thoughts in Acts 17:27, "God did this so that they should seek God, if perhaps they might grope for Him and find Him, though He is not far from each of us."

The simple reality is that God's commitment to human free will limits some of His actions. He can't supernaturally reveal Himself to every single person and say, "Hello, this is God. I'd really like your attention." We would all like greater certainty. However, if God regularly performed miracles or visibly showed Himself to every single person I believe He would violate the very concept of the dignity of free will.

In fact, if God were to prove Himself with certainty, His very presence would overwhelm people. People would not even be able to resist His will. However, God wants people to seek Him in this life without their free choice being violated or coerced. He wants people to be able to choose Him on the basis of their own free will. In other words, He wants people to seek Him freely. God is not interested in violating the dignity of free will.

Biola University Professor Dr. Clay Jones expresses unusual clarity when it pertains to the unique quality of man's free will and its implications regarding God's actions in our world. In one of his lectures he made this observation:

> God doesn't want to interfere with our wills. How many people would be Christians if a flaming sword cut down everyone as a display of His power? How many would be worshippers? What about if every Christian was healed no matter what the situation? Wouldn't everyone want to be a Christian? Would you have any worshippers?[10]

The late Dallas Willard expressed a similar concept when he described the human will and its propensity to choose its own way. Notice his observation:

> Thus no one chooses in the abstract to go to hell or even to be the kind of person who belongs there. But their orientation toward self leads them to become the kind of person for whom away-from-God is the only place for which they are suited. It is a place they would, in the end, choose for themselves, rather than come to humble themselves before God and accept who he is. . . . The fundamental fact about them will not be that they are there, but that they have become the kind of people so locked in their own self-worship and denial of God that they cannot want God.[11]

God designed this world so that you and I would have to exercise faith in the evidence before us. Fortunately, God has left various clues within

---

[10] Clay Jones, "Why God Allows Evil" (class lecture, Biola University, La Mirada, CA, 2013).

[11] Dallas Willard, quoted in Clay Jones, "Why God Allows Evil" (class lecture, Biola University, La Mirada, CA, 2013 2013.)

our universe and throughout history in order to address our doubts. Think about it this way. If our universe points to the likelihood of an eternal, powerful, and personal Creator isn't it likely that He would put within the very fabric of humanity the capacity and desire to pursue Him as part of our free will? Isn't it likely that God would also honor mankind by giving them the single trait that distinguishes humankind from all the rest of creation—free will?

In his tremendously insightful book, *The Enigma of Evil*, John Wenham observes that regardless of proof it ultimately comes down to whether a person is inclined to seek and respond to God. Listen to his observation, "God has given us plenty of evidence if we are willing to believe, and He has given us plenty of perplexities if we want to buttress our disbelief."[12]

TALKING POINT #4: DOUBT IS NOT FATAL

To some degree, all of us wrestle with doubt. It's what we do with those doubts that makes all the difference. It's absolutely necessary that we recognize that doubt has many different faces. In other words, there are many different reasons why people doubt. If we are not sensitive to the different reasons for doubt we will not be able to understand or address the specific reasons for our struggles.

Whether a person is a follower, a seeker, or a skeptic, sometimes doubt is part of their agonizing journey. Dr. Lynn Anderson, one of the great experts on the issue of doubt, puts it this way:

> For years, through these dark, lonely, and frightening periods of my developing faith, I had not the slightest notion that so many others shared my private hell . . . . I gradually learned that admitting my faith struggle does not make doubt worse—as if admitting my doubts would make them come true. Instead, facing up to my doubts somehow opens up the possibility of renewed faith.[13]

---

[12] John Wenham, *The Enigma of Evil: Can We Believe in the Goodness of God?* (Downers Grove: Intervarsity Press, 1985), 84.
[13] Lynn Anderson, *If I Really Believe Why Do I Have These Doubts?* (West Monroe: Howard Publishing, 2000), 14.

All too often a person's resistance toward the Christian faith is a combination of great disappointment and doubt. Those two factors can't always be fixed by presenting an intellectual argument. We must connect with people on an emotional and relational level. They must sense that we truly understand how they look at this world and at God.

Unfortunately, life in this imperfect world is full of disappointments. It's vital that we distinguish disappointment from doubt. Philip Yancey, the gifted Christian author and thinker, makes this observation:

> We tend to think, 'Life should be fair because God is fair.' But God is not life. And if I confuse God with the physical reality of life—by expecting constant good health for example—then I set myself up for crashing disappointment.[14]

CONCLUSION

Too many conversations with people in our unbelieving culture begin and end with a crass and rational approach of arguments and evidence. These arguments often bypass some of the personal and theological issues that prepare us for compelling and effective conversations with our skeptical family and friends. McGrath summarizes his thoughts with this powerful conclusion:

> So how can we best make sense of such clues? What can they prove? In a criminal trial, the jury is asked to decide which explanation of the clues makes the most sense of them—whether that of the prosecution or the defense. They are not expected to accept that guilt or innocence has been proved, merely that they believe they can reach a conclusion beyond reasonable doubt. Apologetics works in much the same way. No one is going to be able to prove the existence of God. . . . Yet one can consider all the clues that point in this direction and take pleasure in their cumulative force. God's existence may not be proved, in the hard rationalist

---

[14] Philip Yancey, *Disappointment with God: Three Questions No One Asks Aloud* (Grand Rapids: Zondervan, 1997), 183.

sense of the word. Yet it can be affirmed with complete sincerity that belief in God is eminently reasonable and makes more sense of what we see in the world, discern in history, and experience in our lives than its alternative."[15]

SUGGESTIONS FOR ADDITIONAL READING

Alister E. McGrath, *Intellectuals Don't Need God & Other Modern Myths: Building Bridges to Faith Through Apologetics*
Alister McGrath is a great apologist who has a burning passion to reach non-Christians. His book presents a very helpful approach for Christians who struggle with doubts or struggle in sharing their Christian faith.

Sean McDowell, General Editor, *Apologetics for a New Generation*
This book is a collection of sixteen articles that provide a very modern approach to how Christians must represent their faith in a secular culture. Each chapter is self-contained and easy to read. The book is geared especially toward a younger generation. It is an excellent overview of key topics and issues that Christians must address as they embrace their faith

---

[15] Alister McGrath, *Mere Apologetics: How to Help Seekers & Skeptics Find Faith* (Grand Rapids: Baker Books, 2012), 95-96.

FOOTPRINT TWO:
HOW CAN FAITH SURVIVE A RELATIVISTIC CULTURE?

Do you ever listen to how people talk? If you listen to a sports fan for five minutes you can easily tell whether they love the Boston Celtics or Los Angeles Lakers. If you listen to someone talk about politics you can tell which way the room is leaning—right or left. If you listen to someone for five minutes you can learn about his or her hobbies, favorite pastimes, or whether the person really loves to travel. The same exact thing happens if you listen to people talk around religion, morality, or truth.

If you try to have a conversation about religion with a skeptic you will eventually hear one of the following statements:

- That's just your opinion.
- That's true for you, but not for me.
- All religions are the same.
- It's all a matter of perspective; everything is relative.

How did this happen? How did we end up living in a country where morality and knowledge are up for grabs? How can people doubt things that you and I believe so very much? This is what I would like to cover with this chapter. I'd like to begin by sharing with you the words of J. Gresham Machen, a great Christian thinker who said something one hundred years ago that was so prophetic it's uncanny. Listen to his words:

> False ideas are the greatest obstacles to the reception of the gospel. We may preach with all the fervor of a reformer and yet succeed only in winning a straggler here and there, if we permit the whole collective thought of the nation or of the world to be controlled by

ideas which . . . prevent Christianity from being regarded as anything more than a harmless delusion.[16]

Over the past one hundred years our culture has dismissed Christianity as a harmless delusion because the secular elite won the battle of ideas. This battle has been controlled by one over-arching idea. It hasn't been advertised on billboards, on the internet, or on public radio, but it has been the driving force behind every conversation and every statement made by the opinion shapers and intellectuals of our secular culture. In fact, it's part of the life-blood of every school of higher education in the United States. I call it,

> Over the past one hundred years our culture has dismissed Christianity as a harmless delusion because the secular elite won the battle of ideas.

THE FACT/OPINION DIVIDE[17]

If there is one thing that you remember from our discussion about relativity it is the concept of the Fact/Opinion Divide. It will make sense of everything you see and hear in our culture, whether it is from books, interviews, the news, or politicians. Time and time again, the opinion shapers in our culture have told people that the only knowledge that can be trusted as fact is information that can be determined by the five senses—things that science can teach us. Science gives us facts. Science gives us real truth.

---

[16] J. Gresham Machen, *What Is Christianity?* (Grand Rapids: Eerdmans, 1951), quoted in J.P. Moreland and William Lane Craig, *Philosophical Foundations for a Christian Worldview* (Downers Grove: InterVarsity Press, 2003), 2.

[17] Dr. Scott Smith, "Ethics" (class presentation, Biola University, La Mirada, CA, 2013). Dr. Smith's original terminology was the "Fact/Value Dichotomy." In order to communicate to my church-based audience I have chosen a slightly less formal expression: "Fact/Opinion Divide." A special thanks to Dr. Smith for his insight into this concept.

Richard Dawkins, who is one of the most vocal and famous atheists in our culture, expresses this sentiment with great enjoyment and conviction. Listen to his perspective:

Science replaces private prejudice with verifiable evidence.[18]

The truth is more magical than any myth or made-up mystery or miracle. Science has its own magic: the magic of reality.[19]

Think of the power of this sentiment. Once you determine the nature of truth, what is everything else? It is simply an opinion or preference. We live in a culture that defines what is true and valuable and determines that anything else can simply be disregarded.

Please allow me to illustrate what Christians are facing within our culture. Imagine if you were approached by a contingent of Hare Krishna followers. Can you imagine the scene? They are all in robes, chanting, and banging on their drums. They begin to tell you why you should become a follower of Krishna. Most people in America—inside or outside the church—would look at them as if they were from outer space. Their worldview is so very different that most people wouldn't even remotely consider their ideas.

> Most of our secular culture looks at Christians as if we just arrived from a different planet. We hold viewpoints and beliefs that are so clearly against the facts of our modern, secular culture.

Now imagine that you approach a graduate student at any major university in America and begin to share that Christianity is the only way to God. You begin to describe the universal problem of humanity's sin and that Jesus is the only solution. This student would look at you in the same exact way—as if you were coming from a different planet. Most of our secular culture looks at

---

[18] Richard Dawkins, "Quotable Quote," *Goodreads*, accessed September 1, 2014, http://www.goodreads.com/quotes/304327-science-replaces-private-prejudice-with-public-verifiable-evidence.

[19] Richard Dawkins, *The Magic of Reality: How We Know What's Really True* (New York: Bantam Press, 2011), 257.

Christians as if we just arrived from a different planet. We hold viewpoints and beliefs that are so clearly against the facts of our modern, secular culture.

Our modern, secular culture is built on three primary pillars or talking points that are so strong that the vast majority of secular thinkers don't believe there is any other way of looking at religious issues. Allow me to suggest a fun yet effective way of looking at these three talking points. Do you remember the famous Clint Eastwood movie entitled *The Good, The Bad and The Ugly*? I'm going to use this movie title to better describe each pillar. These pillars are not bad in themselves. Unfortunately, they've been hijacked by the opinion shapers and power brokers of our culture and turned into negative forces that cause people to resist the Christian faith.

Pillar #1: Pluralism

Pluralism refers to numerous ethnic, religious, or cultural groups tolerated within a society. The following are the positive and negative elements of this pillar:

The Good: The Establishment of Religious Freedom.
Our founding fathers wanted a country that would recognize various religious thoughts and expressions. Our founding fathers didn't want there to be one singular religious viewpoint like they had experienced in England with the Church of England. They didn't want the establishment of the Church of America. Ultimately, this was guaranteed by the First Amendment to the United States Constitution.

The Bad: All Beliefs have Equal Value and are Equally True.
Unfortunately, something has changed in the use of this expression. The opinion shapers and power brokers of ideas within our culture have not been content with simply recognizing different religious communities. Slowly yet surely, they've insisted that living in a culture with many beliefs means that all these beliefs are equally true.

THE UGLY: RELIGIOUS PLURALISM RESISTS CHRISTIANITY.

Religious pluralism has grown so strong that it has evolved into a movement that is dedicated to resisting any belief that insists it is the unique and singular path to God. Whether it is in the media, in conversations, at school, or at work, this is the primary reason why Christianity faces such hostility.

PILLAR #2: TOLERANCE

Tolerance refers to the ability or willingness to tolerate something, in particular the existence of opinions or behavior with which one does not necessarily agree. The following are the positive and negative elements of this pillar:

THE GOOD: CONFLICTING VALUES CAN BE VOICED IN PUBLIC DEBATE.

America has always been a tolerant and open society. Historically, tolerance simply meant that conflicting values could and should be voiced in public debate. This is a good thing. It's wonderful to live without fear of being attacked or shot simply because you embrace a different set of beliefs. Imagine living in modern Egypt, Pakistan, Iran, or Iraq. I welcome the expression of different religious beliefs. I want to live in a place that values the free exchange of ideas and viewpoints.

THE BAD: TOLERANCE ACCEPTS OTHER'S VIEWS AS EQUALLY TRUE.

Unfortunately, the traditional view of tolerance has slowly morphed into something that sounds similar but is as different as night and day. Today the concept of tolerance means that we must accept each other's views because the issues of truth and falsehood are no longer important. The new tolerance goes beyond respecting a person's rights. It demands praise and endorsement of the idea that the beliefs of other people are equally true.

> Today the concept of tolerance means that we must accept each other's views because the issues of truth and falsehood are no longer important.

THE UGLY: SOCIETY EMBRACES THE MODERN NOTION OF TOLERANCE.

Media and education centers have attempted to convince us of the following:

- All beliefs are equal.
- All values are equal.
- All lifestyles are equal.
- All truth is equal.

In his book, *The New Tolerance*, Josh McDowell and his co-author Bob Hostetler describe some of the dangerous implications of this new kind of tolerance. Notice their unique observation:

> Now, rather than responding to the substance of my message, my detractors invariably say things like, 'How dare you say that?', 'You're intolerant!' 'Who do you think you are that you have the corner on truth?' and, 'What right do you have to make a moral judgment on someone else's lifestyle?' The issue is no longer the truth of the message, but the right to proclaim it . . . because any message that challenges the new tolerance—either explicitly or implicitly—constitutes a 'thought crime'! [20]

We live in a climate in which the fundamental message of the Christian faith is increasingly viewed as intolerant and politically incorrect.

PILLAR #3: RELATIVISM

Relativism insists that there are no objective truths. Ultimately all principles are just preferences or opinions. The following are the positive and negative elements of this pillar:

THE GOOD: THERE ARE MANY HARMLESS DIFFERENCES WITHIN CULTURES. It is good to realize that we don't need to impose every aspect of our culture upon the cultures of other people. After all, not all the aspects of culture should be embraced as objectively true or morally superior. Some things are neither good nor bad; they are merely different. If

---

[20] Josh McDowell and Bob Hostetler, *The New Tolerance: How a Cultural Movement Threatens to Destroy You, Your Faith, and Your Children* (Wheaton: Tyndale House Publishers, 1998), 80.

you've ever traveled you've realized this by how people dress, how they talk, various cultural customs, and by the foods they eat.

THE BAD: RELATIVISM INSISTS THERE ARE NO OBJECTIVE TRUTHS.
Unfortunately, while many people believe in mathematical and scientific truth, others insist that this same thing can't be said about religious beliefs. In his book, *The Closing of the American Mind*, American academic Allan Bloom writes:

> Openness—and the relativism that makes it the only plausible stance in the face of various claims to truth and various ways of life and kinds of human beings—is the great insight of our times. The true believer is the real danger. The study of history and of culture teaches that all the world was mad in the past; men always thought they were right, and that led to wars, persecutions, slavery, xenophobia, racism and chauvinism. The point is not to correct the mistakes and really be right; rather it is not to think you are right at all.[21]

THE UGLY: WE NO LONGER SEARCH FOR TRUTH. We no longer have frank dialogues about truth. As a result, the politically correct climate of our culture has imposed limits on the following:

- Religious discussion.
- The pursuit of truth.
- The expression of opinion.

We live within a culture that is diametrically opposed to the central tenets of Christianity. However, we can't just sit back and complain by saying, "Why aren't they like us?"

Allow me to try to explain the significance of the three pillars of modern culture. We live within a culture that is diametrically opposed to the central tenets of Christianity. However, we can't just sit back and complain by saying, "Why aren't they like us?" God has called us to be prepared to connect with people who think this way. This is not an option. It's the calling of our generation.

---

[21] Allan Bloom, *Closing of the American Mind: How Higher Education Has Failed Democracy and Impoverished the Souls of Today's Students* (New York: Simon & Schuster, 1998), 26.

Listen to this wonderful Scripture in Colossians 4:6: "Let your conversation be always full of grace, seasoned with salt, so that you may know how to answer everyone."

- We must be prepared to give people an answer.
- We must be ready to speak to them in a language they understand.
- We must not react negatively to people but develop the tools to create healthy dialogue.

For the rest of this chapter we are going to discover how to converse with people who believe in relative morality and relative truth. We need to learn how to use our conversations to give people answers. Whenever we begin to talk about religion, morality, or truth, far too many people repeat the typical talking points without thinking through their implications. We have to help them engage with the information rather than simply repeating it. We aren't called to simply quote Bible verses because that will cause them to shut down. Our goal should be to assist our unchurched friends to realize their talking points are inconsistent.

> We aren't called to simply quote Bible verses because that will cause them to shut down. We are trying to help them see how their talking points aren't consistent.

Relative Morality

Relative morality is the view that there are no moral absolutes and that right and wrong are determined solely by the individual or by the society. Let's examine three fatal flaws in relative morality. Each of these is an effective way to help our family and friends see that moral relativism simply doesn't work.

Fatal Flaw #1: Moral Absolutes Exist

The most effective way to point out the flaw of moral relativism is by reminding people of those actions that people unequivocally recognize as wrong. After all, there are many actions that shock the senses of the typical person on the street. Look at the following three examples:

- Murder (an unjustified killing of an innocent person) is wrong.
- Torturing babies is wrong.
- Raping another person is wrong.

These actions are clearly seen by most people as wrong by any definition or within any culture. In other words, they are universally wrong. Most people don't really believe in moral relativity. We know this because we watch the shock, horror, and disbelief on people's faces whenever they

> Why is the entire world outraged at some of these things if morality is always just a subjective choice? This only makes sense if there was a genuine moral standard or if some objective absolute was violated.

see heinous and immoral actions happen in the world. If they truly believed in moral relativity they wouldn't be shocked by the following:

- The heinous executions of innocent civilians by ISIS.
- The shootings at the movie theater in Aurora, Colorado where twelve were killed and fifty-eight injured.
- The school shootings at Sandy Hook, Connecticut where twenty innocent children and six teachers were killed.
- The Cleveland man who kidnapped and abused three girls for ten years.
- The Kenyan terrorists who went into a mall and killed over seventy people on the basis of whether they were Muslims or not.

My guess is that people don't really believe in relative morality. They might be playing word games because they don't like the implication of a Moral Law Giver, they react negatively to the moral judgments of religious people, or they've just heard the talking points for too long.

The moment a person admits that there are certain moral absolutes the belief in moral relativism crumbles. The next time you hear someone say, "All morality is relative," your response should be, "Really? I know you don't think it's morally okay if someone were to rape a little girl or torture a baby." If they insist, you might need to make it personal: "What if someone did one of these things to someone in your family? Is that wrong?"

But here's another fatal flaw in moral relativism.

FATAL FLAW #2: GENOCIDE IS UNIVERSALLY WRONG

A central pillar of relativism is that a culture has no moral right to tell other cultures what is right and wrong. But this is exactly what happens when the world tries to stop genocide. Remember, genocide is the intentional eradication of an entire race based upon culture, religion, or nationality. World history is full of examples of individual nations and world organizations banning together to eradicate crimes against humanity. People of every political, cultural, and religious background have seen the horror of genocide. Think of the following examples:

- Nazi Germany exterminated six million Jews in World War II.
- The Killing Fields in Cambodia were the sight of horrible atrocities.
- The Soviet Union established Gulags where millions were imprisoned and brutalized.
- During the 1990s, one out of ten people were killed in the nation of Rwanda.
- ISIS has committed horrible atrocities in Iraq where they threaten entire ethnic or religious minorities.

The Nuremberg War Trials were the most famous war trials in human history. These criminal court trials, which happened in the aftermath of World War II, were based upon the concept that there are universal absolutes that transcend the laws of any given society. The Nuremberg War Trials established a series of universal truths or morals that civilization could embrace as it attempted to stop mass genocide. Although Nazi officials tried to defend themselves by stating that they were just taking orders, the Nazi officials were held to a higher law. This law was based upon a basic set of moral absolutes.

> The Nuremberg War Trials established the concept of a law above the law—a series of universal truths or morality that civilization could embrace as it attempted to stop mass genocide.

FATAL FLAW #3: RELATIVISM CAN'T EXPLAIN MORAL HEROES

Any discussion of history's great moral heroes usually includes Abraham Lincoln, Martin Luther King, and Nelson Mandela. Each of these great men led a revolt in their own country against something deeply immoral.

- President Abraham Lincoln will forever be viewed through the lens of history as the man who stood up against slavery in America. He thought it was so immoral that he was willing to wage civil war to rectify the situation.
- Martin Luther King changed the face of America by addressing civil rights in America in the 1960s.
- Nelson Mandela worked to abolish the policy of apartheid, which was a system of racial segregation in South Africa. He was viewed as a national hero because he spent twenty-seven years in jail, then spent the rest of his life attempting to rid South Africa of its heinous and immoral policies.

Here's the power of this final fatal flaw. Each of these men was working against the prevailing moral viewpoint of their nation or of a large segment of their nation. Why honor someone as a hero if there is no objective standard to uphold or any injustice or lack of virtue to correct?

> These moral reformers tried to change history because they believed that certain things were absolutely right and other things were absolutely wrong.

These moral reformers tried to change history because they believed that certain actions were absolutely right and other actions were absolutely wrong.

RELATIVE TRUTH

Our unchurched family, friends, and neighbors not only embrace relative morality, they also embrace relative truth. As we attempt to better understand relative truth I would like to use three easily understood examples. Each of them is a helpful reminder that the talking points people use don't always make sense. After all, we want to prepare our family and friends to take a fresh look at the evidence for Christianity.

EXAMPLE #1: THE PLANET TEST

In AD 1500 almost everyone believed that the sun and planets revolved around the earth. By AD 1700, almost every educated person believed that the earth and planets revolved around the sun. What changed and what didn't change?

- Did reality change? In other words, did the motions of planets change from earth-centered (AD 1500) to sun-centered (AD 1700)? No.
- Did the truth change? No. If truth is defined by reality, then what was true in AD 1500 (the earth and planets really moved around the sun) was also true in AD 1700.

Let's be very clear about this—reality and truth did not change between AD 1500 and AD 1700. Truth is not dependent upon whether or not you

> Truth is not dependent upon whether or not you believe in it. Truth is defined by reality.

believe in it. Truth is defined by reality. People say, "It may be true for you but it's not true for me," because they want to dodge the issue of truth. Using this example reminds people that the quest for truth is objective and not subjective. Reality itself doesn't change from person to person.

EXAMPLE #2: THE RELIGION TEST

Allow me to give you another example—the religion test. This is absolutely necessary because if there is one talking point that is repeated over and over again in our culture, it's the following: "All religions are the same," or "All religions are equally true."

When your family and friends say this you could choose to quote the famous verse from John 14:6, "I am the way, the truth and the life—no man comes to the Father except through me." Unfortunately, for our unchurched or unsaved friends who don't believe in the authority of

Scripture, this will probably have very little impact. I believe there is a better way to illustrate this. The next time your friends try to tell you that all religions are the same or equally true, you may ask, "How can this be true if the two major religions (Islam and Christianity)—which represent close to four billion people (1.6 billion Muslims and 2.1 billion Christians)—are so fundamentally different?"

For example, Islam claims that the crucifixion of Jesus never happened. The holy book of the Islamic religion, the Qur'an, states emphatically that Jesus did not die on the cross. In fact, the Islamic religion teaches there is no need for a Savior to die on the cross.

> How can this be true if the two major religions (Islam and Christianity)—which represent close to four billion people (1.6 billion Muslims and 2.1 billion Christians)—are so fundamentally different?

Christianity claims that the crucifixion did happen. The Bible distinctly teaches that Jesus died on the cross. His death is central. It's the linchpin of the Christian faith.

It is important to note that few reputable historians dispute the historical fact that Jesus of Nazareth was publicly crucified. Of all the facts about Jesus, the fact of his crucifixion is beyond doubt. However, even if a person does not want to accept these clear facts, the following is obvious: one of these two religions is right and one is wrong. The crucifixion of Jesus Christ either happened or it didn't happen. All religions are not equally true.

It might also be helpful to think about this issue from another perspective. The next time someone says, "All religions are true," think for a moment about the logical implications of this statement. If all religions are true then Christianity must be true, but Christianity teaches that all religions are not true, so it can't be true. In other words, if all the religions are true then all the religions can't be true. This statement is self-refuting.

Example #3: Truth Doesn't Need to be Certain Just Reasonable

All too often, faith is placed in opposition to fact. Faith is viewed by skeptics as the option for the weak-minded or ill-informed. Unfortunately, we have been so influenced by our skeptical culture that we routinely doubt anything that cannot be scientifically proved with absolute certainty. Think about all the information we know—all the facts we regularly count on—not because it is certain but because it is reasonable!

- **Moral Truths** - We know that it is wrong to murder someone, torture a baby, or rape someone.
- **Human Rights** - We know that human beings have fundamental human rights—our moral intuition is shocked when people are not shown basic human kindness.
- **Historical Events** - We know that certain things happened—that a person by the name of Jesus lived and died. We know that the Bible is the most attested book of antiquity known to man.
- **Existence of God** - We can look at a handful of evidences that clearly point to the reasonableness of God's existence.

I'm sure all of us would like greater certainty in certain issues. We would love for God to knock on our door and shed perfect light on every issue. However, in a world where God has granted humanity the dignity of free will we must allow enough room for people to express faith in God; certitude would remove the need for the expression of free will.

God doesn't personally knock on every person's door and say, "Hello, this is God, I'd really like your attention." In fact, if God were to do this, His very presence would overwhelm people. People would not even be able to resist His will. However, God doesn't want that—He wants people to seek Him in this life. God wants people to seek Him freely. If He compelled people to respond to Him with overwhelming proof He would violate the very concept of the dignity of free will.

Conclusion

Allow me to finish this chapter with a final insight from Scripture:

> Always be prepared to give an answer to everyone who asks you to give the reason for the hope that you have. But do this with gentleness and respect.
> 1 Peter 3:15

Think for a moment about the implications of this one passage. We must be ready to give people evidence that Christianity is not contrary to reason. Ultimately, we must always do it with respect. We must genuinely respect how people have come to their viewpoints. They may never have been questioned before. They may have strong negative feelings toward Christianity. We want to provide our unchurched friends with convincing proof that relativism doesn't work. We want to show them that Christianity is actually a reasonable worldview.

> We want to provide our unchurched friends with convincing proof that relativism doesn't work. We want to show them that Christianity is actually a reasonable worldview.

SUGGESTIONS FOR ADDITIONAL READING

Paul Copan, *True For You But Not For Me: Overcoming Objections to Christian Faith*

This book is one of the best overviews of our culture's belief in moral relativity and relative truth. Copan uses two entire sections to address the twin concerns of relative truth and moral relativism. This is an intriguing, thoughtful, and helpful book.

Francis J. Beckwith and Gregory Koukl, *Relativism: Feet Firmly Planted in Mid-Air*

This is another wonderful book that correctly identifies and addresses the profound relativity of our secular culture. Both Beckwith and Koukl are extremely gifted philosophers and tacticians who attempt to make all of the content in their book accessible.

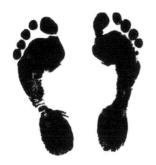

HOW TO DISARM YOUR DOUBTS

Everyone struggles with doubt. It creeps into our minds and sneaks into our lives. Events and issues come into our life and overwhelm us with seasons of doubt.

- We face situations so difficult that we wonder whether God is still all-loving and all-good.
- We witness events or are challenged to think about issues that cause us to question our trust in the Lord.
- We face intellectual issues that cause us to question whether or not our faith is true.

There are many different issues that systematically raise doubts within the hearts and minds of people. When the storm clouds of doubt float into the lives of believers, we naturally question whether these doubts disqualify us as followers of Christ. We wonder if it's okay to express this uncertainty to God. We question how long we can keep our faith afloat.

Unfortunately, dealing with doubt is not a badge of honor within the Christian community. All too often, Christians are embarrassed to admit they have doubts. Reflect on the perspective from a former-pastor-turned-atheist, Dan Barker:

> In their most inner thoughts, even the most devout Christians know that there is something illegitimate about belief. Underneath their profession of faith is a sleeping giant of doubt. In my experience, the best way to conquer doubt is to yield to it.[22]

---

[22] Dan Barker, *Losing Faith in Faith: From Preacher to Atheist* (Madison: FFRF Inc., 2006), 26.

Several years ago my son entered a competition to win season tickets for UCLA basketball. The competition was simple—the person who dressed up as the craziest fan would win season tickets for the next season. When he told me he was going to do it I said what any supportive and loving father would say, "You're crazy. You won't win." I thought of the hundreds of students who entered the competition and would be desperate for free season tickets, and I knew it wasn't going to happen.

For weeks he talked about it, and I thought to myself: "There is no way he's going to win. The odds are totally against it."

On the day of the game I was absolutely convinced that it wasn't going to happen. When he didn't call me at halftime I knew it for sure. I began to think about how I could encourage him in the midst of his disappointment.

Sometime after the game I received a call and all I could hear was him screaming, "I won. I won. I won." I repeatedly told him, "You didn't win. You're kidding me aren't you?" Eventually he sent me a picture of him winning the competition during half-time, and I no longer doubted.

Unfortunately, doubt isn't just about a funny story. Our struggle with doubt threatens our faith. Everyone has moments when a question, doubt, or uncertainty enters our life. You may doubt whether God can

> Doubt isn't just about a funny story. Our struggle with doubt threatens our faith.

get you through a difficult season with your family. You may doubt whether God can provide for you financially.

Of course, our doubts don't always stop there. Sometimes they seep into our Christian faith.

- We may doubt whether we are truly saved.
- We may question why God has allowed so many bad things to come into our life or why He allows so much evil and suffering.
- We may wonder whether we can continue to trust the Bible in light of the theory of evolution or discoveries of science.

- At times, we may even doubt His presence in our life or whether prayer really works.

I've been a pastor for over thirty years and I have had moments in my own spiritual journey when I've come face to face with doubt.

- I know what it's like to lose a parent or close friends and ask the question, "Why?"
- I know what it's like when disappointment and doubt come uninvited into my life and hit me like a freight train.
- I know what it's like to cry out to God when I feel like I am drowning in a sea of hurt.
- I know what it's like to wrestle with weighty intellectual issues that seemed to threaten my faith.
- I know what it's like to experience so much overwhelming loss and trauma that I seriously considered leaving ministry.

Everyone is touched in some way by doubt. Some people are overwhelmed by doubt. Others desire more than anything in the world to get rid of doubt. Still others know someone who is eaten up on the inside with doubt. Despite the fact that everyone is touched by doubt in some way, it's a topic rarely addressed in church.

> Despite the fact that everyone is touched by doubt in some way, it's a topic rarely addressed in church.

Let's take a quick look at some select Scriptures that address the topic of doubt. Jesus longed for his disciples to be free from the control of doubt. Do you remember what Jesus said when Peter began to sink as he walked out on the water to Jesus? "You of little faith," he said, "why did you doubt?" (Matthew 14:31). In one of the most memorable stories of Jesus and His disciples in the aftermath of the resurrection of Jesus, Thomas sincerely doubted the reality of Jesus coming back to life. Remember what Jesus told Thomas, "Put your finger here; see my hands. Reach out your hand and put it into my side. Stop doubting and believe." (John 20:27)

Throughout the Scriptures we continue to learn very important things about the nature of doubt. James, the half-brother of Jesus, recognized that doubt can undermine the very essence of a person's faith. He expressed the power of the waves of criticism and confusion this way:

> 5 If any of you lacks wisdom, he should ask God, who gives generously to all without finding fault, and it will be given to him. 6 But when he asks, he must believe and not doubt, because he who doubts is like a wave of the sea, blown and tossed by the wind.
> James 1:5-6

Jude, the half-brother of Jesus, cautions the church to be careful with those who may have been troubled by the false teachers of the day. Here are his words:

> 22 Be merciful to those who doubt; 23 snatch others from the fire and save them; to others show mercy, mixed with fear—hating even the clothing stained by corrupted flesh.
> Jude 22-23

People who go through a season of doubt should not be slandered or criticized. They should be surrounded by love and mercy. We should be merciful to them because that is how Jesus treated folks. Jesus faced people with doubt all the time; he was not threatened by or hostile toward those who admitted their doubt. He had solutions for their doubt.

Let me briefly relate two powerful stories that illustrate how Jesus responded to people struggling with doubt. As you read the heartbreaking story of a father whose son was demon-possessed try to imagine the anguish:

> 17 A man in the crowd answered, "Teacher, I brought you my son, who is possessed by a spirit that has robbed him of speech. 18 Whenever it seizes him, it throws him to the ground. He foams at the mouth, gnashes his teeth and becomes rigid. I asked your disciples to drive out the spirit, but they could not." . . . 21 Jesus asked the boy's father, "How long has he been like this?" "From childhood," he

answered. [22] "It has often thrown him into fire or water to kill him. But if you can do anything, take pity on us and help us."
Mark 9:17-18, 21-22

This father has been experiencing a nightmare since his son's earliest days as a child. His son was controlled by a demonic spirit that would take control of his life and render him powerless. The traumatic impact of this situation is not that different than modern day accounts of a person suffering from bipolar disorder, a psychotic break, or some other debilitating disease. Each of these situations renders a family helpless as they watch a child or loved one suffer. Don't miss what happens next. The father brings his son to a miracle worker from Nazareth, but he doesn't know that Jesus is the Son of God. In other words, this father doesn't know that the creator of the universe is standing in front of him.

Listen to Jesus' response:

[23] "If you can?" said Jesus. "Everything is possible for him who believes." [24] Immediately the boy's father exclaimed, "I do believe; help me overcome my unbelief!"
Mark 9:23-24

Look at the man's amazing honesty as he says, "I do believe; help me overcome my unbelief!" This father knew that he didn't possess perfect belief. Jesus knew it too. But notice that Jesus didn't rebuke him. Jesus didn't say, "Stop the presses. I want more belief. I want perfect faith." He simply challenged him by enlarging the man's horizons. Notice what Jesus said: "Everything is possible for him who believes." Jesus saw an element of faith, and He understood the reality of doubt.

> Jesus saw an element of faith but He understood the reality of doubt.

Allow me to show you another example illustrating that doubt doesn't play favorites. Doubt even touched one of the central figures in the New Testament. We all know the story of John the Baptist. His job was to get people's attention and point them to Jesus as the Messiah. John the Baptist had a short yet remarkable career. In the twilight of his career he found himself in jail. What's interesting is after John heard the incredible accounts of the ministry of Jesus, he asked a couple of his disciples to find Jesus and ask him a question:

> 18 John's disciples told him about all these things. Calling two of them, 19 he sent them to the Lord to ask, "Are you the one who was to come, or should we expect someone else?" 20 When the men came to Jesus, they said, "John the Baptist sent us to you to ask, 'Are you the one who was to come, or should we expect someone else?'"
> Luke 7:18-20

Does John's question surprise you? John expected that when Jesus, the Messiah, came on the scene, he would immediately set up the kingdom. John the Baptist was waiting for the arrival of the kingdom of God and for things to change dramatically. John found himself in prison and in danger of being put to death, and still the kingdom had not come in the way he had expected. John sent his followers to Jesus with a simple question "Are you the One?" Here are my observations on what John was thinking,

- John wasn't sure.
- John had questions.
- In other words, the great John the Baptist had a genuine moment of doubt regarding whether Jesus truly was the intended Messiah.

Please don't miss the response from Jesus. Jesus didn't rebuke John. He didn't chastise him. Listen to His words:

> Go back and report to John what you have seen and heard: The blind receive sight, the lame walk, those who have leprosy are cured, the deaf hear, the dead are raised, and the good news is preached to the poor.
> Luke 7:22

Jesus simply reminded John's disciples of the miracles He was performing, and then he quoted Isaiah 61:1-2 to show that He was fulfilling prophecy. In other words, He gave John the Baptist evidence designed to bolster John's faith. Jesus didn't insist on blind faith. He supplied evidence.

> The evidence was designed to bolster the faith of John the Baptist. Jesus didn't insist on blind faith. He supplied evidence.

Have you noticed something about all of the Scriptures that we've looked at? There are many different responses to doubt.

- To some, Jesus called for more faith.
- To others, Jesus extended mercy.
- To still others, Jesus gave evidence.

For some reason, we don't think it is okay to express doubts; we don't think that God-fearing followers ever have moments when they question their beliefs. We think that we are the first generation in the history of the church to ever deal with doubt head on.

In this chapter I'm going to give you an approach you can use to disarm the doubts that come into our lives. This approach will involve three distinct steps. First, I'd like to look at the different kinds of doubt. Second, I'd like to look at some misunderstandings about doubt and faith. Third, I'd like to make some suggestions regarding how we're supposed to work through these difficult seasons.

Most importantly, I've made these three steps easy and helpful enough that you can begin to help other people who struggle with doubt. You can use these in helping yourself, your spouse, kids, grandchildren, friends, neighbors, or the person sitting next to you in church.

STEP #1: SEE THE FACES OF DOUBT

There is not just one face of doubt or one reason why people doubt. There is not a simple solution for one kind of doubt because there are many faces of doubt. Each of these "faces" has a different reason and requires a different response. Dr. Larry Anderson, who is one of the foremost Christian experts on doubt, identifies four general categories or faces of doubt. Let's look at the four general categories of doubt and the response that is most helpful in supporting our family and friends during a season of doubt.

Genetic Doubters: Many people come out of the womb doubting.

- Some are melancholy and think the cup is always half empty. They are truly walking "Eeyores."
- Other folks are simply analytical by nature and feel comfortable questioning and doubting issues they are told.
- Other folks are doubters by virtue of their training (e.g., engineers, accountants, etc.). They are drawn to uncertainties and are trained to question everything. They constantly address an issue asking the question, "How do you know?" or, "But what if?"

Response to Genetic Doubters: Don't overreact. Some people are simply predisposed to doubt more than others. It's our obligation to be patient with them. Something may sound like doubt when in reality it is simply a question—a desire to better understand something. A genetic doubter's questions may actually help us. They may help us to better understand an issue or to help someone build a stronger faith.

Rebellious Doubters: Other people express their doubt as a function of an attitude of independence.

- They don't want someone telling them what they can or cannot do.
- They want to question the person giving them the rules.
- Sometimes you can discern this quality within your children from the earliest age.
- Sometimes this is particularly evident as people progress through different stages of their religious faith.

Response to Rebellious Doubters: Distinguish independence from rebellion. Some need to learn on their own; they need to package information themselves rather than receiving everything pre-packaged. Pray for wisdom. It is not an easy task to distinguish independence from rebellion. We must pray for wisdom so that we can determine whether people just want to learn on their own or whether they struggle with a rebellious spirit.

Disappointed Doubters: This refers to people who are disappointed with God.

- Something happened which has caused a person to doubt whether God is real.
- Sometimes these events are life-changing or dramatic or so ongoing that they challenge a person's belief in God.
- Sometimes they lament, "If there's a God, why is this stuff happening to me?" or "God, enough already."
- Sometimes they lament, "Why is this conflict happening at church? I don't understand it."
- Sometimes a person has never doubted God once in his or her entire life, but then everything goes wrong and the person is overwhelmed by loss and hurt. For the first time the person begins to doubt whether God is good.

Response to Disappointed Doubters: Be sensitive to a person's emotional hurt. Pain and sorrow are the real issues. Sometimes hurt disillusions people and their perception of God is challenged. It is very important to learn the powerful words, "I'm so sorry . . . I can only imagine how you feel!" This is especially important to say to our brothers and sisters in Christ within the church. Every person processes loss, disappointment, fear, or frustration in a different way and at a different pace.

Intellectual Doubters: These are people who have to overcome genuine hurdles.

- They look at the issues and genuinely want answers to certain questions which appear to block their path to understanding or embracing the Christian faith.
- They may think that smart people have thoroughly ruled out faith until they find out that many really intelligent people have provided reasonable answers to the profound questions of our age.
- Some folks don't need all their questions answered. Other folks need to be convinced of the intellectual basis of their faith.

Response to Intellectual Doubters: The church must create an environment that is conducive to asking deep questions of faith. The church must also determine an overall strategy to address those issues which are most significant for their people. If we as Christians are ever going to get the upper hand against doubt, we have to discover the reasons for our doubt and learn how to respond to it. In other words, we have to see ourselves in one of these faces. We need to understand why a family member, friend, child, or grandchild is struggling with doubt. We also need to master our response to that particular kind of doubt. Without discovering the reason and response, we will never be able to get the upper hand on disarming doubt—never!

STEP #2: BALANCE FAITH AND REASON

A major part of the reason why we doubt is that we don't understand the divine balance that God has created between faith and reason. Most churches never give Christians the tools to understand this delicate balance. Most Christians can't remember hearing a sermon that attempts to explain the Christian balance between faith and reason. As a result, too many Christians have opted for a very naïve and hurtful approach that fails to appreciate this balance. Allow me to briefly illustrate the difficulty:

> Most Christians can't remember hearing a sermon that attempts to explain the Christian balance between faith and reason.

- Some Christians rely exclusively on faith and think it's immature to seek out answers or evidence. In other words, they minimize reason.
- Other Christians are looking for absolute certainty in every question or situation. In other words, they minimize faith.

Neither approach is right. Christian thinkers have always attempted to provide a balance between faith and reason. Seventeenth century French philosopher Blaise Pascal put it this way, "In faith there is enough light for those whose only desire is to see and enough darkness for those of the opposite disposition."[23] Modern-day thinker Ravi Zacharias

---

[23] Blaise Pascal, *Pensées and Other Writings* (New York: University Press, 2008), 81.

expressed the importance of achieving a divine balance between faith and reason this way,

> God has given enough reason in this world to make faith in him a most reasonable thing. But he has left out enough to make it impossible to live by sheer reason and observation alone.[24]

Of course, the Scripture has always been very clear that God has a specific role for faith and a specific role for reason.

The Role of Faith

> And without faith it is impossible to please God, because anyone who comes to him must believe that he exists and that he rewards those who earnestly seek him.
> Hebrews 11:6

Role of Reason

> Always be prepared to give an answer to everyone who asks you to give the reason for the hope that you have. But do this with gentleness and respect.
> 1 Peter 3:15

Scripture makes it clear that faith and reason are important from God's vantage point. We have enough evidence to make Christianity reasonable but not so much that we never need faith. But the million dollar question that very few people attempt to answer is, "How are we supposed to balance faith and reason?" Before we attempt to give a detailed answer

> We have enough evidence to make Christianity reasonable but not so much that we never need faith.

to this question I would like us to look at a fascinating passage in 1 John 5:6-10. Most Christians have never read these verses within the context of the relationship between faith and reason. This passage can be a little confusing, so read carefully the words of the Apostle John:

---

[24] Ravi Zacharias, *The Real Face of Atheism* (Ada: Baker Books, 2004), 112.

> 6 This is the one who came by water and blood—Jesus Christ. He did not come by water only, but by water and blood. And it is the Spirit who testifies, because the Spirit is the truth. 7 For there are three that testify: 8 the Spirit, the water and the blood; and the three are in agreement. 9 We accept man's testimony, but God's testimony is greater because it is the testimony of God, which he has given about his Son.
> 1 John 5:6-9

This passage was written by John to confront a false teacher by the name of Cerinthus who taught in the first century. Cerinthus taught that the divine Christ descended on the man Jesus at His baptism but left Him before His crucifixion. In other words, Jesus was made to look like Superman at His baptism, but when it came to Jesus dying on the cross, he was just a man. He was not God incarnate—God in the flesh.

John wanted to make absolutely sure that everyone knew that God the Father declared Jesus to be the Son of God at both His baptism and His crucifixion. That's why he wrote the following verse:

> This is the one who came by water and blood—Jesus Christ. He did not come by water only, but by water and blood.
> 1 John 5:6

The water referred to Jesus' baptism and the blood referred to Jesus' crucifixion. This was John's way of pointing to the two central public moments in the ministry of Jesus Christ—His baptism and His crucifixion. It was the clearest way for John to say, "Jesus was truly the God/man from the very beginning."

Please don't miss how this passage relates to the topic of doubt. John was trying to reassure the first century Christians that what they believed was really the truth, so he began to act like a

> These three witnesses can be placed into two basic categories—internal witness and external witness.

lawyer before a judge. He reminded his readers that he possessed a handful of reliable witnesses to the truthfulness of what he had just spoken. Listen to the next step in his argument:

[7] For there are three that testify: [8] the Spirit, the water and the blood; and the three are in agreement.
I John 5:7-8

Folks, do you see the three witnesses that he brings before the judge in the courtroom? They are the Spirit, the water, and the blood. These three witnesses can be placed into two basic categories—internal witness and external witness. Allow me to explain what John is trying to say. All three witnesses have been given to us by God to establish the truthfulness of what we believe.

- The Spirit by faith or the internal witness - The Holy Spirit is a divine GPS that consistently points us to the truth of Christianity.

- The water and the blood or the external witnesses - These are real historical events that people could touch and see that remind believers that Christianity is true.

However, it is very important to realize that the Apostle John understood that there should be a certain relationship between faith and reason. Listen to the last thing that the Apostle John reveals:

We accept man's testimony, but God's testimony is greater because it is the testimony of God, which he has given about his Son.
I John 5:9

Gifted philosopher and apologist William Lane Craig has effectively captured this balance by using two simple questions:

- How do we know our faith is true?
- How do we show our faith is true?

These questions sound similar but they are as different as day and night. They illustrate the balance between faith and reason.

As Christians, the first question that we must answer is, "How do we know our faith is true?" In other words, "How are we supposed to re-assure ourselves that our faith in Christianity is true? How do we resolve doubts?"

As Christians, the second question that we must answer is, "How are we supposed to demonstrate to others that our faith in Christianity is reasonable?" It's not just, "How do we know for ourselves?" it's, "How can we show or demonstrate to those around us that Christianity makes sense?" These two questions and how we should respond to each are illustrated through the following graphic:

KNOWING OUR FAITH IS TRUE　　　SHOWING OUR FAITH IS TRUE

INTERNAL WITNESS	*EXTERNAL WITNESS*
SPIRIT BY FAITH	REASON/ARGUMENT
EXTERNAL WITNESS	*INTERNAL WITNESS*
REASON/ARGUMENT	SPIRIT BY FAITH

HOW DO WE KNOW OUR FAITH IS TRUE?

First, we know our faith is true because of the inner witness of God's Spirit. Our primary confidence is by the Spirit through our faith.

- The Holy Spirit reassures us that we are children of God. I John 2:20 tells us, "You have an anointing and you all know."
- The Holy Spirit points us to the truth. 1 John 5:7 tells us, "It is the Spirit who bears witness, because the Spirit is the truth."
- The Holy Spirit protects us from error. John 14:26 and John 16:23 tell us, "He will guide you into all truth."

We must reaffirm to believers within the church that our confidence in our Christian faith is not primarily linked to the ups and downs of apologetic arguments, whether a Christian scholar wins a debate against a secular atheist, or whether a book really answers all of our questions. Second, we also know our faith is true through reason and evidence. God has given us the ability to think and see all the evidence for our faith. I believe He wants us to use that ability. There are evidences all around us that point to the truthfulness of the Christian faith. We can use philosophy, science, logic, and historical events to provide reasons for our faith.

> God created us with the ability to think. I believe He wants us to use that ability. There are evidences all around us that point to the truthfulness of the Christian faith.

Jesus of Nazareth clearly re-affirmed the role of the mind in the life of the believer. In Matthew 22:37, Jesus made the following observation, "Love the Lord your God with all your heart and with all your soul and with all your mind."

HOW DO WE SHOW OUR FAITH IS TRUE?

As Christians we show our faith is true by reversing the order of how we answered the first question. First, we use the apologetic evidence, the compelling case of reason, and sharp arguments to make a case for the reasonableness of the Christian faith. Paul reasoned in the synagogue wherever he went (Acts 17:2). We are told to give a reason for the hope that is within us (1 Peter 3:15).

> Our role is to make a compelling case for why Christianity should be included as a viable worldview.

It is our obligation to demonstrate the reasonableness of our Christian faith to our skeptical family and friends. Our role is to make a compelling case for why Christianity should be included as a viable worldview. In addition, we have a chance to show Christians that we really have a lot of tremendous reasons that we can use to show that our faith is true.

Second, we appeal to the Holy Spirit to show the truth of what we are saying to the people we are addressing. We ask for the Spirit of God to use what we say and to help it make sense to our friends. We also ask our friends to look inside themselves to see if the explanation resonates with their intuition—whether or not it makes sense.

Notice something—we don't go to our non-churched friends and ask them to believe us because the Holy Spirit tells us that this is the truth. They would think you're crazy. Unfortunately, this is the consistent approach that the Mormons use when they say to us, "You should believe Mormonism because we have prayed and God gave us a burning in the bosom." Actually, too many Christians utilize a similar approach when trying to appeal to non-Christian friends. It's time that we use solid evidence and reason to help our family and friends to place the Christian faith back on the table as a viable option.

WHAT HAPPENS WHEN YOU DON'T HAVE BALANCE?

Too many people hide behind blind faith. In other words, they don't think through issues—they don't think they should. However, when doubts eventually come into their lives, and they will, it creates deep inner tension that causes a person to live a split life in which there are things they believe and things they don't believe.

Other people have weak faith because they never really exercise their faith. You see, some folks are always on a quest for certainty. They need one hundred percent proof for everything and anything. As a result, they never have a chance to exercise their faith muscle.

Still other people have timid faith because they don't ever share their faith and/or don't have the confidence in their faith to want to share. They are afraid of what others will say because deep down they don't think their faith is reasonable.

STEP #3: LEARN TO DISARM YOUR DOUBT

We all face doubt at different moments in our lives. When doubt, uncertainty, and questions threaten to overwhelm us it's absolutely necessary that we learn to disarm our doubt. The doubt may be about your faith, or it may be about whether you trust God with things in your own personal life or in the life of your church. It may be that you've never struggled with doubt in your life until this season in your life, or you may have struggled with it your entire life.

Here are four very practical suggestions on how to disarm the doubt in your life. Each of them is a practical way to help yourself or someone close to you.

VERBALIZE YOUR DOUBTS

- Have you ever felt like you were all alone with a physical sickness?
- Have you ever felt like you were all alone because no one really understood what you were facing in life situations?
- Have you ever felt you were by yourself in something you were thinking or facing?

Being alone in our struggles is awful isn't it? The same is true when we face doubts; it's horrible to feel alone with our doubts. Unfortunately, too many churches don't foster a safe place where people can say, "I struggle with this issue—I have doubts about this." The church frowns upon people who express their doubts. We feel uncomfortable when people

> Unfortunately, too many churches don't foster a safe place where people can say, "I struggle with this issue—I have doubts about this."

express their uncertainties about a certain aspect of our faith. It's as if our faith is on trial and is being attacked or diminished. But something powerful happens when we verbalize our doubts. We realize the following things:

- We are not alone. Other people have doubts also, maybe regarding the same exact issue.
- There are answers to our questions and resources that can really help our faith. It's awesome to ask a question out loud and very quickly realize that other people have answers.
- Even if we can't get all the answers, our faith can still be strong.

DISTINGUISH DISAPPOINTMENT FROM DOUBT

Life is full of disappointments. The world and everything about it is flawed and imperfect. Disappointment can lead to doubt, but it's very different from doubt. Philip Yancey, who is a gifted Christian author and thinker, makes this observation:

We tend to think, 'Life should be fair because God is fair.' But God is not life. And if I confuse God with the physical reality of life—by expecting constant good health for example—then I set myself up for crashing disappointment.[25]

During this latest season in my life I have been surrounded by disappointment. I faced some pretty big issues—issues that challenged me emotionally and professionally. During this time, two influential friends in ministry faced agonizing end-of-life challenges. During my struggles I have repeatedly cried out to God. Here's what I have had to remember: disappointment is part of living in a flawed and fallen world, but it is not the same as doubt and doesn't have to lead to doubt.

> Disappointment is part of living in a flawed and fallen world, but it is not the same as doubt; and doesn't have to lead to doubt.

This is tremendously freeing as a Christian. You see, I can explain my disappointment with the fact that I live in a fallen and broken world. Like Job, I have learned that we are able to re-discover God in a deeper way than we ever thought possible through disappointment. I have found that God hears my voice in disappointment. Being disappointed with life—even being disappointed and confused by God—is not fatal.

RESOLVE DOUBTS ONE AT A TIME

This might be one of the most important steps in disarming our doubts. We live in an information age. We have 24/7 access to every question, criticism, or skeptical thought that has ever been expressed about Christianity. People hear a sound bite on cable news, they talk to a friend, read a review of a book, or listen to a guest speaker on TV. Before we know it we feel neck deep in doubt or skepticism. Before we can catch our breath it seems as if the entire world is an obstacle to

---

[25] Philip Yancey, *Disappointment with God: Three Questions No One Asks Aloud* (Grand Rapids: Zondervan, 1997), 183.

Christianity and that only people with half a mind believe in the Christian faith.

There is only one approach that works. We must resolve our doubts one at a time. Take them issue by issue. We should use the same advice that Christian financial expert Dave Ramsey gives to Christians as they attempt to eliminate credit card debt. He advises them to take care of one debt at a time. Get the momentum going in a positive direction. Experience some success. Release some additional capital to address other debt. Get some positive history under your belt.

It is impossible to resolve all these feelings and issues at once. Each of these feelings is connected to a different issue and a different train of thought or answer.

Here's the really great thing that happens when we use this approach. Once we resolve one issue of doubt, it creates hopefulness and momentum for the next issue. Here's how this can work:

- If you have a problem with a verse in the Bible, study it until it is resolved in your head.
- If you have a problem with a particular issue, study it until you feel that you have a reasonable explanation.
- If you are overwhelmed by the questions of skeptics, take one question a time and find a reasonable answer.

The church simply needs to be intentional with the big intellectual or emotional problems/questions that weigh on your faith. Figure out the issues that the people in your church struggle with and systematically and intentionally begin to address them. Take them one at a time. Use a resource like this book to get some expert analysis or bring someone into your church to address key issues. Keep wrestling with these topics until you really begin to feel comfortable within your own skin. Make sure you feel a greater degree of confidence in addressing this question. Help everyone feel more comfortable in the give and take with those outside the faith. Model how you can talk through an issue.

DON'T MINIMIZE THE BATTLE

I would like to finish this chapter by simply stating that we dare not minimize the battle that we are in as Christians. There is nothing that the evil one would want more than for individual Christians to be overwhelmed, isolated, and defeated by doubt. Don't be mistaken—we are in a battle! The battle is being waged on two fronts: the battle for our souls and the battle for our minds.

BATTLE FOR OUR SOULS

Listen to a description of this battle from the pages of Scripture,

> [3] For though we live in the world, we do not wage war as the world does. [4] The weapons we fight with are not the weapons of the world. On the contrary, they have divine power to demolish strongholds. [5] We demolish arguments and every pretension that sets itself up against the knowledge of God, and we take captive every thought to make it obedient to Christ.
> 2 Corinthians 10:3-5

The Apostle Paul describes the spiritual struggle that occurs in the life of the Christian. A quick survey of these verses tells us the following:

- We are fighting a spiritual battle in which spiritual darkness blinds people—it's not a level playing field.
- We are fighting for the hearts of the unsaved.
- We are talking with folks who resist God for a lot of reasons—emotional, spiritual, and relational.

BATTLE FOR OUR MINDS

Our job as Christians is to battle in the world of ideas. We must stand up for the truth of the Christian faith and show the reasonableness of our faith. We are in an intellectual struggle wherein the opinion-shapers and power-brokers of the world have already won the battle—it's not a level playing field. However, the church must do a better job of providing an atmosphere in which believers feel comfortable expressing and resolving the doubts in their Christian faith.

CONCLUSION

If friends in your church have doubts about their faith we must reassure them that they are not alone. If they doubt whether they can trust God during seasons of doubt, the church must collectively create an environment in which they sense they are not alone. If they wrestle with questions they must be able to find answers.

> God hasn't promised so much evidence that we will have absolute certainty and no need for faith.

Having doubts is not the end of the road. Doubt is not fatal. God hasn't promised that we'll always see Him with absolute clarity in our lives. Sometimes, we face situations in which we must believe certain things about God even though we are faced with very real questions and disturbing doubts. God hasn't promised so much evidence that we will have absolute certainty and no need for faith.

As we try to come alongside of our family, friends, and fellow Christians, it is helpful to remember the following observation that Sir Francis Bacon, a seventeenth century English philosopher and statesman, made:

> If we begin with certainties, we shall end in doubts; but if we begin with doubts, and we are patient in them, we shall end in certainties.[26]

Let's be patient with doubting people. They are at a crossroads; they need us.

---

[26] Francis Bacon, *The Advancement of Learning Book I* (New York: Whiley Book, 2012), 22.

SUGGESTIONS FOR ADDITIONAL READING

Dr. Lynn Anderson, *If I Really Believe Why Do I Have These Doubts?*

This is one of the best books that talks exclusively on the topic of doubt from both an emotional and spiritual perspective. It is easy to read and uses real life stories of people who have struggled with doubt.

William Lane Craig, *Hard Questions, Real Answers*

This short book by one of America's great Christian thinkers lays a brief foundation for addressing doubt, unanswered prayer, and the question of evil and suffering. Of all William Lane Craig's works this is easily the most readable. It's helpful as a brief overview of several key issues.

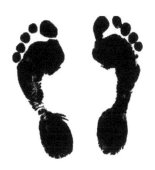

FOOTPRINT FOUR:
WHERE IS GOD WHEN IT HURTS?

I can still remember the day that I lost my mother to a ruptured brain aneurysm. She had suffered a mild heart attack the day before, but the doctors assured us that everything about her prognosis looked positive. This was supposed to be a minor health hiccup that could easily be treated with medication. Unfortunately, in the aftermath of her heart attack the hospital staff gave her a routine dose of blood thinning medication. That's all it took for the aneurysm to burst. On that day my world changed.

Eighteen years ago for the very first time, the reality of living in an imperfect and flawed world came crashing into my insulated life. Pain, suffering, loss, and hurt became emotional realities that forever changed how I looked at the world.

You see, for most of my life I lived in a bubble that protected me from some of the harsher realities of life. Nothing too bad or hurtful ever seemed to come my way. In many ways you can describe my early years as idyllic. I can't remember hearing the issue of trials, difficulties, or pain discussed at church. I don't ever remember taking a course at seminary that prepared me for the harsh realities of living in a fallen world. Ultimately, nothing prepared me for the tidal wave of grief and shock that hit my Christian faith.

Since that moment my family has faced a number of issues that have severely shaken our foundation as a family. We have faced the tragic reality of Alzheimer's, debilitating chronic pain, and emotional issues. We have witnessed close family friends who have been ravaged by ALS and cancer. We have faced job losses, career changes, and traumatic events that overwhelmed us and caused us to experience tremendous loss, grief, and hurt.

Everywhere I go and at every church I visit, I ultimately encounter people who have faced hurtful times. I talk to people who have:

- Lost a job.
- Experienced a horrible illness.
- Gone through reversals in finances.
- Lost a loved one.
- Experienced uncertainty and confusion over the future.

Sometimes you see in a person's face or hear in his or her voice that they are about to give up. Life has become too much. In those moments you realize that no one is immune to pain's touch.

For many people these difficult seasons result in feeling increasingly distant from the Lord. We question His motives or His plan. Sometimes, we even find ourselves questioning His love or presence. One of the most famous Christians of all time, C.S. Lewis expressed some of these sentiments in the aftermath of his wife's death of bone cancer:

> Meanwhile, where is God? . . . When you are happy, so happy that you have no sense of needing Him, if you turn to Him then with praise, you will be welcomed with open arms. But go to Him when your need is desperate, when all other help is vain and what do you find? A door slammed in your face, and a sound of bolting and double bolting on the inside. After that, silence. You may as well turn away.[27]

Although Christians throughout the ages have faced the difficulties and disappointments of life, most modern-day churches don't prepare people for those moments. Most churches never give Christians the tools to face times of suffering and pain. As I found myself immersed in the intellectual and philosophical issues of evil and suffering I was acutely aware that I didn't have the necessary tools to cope with the emotional and spiritual upheaval going on within me. I found that no one had prepared me for integrating these difficult times into my faith. No one

---

[27] C.S. Lewis, *A Grief Observed* (San Francisco, CA: Harper House, 1961), 6.

had prepared me to look through the maze that comes into everyone's life whenever they ask the question, "Where is God when it hurts?"

People are hurting! People are struggling to integrate their faith in a loving and powerful God with what they are feeling and experiencing during

> Most churches never give Christians the tools to face times of suffering and pain.

difficult seasons in life. This is a major reason why this is one of the longest chapters in my book. If Christians are going to leave a tangible footprint that represents a legacy of their Christian faith, they must possess the emotional and spiritual tools to survive the difficult seasons in life.

The purpose of this chapter is very straightforward. I am going to share with you five reasons for why God allows hardship, pain, and struggle into the life of the Christian. They may not be the reasons for what you are going through in your life right now. They are not an attempt to provide a thorough theodicy for the question of evil and suffering. They will not answer every question you have for God, nor will they remove the emotional heartache you may be facing. However, I believe it's reassuring to know that God has left us reminders that are scattered throughout the Word of God.

Think about it: if God never gave a single reason why we face bad things we might have reason to doubt whether He has a plan. But God has left us reminders regarding how He is able to use bad things to

> If God never gave one single reason why we face bad things we might have reason to doubt whether He has a plan.

lovingly remind us, "I'm with you. I have a purpose for this season in your life."

It's very important that I make this disclaimer. The journey of grief, loss, and pain is very complicated. If you've been devastated by a traumatic event, the significant loss of a loved one, or some unexplained tragedy, you may not be ready to see the big picture. All you can think about is,

"Why?" Your emotions may be too raw. Quite frankly, you are so heartbroken that you are just trying to keep it together.

If you feel this way my prayer is that you would remember that God is with you and He will get you to the other side. The Lord saw me through the most difficult and traumatic season in my life. He can do the same for you.

REASON #1: GOD MAY ALLOW HURTFUL TIMES TO ACCOMPLISH HIS PURPOSES

> You intended to harm me, but God intended it for good to accomplish what is now being done, the saving of many lives.
> Genesis 50:20

If there is a poster child for undeserved difficulties and trials in a person's life it is Joseph. Whenever I think about Joseph, whose story is told in the Old Testament, I cringe. I can't help but feel his anguish and pain. Just think of all the things that came uninvited into his life:

- Hardship of being hated by his own brothers.
- Injustice of being sold into slavery.
- Heartache of being removed from his father and family at a relatively young age.
- False accusations by Potiphar's wife that sent him to prison.

Joseph lived in a fallen world. His world, like ours, was a place where the evil choices of people and the difficult circumstances of life come uninvited into our lives. It is important for all of us to recognize that when God created a world in which people possess the dignity of free choice, there existed the possibility that some people would use that free choice for evil.

> When God created a world where He gave people the dignity of free choice, there existed the possibility that some people would use that free choice for evil.

Please don't miss the implication of this observation. God didn't cause Joseph's brothers to hate him or to sell him into slavery. Flawed people within the sphere of Joseph's life made these choices. As you read the Biblical account in Genesis 50 it is abundantly clear that Joseph did not blame God. The blame fell squarely on the shoulders of his brothers. However, it is also very clear that in His ultimate wisdom God decided to use those tragic events for something greater.

Think about all that we can learn from Joseph's story. First, God's purposes can extend past our own lives. In other words, God's objective and plans extend well past the scope of our personal experience. At any given moment in our lives the Lord is trying to weave a global montage that achieves His bigger purposes. It's not always about us. In our Facebook age in which people have a forum to let the entire world know what is happening in their life some folks believe that everything is about them. Nothing could be further from the truth. For example, Joseph's story was bigger than Joseph because it involved the fate of Egypt and eventually the surrounding nations.

Second, God may be preparing us for something greater in the future. The simple reality is that the purpose of our life is not to achieve our happiness. God has and will sometimes allow affliction and difficulty in the life of the Christian as the foundation for something greater He wishes to accomplish.

Alexander Solzhenitsyn, the famous Soviet dissident, endured years in the awful Gulag prisons of the former Soviet Union. Despite the loneliness, persecution, and awful conditions, he eventually recognized that God had somehow been able to use these events for his good. Listen to his observation:

> It was only when I lay there on rotting prison straw that I sensed within myself the first stirrings of good. Gradually it was disclosed to me that the line separating good and evil passes not through states, nor between classes, nor between political parties either—but right through every human heart—and through all human hearts. . . . That is why I turn back to the years of my imprisonment and say, sometimes to the astonishment of those about me: "*Bless you,*

prison!" I nourished my soul there, and I say without hesitation: *"Bless you, prison*, for having been in my life!"[28]

Despite the horrific experiences of his life, Solzhenitsyn was able to turn and find God. His life illustrates one of the most difficult juggling acts we'll ever face—reconciling our faith with the realities of a fallen world. Tough times can drive a wedge between us and the Lord. They can cause us to doubt whether or not God really is in control of this world. They can cause us to doubt whether or not God is actually as loving as He claims.

> God doesn't cause the horrible things to come into our lives, but in His knowledge of everything that will happen in the past, present, or future He is able to take those darker moments and weave them into something greater for the future.

God doesn't cause the horrible things to come into our lives, but in His knowledge of everything that happened in the past, is happening in the present, or will happen in the future He is able to take those darker moments and weave them into a greater purpose for our future.

God was preparing Joseph for a huge task. Joseph never could have imagined the task that God had in store for him. The only way that Joseph could be in the position to be used for future greatness was for those bad things to happen to him. It was the only way.

The really difficult part of this entire process is that we don't always see how God will use something in the future or how He desires to use us. Sometimes all we see is the hardship, agony, or frustration. In those moments, we can't see everything that God is trying to accomplish. We may not see it for months or years. Here are some of the things that we won't always see:

---

[28] Alexander Solzhenitsyn, *The Gulag Archipelago: 1918-1956: An Experiment in Literary Investigation, Vol. 2* (New York: Harper & Row, 1973), 615-617.

- How the tough season prepares us for a greater season.
- How we will touch people with similar experiences.
- How His character or His power will be shown through trials.
- How God's future work will eventually become crystal clear.
- How our life might be used as the impetus for something great.

Folks, despite how difficult things are or how confused we might be, we must remind ourselves that God sees things that we'll never be able to see! He sees:

- The future direction of our lives.
- The preparation of our character.
- The lessons which may be learned.
- Our dependency upon Him.
- How the events of our lives work as part of His master plan.

The Apostle Paul put it this way:

> 33 Oh, the depth of the riches of the wisdom and knowledge of God! How unsearchable his judgments, and his paths beyond tracing out! 34 Who has known the mind of the Lord? Or who has been his counselor?
> Romans 11:33-34

I can't begin to tell you how often I've told the Lord, "God, I don't get it. I don't see how this will work out." Some of my biggest disappointments were those moments when I questioned God's game plan for me. However, I've learned a lot from those moments. As I look back on those times when I questioned God's plan for my life, I have realized that He's been right. God's vision of the future was a lot better than mine. In fact, I'm so very glad that He didn't do everything I asked of Him.

No one likes the tough things we go through, but at least we know that the things they produce inside of us are eternally pleasing to God.

If we turn away from God in the midst of affliction, we communicate to those watching us that at times of stress, Christianity offers no more of an answer than any other religion or ideology. God still needs people today who will show others that even when life brings the unexpected and the tragic, they will continue to love and serve God. Not because it pays to do so, but because he is worthy of devotion.

You may be in a season when you must bend your knee before God's purposes and say, "Not my will, but yours." You may need to say, "God, I want my life to reflect anything that brings you pleasure and advances your purposes." You may need to say, "God, being where you want me is more important than being where I want to be."

REASON #2: GOD MAY ALLOW HURTFUL TIMES TO REMOVE OUR SELF-SUFFICIENCY

> To keep me from becoming conceited because of these surpassingly great revelations, there was given me a thorn in my flesh, a messenger of Satan, to torment me.
> 2 Corinthians 12:7

In the book of 2 Corinthians, the Apostle Paul reveals a clear example of how God can take tough times and use them in a positive fashion. We aren't specifically told the identity of Paul's "thorn in the flesh," but we know that there was something in Paul's physical body that wasn't pleasant. It was painful, it was annoying, and it was confusing.

It seems that God's purpose in the grand scheme of events was to keep Paul from having an elevated perception of himself. God used this physical malady to keep Paul's feet on the ground and to remind him that God was in control and that Paul wasn't God. Remember, Paul had tremendous spiritual and religious experiences. His conversion experience involved a divine revelation on the road to Damascus (Acts 9). Later in his life, he referred to a time when he had divine revelations of the third heaven (2 Cor. 12:1-5).

Here's how the Apostle Paul's situation relates to each of us. The simple reality is that we (citizens of the United States) live in one of the most affluent eras and countries in the history of humanity. Every night on CNN or Fox News we are routinely reminded of our good fortune. Horrific images of people suffering in Iraq, Syria, Gaza, or Ukraine remind us of our good fortune.

Unfortunately, our affluence and ease of life can easily reinforce that part of the human spirit that desires comfort, ease, and self-reliance. We are used to things going smoothly in life and to having control of what is happening in our life. The down side of all this is pretty simple. Affluence prevents us from being totally and completely dependent on God. We can go weeks or even months without really needing God. God is interested in fostering our dependence upon Him. He desires that we do everything with reliance upon Him. He knows that circumstances work best when we depend upon Him for everything in our lives.

Cheri and I have been blessed with three wonderful grandchildren. One of the things I've observed in my brief journey as a grandparent is that those beautiful children are utterly dependent upon their parents and grandparents for everything. We can't just wind them up like toys and let them go. They are dependent upon us for food, diaper changing, decision making, baths, dressing—everything.

> God is interested in fostering our dependence upon Him. He desires that we do everything with reliance upon Him. He knows that things work best when we depend upon Him for everything in our lives.

Somehow, we have been given the impression that we are supposed to grow out of this toddler phase. This is wrong! Don't miss this simple yet powerful truth. The whole Christian life is meant to look like the toddler phase in terms of dependency. We are to always depend on God for everything.

It's important to remember that God doesn't take delight in seeing us agonize during these difficult times. However, God is interested in removing our self-sufficiency and in nudging us toward a greater dependence upon Him. Jesus reflected this sentiment beautifully:

> [4] Remain in me, and I will remain in you. No branch can bear fruit by itself; it must remain in the vine. Neither can you bear fruit unless you remain in me. [5] I am the vine; you are the branches. If a man remains in me and I in him, he will bear much fruit; apart from me you can do nothing.
> John 15:4-5

Since God has designed us to be dependent upon Him for everything, I believe the following questions are always appropriate for us to ask ourselves:

- Have we been too self-sufficient in our life?
- Have we lived a fairly affluent and undisturbed life?
- Do we have our entire life already mapped out for months or years in advance?
- Are we able to go for weeks and months never seriously thinking about our utter dependence upon God?

REASON #3: GOD MAY ALLOW HURTFUL TIMES TO DEVELOP OUR FAITH

> 6 In this you greatly rejoice, though now for a little while you may have had to suffer grief in all kinds of trials. 7 These have come so that your faith—of greater worth than gold, which perishes even though refined by fire—may be proved genuine and may result in praise, glory and honor when Jesus Christ is revealed.
> 1 Peter 1:6-7

I think most people would just as soon pretend that certain verses were never in the Bible. In fact, I think it is human nature for people to look for loopholes in those passages of the Bible that are difficult to understand or hard to swallow. As you first read this verse it is human nature to see if you might be able to find some wiggle room. After all, no one wants to go through trials. No one wants to experience hardship or difficulties.

Allow me to show you that the actual meaning of this passage provides no wiggle room. Take a moment and look at verse six from the New American Standard Version, which attempts to capture more literally the essence of the Greek text.

> Even though now for a little while, if necessary, you have been distressed by various trials,
> I Peter 1:6 NASB

In Greek, the phrase, "if necessary you have been distressed by various trials" should literally be translated "if necessary, as it is." This verse isn't just telling us that we live in an imperfect world. It teaches that God has placed us in an imperfect world because He values the growth of our faith. The idea is that hurtful times, difficult times, and disappointing times are part of the natural development in our spiritual life. They are not fun or enjoyable but absolutely necessary.

Allow me to give you an example of this Scriptural principle that comes from the Cold War Era of the Soviet Union. For years, Soviet cosmonauts struggled in the aftermath of space voyage. It was not uncommon for the cosmonauts to spend 200 to 300 days in space. Upon their return to Earth they suffered from dizziness, high pulse rates, and heart palpitations. They couldn't walk for a week and after 30 days they were still undergoing therapy for weakened muscles and hearts.

The problem was simply that at zero gravity, the muscles of the body begin to waste away because there is no resistance. It became necessary for scientists to design something that would provide continual resistance to the muscles of the body. As a result of their observation and desire to assist their cosmonauts, Soviet scientists invented the penguin suit, which is a running suit laced with elastic bands. It resists every move the cosmonauts make and forces them to exert

> God has allowed this imperfect world to function as our very own penguin suit.

their strength. God has allowed this imperfect world to function as our very own penguin suit.

Folks, we must embrace all the experiences of life, not just the good and happy ones, but the bad ones, the shameful ones, the wrong ones, and the sad ones too. Although none of us enjoy times of pain we still have the opportunity to benefit from those events. Many of us have a human tendency to run away from our past. Please don't. God can use every experience in our lives for good, but we've got to stop running from them. As painful as they might be we must embrace and process the emotions of these experiences. We must own and learn from these difficult experiences.

Victor Frankl, a Jewish psychiatrist, was imprisoned by the Nazis during World War II. His parents, brother, and wife either died in the camps or were sent to the ovens. One day, as he was naked and alone in a small room he became aware of the one freedom his Nazi captors could not take away. In his work entitled *Man's Search for Meaning* he made this observation:

> Everything can be taken from a man but one thing; the last of human freedoms—to choose one's attitudes in any given set of circumstances, to choose one's own way.[29]

My wife and I have had a number of difficult seasons in our lives. The births of our children were incredibly dangerous and stressful. We've lost three of our four parents. Recently, we've faced one of the most stressful and traumatic moments in our more than thirty years of pastoral ministry. Sometimes, the overwhelming trauma, loss, and pain were almost too much too bear. In 2013, Pastor Rick Warren and his wife, Kay, of Saddleback Community Church experienced the unbelievable heartbreak and tragedy of losing their son,

> Don't let the bad things in life destroy you. Don't let them define you. Let God use them to develop you.

Matthew, who committed suicide. Throughout this very painful and personal journey Rick regularly reminded millions of Christians who are exposed to his teaching ministry of a universal principle. It's a principle that has given me hope in some of my darkest and traumatic times. Don't let the bad things in life destroy you. Don't let them define you. Let God use them to develop you.

REASON #4: GOD MAY ALLOW HURTFUL TIMES SO THAT WE CAN COMFORT OTHERS

> [3] Praise be to the God and Father of our Lord Jesus Christ, the Father of compassion and the God of all comfort, [4] who comforts us in all our troubles, so that we can comfort those in any trouble with the comfort we ourselves have received from God. [5] For just as the

---

[29] Victor Frankl, *Man's Search for Meaning* (Cutchogue, NY: Buccaneer Books, 1992), 75.

sufferings of Christ flow over into our lives, so also through Christ our comfort overflows.
2 Corinthians 1:3-5

In the book of 2 Corinthians, the Apostle Paul makes a tremendous observation about God's master plan in using the difficulties that come into our lives. In the space of a handful of verses, the Apostle Paul uses the Greek word for comfort ten times. The word "comfort" means much more than mere sympathy. It communicates the idea of one person standing alongside another to encourage and support his friend. It illustrates someone who is willing to stand with a person until a particular need is met.

Unfortunately, during traumatic events in a person's life, many people don't feel or sense God's presence or comfort. Sometimes God seems distant. Sometimes God seems uncaring. Before you jump to the conclusion that God isn't intervening and changing difficulties because He doesn't care, soak in the sage observation of gifted Christian author, Philip Yancey:

> The image Jesus left with the world, the cross, the most common image in the Christian religion, is proof that God cares about our suffering and pain. He died of it. Today the image is coated with gold and worn around the necks of beautiful girls, a symbol of how far we can stray from the reality of history. But it stands, unique among all the religions of the world. Many of them have gods. But only one has a God who cared enough to become a man and to die.[30]

History reminds us that God does indeed care. The painful steps of Jesus in this world give ample testimony to how much He cares. He took suffering upon Himself. He was willing to go through the same kind of unfair world that each of us experiences.

In his humanity, Jesus Christ experienced suffering exactly like we do. He didn't sidestep this aspect of life. He totally embraced it. Because He

---

[30] Philip Yancey, *Where is God When it Hurts?* (Grand Rapids: Zondervan, 1977), 161.

became a man, He can truly empathize with us. Dorothy Sayers put it this way:

> For whatever reason God chose to make man as he is—limited and suffering and subject to sorrows and death—He had the honesty and courage to take His own medicine. Whatever game He is playing with His creation, He has kept His own rules and played fair. He can exact nothing from man that He has not exacted from Himself.[31]

Don't miss what I am about to say because I think it can be life-changing. Part of God's master plan to prove to people that He actually cares is to prepare us with life experiences so that we can care for other people in times of hurt and suffering. In other words, God wants you to be His agent to care for people in our world. Listen once more to Philip Yancey, this time as he addresses our role as God's agents of comfort:

> This plan of the body meshes with the way God is working in the world. Sometimes He does enter in, occasionally performing miracles, often giving supernatural strength to those in need. But mainly He relies on us, His agents, to do His work in the world. We announce His message, work for justice, pray for mercy . . . and suffer with the sufferers. We are to comfort each other and bring healing; by doing so we will be recognized as Christ's body.[32]

I realize that some of you are saying, "You've got to be kidding me. I'm so far down that I can't even see the top of the hole that I'm stuck in. There is no way I could comfort anyone." This might describe you right now, but God's not done with you yet. During a particularly difficult season in my life when I experienced tremendous trauma and loss, it took seven months before I could even start to believe that God still had a purpose for my life. Until that moment I wasn't able to see how God

---

[31] Dorothy Sayers, *Christian Letters to a Post-Christian World: A Selection of Essays* (Grand Rapids: Eerdmans Publishing Company, 1969), 14.
[32] Philip Yancey, *Where is God When it Hurts?* (Grand Rapids: Zondervan, 1977), 171-172.

might open up doors or to imagine how He would be able to once again use my giftedness. Finally, I reached the point when I was able to see God's hand through the bad events and believe that He had a new and brighter future for me. It was at that time that I could begin to see how to comfort other people just by telling my story.

All of us have a ministry waiting for us. It is a ministry born out of our very own difficulty, out of our very own challenge, and out of our very own hurt. God has given us the unique chance to pass on His comfort to someone else. He's given us

> We are now God's agents to bring comfort. It's God's ministry for our lives.

the chance to pass on His divine care and compassion. We are now God's agents to bring comfort. It's God's ministry for our lives.

- If you've been comforted you can extend comfort to someone else.
- If you've experienced loss you can sympathize with other people who feel that emptiness.
- If you've survived being emotionally wounded you can show the path of survival to someone else.
- If people have extended empathy to you, you should want to share it with others.

> You can take your worst moments and transform another person's life.

- If you've faced a financial reversal you can encourage another person that there is life after bankruptcy.
- If you've faced a major illness you can walk another person through that overwhelming feeling of uncertainty.

The powerful truth for anyone who has faced difficulties and challenges in their life is a simple one—you can take your worst moments and transform another person's life.

REASON #5: GOD MAY ALLOW HURTFUL TIMES TO BRING US CLOSER TO HIM

> 2"I know that you can do all things; no plan of yours can be thwarted. 3 You asked, 'Who is this that obscures my counsel without knowledge?' Surely I spoke of things I did not understand, things too wonderful for me to know. 4 "You said, 'Listen now, and I will speak; I will question you, and you shall answer me.' 5 My ears had heard of you but now my eyes have seen you. 6 Therefore I despise myself and repent in dust and ashes."
> Job 42:2-6

We all remember the horrific story of Job, the Old Testament saint. For a protracted period of time, everything bad that could happen did. Job got no answers from God and no explanations. He heard absolutely nothing. We aren't told exactly how long Job went through this. We can only imagine the duration of Job's extraordinary pain. For a major season in his life Job struggled with trying to understand what God was trying to teach him and why He was allowing such difficult things into the life of his family. He uttered the same exact questions that we ask:

> If only my anguish could be weighed and all my misery be placed on the scales! It would surely outweigh the sand of the seas.
> Job 6:3

> 8 Oh, that I might have my request, that God would grant what I hope for, 9 that God would be willing to crush me, to let loose and cut me off!
> Job 6:8-9

> If only there were someone to arbitrate between us, to lay his hand upon us both, someone to remove God's rod from me, so that his terror would frighten me no more.
> Job 9:33

Although the entire book of Job is a series of laments and pleas for answer, God deliberately sidestepped the issue. He never explained the cause of Job's suffering. Instead, God reminded Job that if He was wise enough to rule the universe He was wise enough to watch over Job, regardless of how things seemed in the bleakest moments.

Ultimately, after God began to explain Himself as the Creator of the world, Job forgot his cry for vindication. As bizarre as it sounds, Job eventually stopped asking, "Why?" There came a point when Job was finally content to live in a world where he wasn't going to get all the answers to his questions. It was a point when he actually received something better than answers. He caught a glimpse of God Himself.

After listening to example after example of how profoundly powerful and wise God is as the Creator of the world, Job forgot his cry for vindication since he had received something much better: a revelation of the person of God and renewed fellowship with

> There came a point when he actually received something much better than answers. He caught a glimpse of God Himself.

God. He had lost everything, but in that moment he was reminded that he had found God Himself.

This may be one of the most difficult lessons for any of us to learn. Our pain seems to cry out for closure in which we want some kind of explanation. However, God is eager for something else. He wants our pain to draw us closer to Him. He wants us to connect with Him on the deepest level possible.

Christian Reger, a Dachau concentration camp survivor expressed the principle this way:

> Nietzsche said a man can undergo torture if he knows the why of his life . . . But I, here at Dachau, learned something far greater. I learned to know the Who of my life. He was enough to sustain me then, and is enough to sustain me still.[33]

---

[33] Christian Reger, quoted in Philip Yancey, *Where is God When It Hurts?* (Grand Rapids: Zondervan, 1977), 97.

No matter the season we are facing, whatever our pain and hurt, whatever the sense of loss we are trying to process, I believe God is waiting for us to see Him on a deeper level. He wants us to come to Him with our pain and loss. Most importantly, He wants us to sense His love. God is the Who in our life. There is no safer person than Him.

LIFE PRINCIPLES

Allow me to finish this chapter by taking a step back and describing the big picture of what is happening during those tough seasons in our lives. Sometimes it is vital that we don't simply look at reasons for why God occasionally allows trials into the life of the believer. Sometimes we should evaluate the lens or perspective by which we look at the world around us. Sometimes it's how you look at life that makes all the difference.

LIFE PRINCIPLE #1: GOD HAS DESIGNED OUR FUTURE TO BE CONCEALED

> 13 Consider what God has done: Who can straighten what he has made crooked? 14 When times are good, be happy; but when times are bad, consider: God has made the one as well as the other. Therefore, a man cannot discover anything about his future.
> Ecclesiastes 7:13-14

Solomon understood that it is human nature to ask why. He understood that many times we would like to sneak a peek at the future. But he tells us very clearly that God has hidden our future. By using the phrase, "who can straighten what he has made crooked," Solomon is trying to stress the point that no one can overturn what God does. Regardless of what happens we must ultimately submit to God's providence. In God's sovereign plan, the events of our lives can be divided into good things and bad things.

It's clear that the ancient author says, "When times are good be happy and rejoice." But please notice that the author doesn't say, "when times are bad be sad." Why? The reason isn't that complex. Solomon understood that sadness is a natural emotion. You don't have to be told to be sad. Instead, the text tells us to consider. Solomon urges his

WHERE IS GOD WHEN IT HURTS?

readers to consider that God has made both the good and the bad so that we don't know what will happen in the future.

God structures our personal histories in a way that conceals the future, but don't miss what this passage is saying. God has hidden our future because He is compassionate. Allow me to explain the implications of this.

Knowing all the good in our future would remove the joy of discovery and the joy of anticipation. Would we trust God if He just revealed in advance that our life over the next two years would be a series of successes and good times? Would we enjoy life or go after our goals with as much passion if we already knew they were going to happen? It would bring us to the point when we felt we were just going through the motions of a preset path. We might even instinctively compare our goodness with the goodness given to others and complain.

> Knowing all the good in our future would remove the joy of discovery and the joy of anticipation. Knowing all the bad in our future would totally overwhelm us and terrify us.

Knowing all the bad in our future would totally overwhelm us and terrify us. Imagine if God told you everything negative that was going to come into your life. Imagine if as part of your preparation for the New Year, God would tell you what He had in store for you. Many of us would give up, become mentally paralyzed, or simply stop living in the present. In His compassion, God withholds much of our future.

> If we insist on getting the answers to why at every juncture in life we will create a constant sense of tension between God and ourselves.

I realize that if you are in the initial stages of grief and loss, your pain requires you to ask "Why?" over and over again! However, as you move forward in your journey you will eventually see that God has intentionally shrouded much of your future in mystery. If we insist on seeing our entire life with perfect clarity, and if we insist on getting the answers to why at every juncture in life, we will create a constant sense of tension between God and ourselves.

Can I suggest something that I know will help you whenever your future is clouded in uncertainty? Write down at least three things that you are thankful for every single day. Leading psychologists and therapists are increasingly coming to the conclusion that giving thanks regularly is absolutely key to mental health. Psychologists are saying what Scripture has always said, "In everything give thanks for this is the will of God" (1 Thessalonians 5:18).

When the well-known British Methodist preacher William Sangster learned that he had progressive muscular atrophy he embodied this very principle. When he realized that he could not get well, he made four resolutions and kept them to the end:

- I will never complain.
- I will keep the home bright.
- I will count my blessings.
- I will try to turn it to gain.

LIFE PRINCIPLE #2: GOD HAS DESIGNED LIFE TO BE LIVED IN COMMUNITY

> [9] Two are better than one, because they have a good return for their work: [10] If one falls down, his friend can help him up. But pity the man who falls and has no one to help him up! [11] Also, if two lie down together, they will keep warm. But how can one keep warm alone? [12] Though one may be overpowered, two can defend themselves. A cord of three strands is not quickly broken.
> Ecclesiastes 4:9-12

King Solomon used a series of Eastern proverbial sayings to illustrate a universal truth—God designed life to be lived in community. Look at the images that he uses:

- Two are better than one at maximizing their talents and energy.
- Two are better than one in times of difficulty because someone will be there to pick up the other.
- Two are better than one in facing hardships.

- Two are better than one because their strength is increased.

Through most of my early adult life I was pretty self-sufficient. I lived pretty independently of other folks. However, in my early 30s I began to realize that despite a person's giftedness, personality, and confidence, God has designed the spiritual life to be lived in community.

Over the last several years I survived because I had a community of family and close friends who took care of me. They believed in me, listened to me, supported me, and loved me unconditionally. Each of us needs people who will truly understand us, rally around us, and stand in solidarity with us. This is never more crucial than when we face hurtful and devastating moments in our lives.

LIFE PRINCIPLE #3: GOD HAS DESIGNED LIFE TO BE LIVED IN HIS SHADOW

> [1] Remember your Creator in the days of your youth, before the days of trouble come and the years approach when you will say, "I find no pleasure in them" . . . [6] Remember him—before the silver cord is severed, or the golden bowl is broken; before the pitcher is shattered at the spring, or the wheel broken at the well, [7] and the dust returns to the ground it came from, and the spirit returns to God who gave it.
> Ecclesiastes 12:1, 6-7

The Hebrew word "remember" doesn't just mean to remember that God exists. It means to live your life with what you know about God clearly in view. In other words, "live your life in His shadow."

In order to make his point, the author of Ecclesiastes intentionally begins to describe the final years of a person's life. His point is clear. There is coming a day when the sorrow and difficulty of advancing age outweigh the joy of discovery and the joy of anticipation.

Death is pictured by the extinguishing of light:

- The golden bowl holds a flame.
- The silver cord that holds it breaks.
- The bowl crashes to the floor and the light goes out.

Death is also pictured by the image of water:

- The pitcher that holds water is shattered.
- The wheel by which water is drawn from the well is broken.

As Solomon describes death in these poetic phrases, he twice uses the Hebrew word "remember." His point is quite simple. Everything we do as Christians we must do before an audience of one. God Himself is our audience.

If you and I live in the shadow of a God who is watching and waiting to reward the way we live life in this present world, it will make all the difference. We must make value judgments and choices and place our trust in Him while realizing that His shadow should be over everything we do. Whether the things that come into your life are good or bad, deserved or undeserved we are to live in His shadow. It's the only way to leave footprints that others will follow.

CONCLUSION

God has used the temporary nature of life on Earth as a divine compass that points to our true eternal home. Our life is a divine alarm clock that constantly reminds us of God's desire that our eternal destiny have a profound bearing on our lives. C.S. Lewis described for us the necessity of allowing God's perspective to dominate our daily experience:

> The moment you wake up each morning, all your wishes and hopes for the day rush at you like wild animals. And the first job each morning consists in shoving it all back; in listening to that other voice, taking that other point of view, letting that other, larger, stronger, quieter life come flowing in.[34]

We ought to listen to the small still voice, because every day His voice reminds us:

---

[34] C.S. Lewis, *Mere Christianity* (New York: Harper Collins, 2002), 199.

- Of our true course.
- That there are eternal rewards for our actions.
- That there are eternal objectives at stake.
- That there are eternal standards.
- Of our true bearings.

His voice reminds us that not until we reach heaven's doors will we totally and finally understand God's plan for our life and the many difficult seasons that will come into our experience.

SUGGESTIONS FOR ADDITIONAL READING

Philip Yancey, *Where is God When It Hurts?*

Yancey's classic book deals with the issue of evil and suffering from a practical viewpoint. Yancey doesn't present a formal defense of the Christian God in the face of evil and suffering, but more of a pastoral treatment of how the believer should respond to our God in the midst of hardships and trials. It is a very encouraging read.

Mike Fabarez, *Lifelines for Tough Times*

Mike Fabarez is a gifted preacher at Compass Bible Church in Southern California. His book is designed to help Christians better relate to God and to walk with Him when things go wrong. It offers tremendous insights for the follower of Christ who is trying to make sense of the Christian journey.

Charles F. Stanley, *How to Handle Adversity*

Charles Stanley is one of the greatest preachers who has taught in America over the last forty years. His insightful and compassionate advice is akin to that of a wise grandfather who has lived through difficulties and wants to help those around him. This book is short and a very easy read.

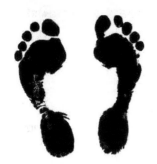

FOOTPRINT FIVE:
WHY DOES GOD ALLOW EVIL & SUFFERING?

If Christians are going to leave indelible footprints for family and friends to follow, we must address one of the great questions of our day—why does God allow evil and suffering? About five years ago, I was reminded of the pressing nature of this question when I got a phone call from my dad. His words were simple yet heartbreaking, "Tom has ALS."

What followed was a two year journey during which my spiritual mentor and former pastor slowly yet surely lost all control of his body, speech, and ultimately his ability to breathe. It was cruel and heart-wrenching. In fact, I had private moments when I secretly asked God, "Why? Why?"

It shouldn't surprise anyone that millions of people are deeply distressed by the presence of evil and suffering in the world. Many people are so distressed that they routinely blame God and the Christian faith. Charles Templeton, who is one of biggest critics of the Christian faith, expressed what so many feel:

> A loving God could not possibly be the author of the horrors we have been describing—horrors that continue every day, have continued since time began, and will continue as long as life exists. It is an inconceivable tale of suffering and death, and because the tale is fact—is, in truth, the history of the world—it is obvious that there cannot be a loving God.[35]

This chapter helps defend the Christian belief in an all-powerful and all-loving God. As I attempt to explain this defense, I want to include insights from the wisest man who ever lived—Jesus of Nazareth.

---

[35] Charles Templeton, *Farewell to God: My Reasons for Rejecting the Christian Faith* (Toronto: McClelland & Stewart, 1999), 201.

Luke 13 records a conversation where Jesus was asked about a collapsed tower that killed eighteen men. Most likely, this tower was an aqueduct built by Romans who were employing local Jews in its construction. In the aftermath of this tragedy, many within the religious establishment began to point fingers. In response to this swirling controversy, listen to what Jesus said:

> 4 Or those eighteen who died when the tower in Siloam fell on them—do you think they were more guilty than all the others living in Jerusalem? 5 I tell you, no! But unless you repent, you too will all perish.
> Luke 13:4-5

INSIGHT: DON'T TRY TO CONNECT THE DOTS

Jesus used the incident to point out a very simple truth. We live in an imperfect world where evil, pain, suffering, and injustice come uninvited into our lives. Jesus was shocked that people would attempt to claim that they knew precisely what God's purposes were for this event. With his emphatic statement of, "No," Jesus made it very clear that we live in an imperfect world where tragic events fall on the righteous and unrighteous alike. Evil, suffering, disease, and tragedy defy easy explanation. Gifted evangelical pastor Erwin Lutzer in his insightful book, *Where Was God?* offers this caution: ←

> We live in an imperfect world where evil, pain, suffering, and injustice come uninvited into our lives.

> We must be warned to not quickly read into these events our own specific view of what God is up to. We've already learned that people will always give these disasters an interpretation compatible with their religion, their understanding of sin, and their own convictions of what they think God should do. Let's avoid these extremes.[36]

---

[36] Erwin W. Lutzer, *Where Was God? Answers to Tough Questions About God and Natural Disasters* (Carol Stream: Tyndale House Publishers, 2006), 17.

As Christians, we might be tempted to use this chapter to explain every specific event or to communicate to people that we know exactly why this happened. We should not do this. Jesus didn't try.

- We aren't obligated nor should we try to give people the exact answer to why something happened to them.
- We simply aren't smart enough to answer these questions.
- We should be more concerned about showing compassion while supporting people through their difficulties.

Remember, Job felt compelled to find an answer for all the issues that came into his life. He wanted to figure everything out. Notice this observation by Alvin Plantinga, the gifted philosopher: ✔

> When God replies to Job, he doesn't explain his reasons for permitting Job's suffering. Instead he attacks Job's unthinking assumption that if he, Job, can't see what God's reasons might be, then probably God doesn't have any reasons. . . . Job can't see what God's reasons might be; he infers that probably God doesn't have any. God's reply, in essence, is that Job knows far too little to draw such a conclusion.[37]

With this as a backdrop, let's begin by using a crazy example to illustrate what I'm going to try to accomplish in this chapter. Imagine for a moment that the police come to your house and accuse you of driving ninety miles per hour on Thanksgiving Day. The officers say that you were seen driving like a madman and that everyone in your car was screaming, "We want turkey and we want it now."

After you call a lawyer, what do you think you would start doing? You would begin to outline the various reasons for why you weren't driving the car that was allegedly speeding. In other words, you would begin to build a defense.

---

[37] Alvin Plantinga and Michael Tooley, *Knowledge of* God (Malden: Blackwell Publishing, 2008), 182.

- You weren't on the road at that time.
- You have a twin who likes to pretend to be you.
- You have a home video of you and your family enjoying turkey at the very time of the alleged speeding.

When it comes to preparing ourselves to have meaningful conversations with our skeptical family and friends, it is essential that we build a defense. Remember, it's not our goal to explain the precise reason why God allows every single act of evil or suffering. In

> It's not our goal to explain the precise reason why God allows every single act of evil or suffering.

fact, I'm not sure if there is a more futile pursuit. How could any human mind comprehend all the specific reasons God might have for every instance of pain and sorrow? It is simply impossible for finite human beings to provide a systematic and exhaustive explanation for all the evil in the world. Lutzer offers his perspective on this approach:

> My intention is not to pry into God's diary and pretend that I can see all of His purposes; indeed, there are plenty of His purposes in these disasters that will never be known to us. Ultimately, only God knows all the whys and the wherefores. Rather, I want to show that natural evil is not incompatible with a good and caring God.[38]

The goal of the Christian defense for our belief in an all-powerful and all-loving God is to prove that the mere presence of evil in this world does not disprove the existence of God. Unfortunately, people see all the evil and suffering in the world and think that it absolutely proves that God is not really loving or that He's impotent. We must demonstrate that this isn't true.

---

[38] Erwin W. Lutzer, *Where Was God? Answers to Tough Questions About God and Natural Disasters* (Carol Stream: Tyndale House Publishers, 2006), xv.

THE CHRISTIAN DEFENSE

As we begin to build the Christian defense of an all-powerful and all-loving God it is vital that we understand the concept of human free will. →Free will is simply the freedom to do otherwise. In any given decision we can choose to do anything we desire. Think about it this way. Every week after church a person has a choice to do different things:

- Some will go directly home.
- Some will begin to watch God's sport—football.
- Some will eat massive quantities of food.
- Some will take a nap.
- Some will go shopping.

No one compels a person to make choices. No one hypnotizes us and causes us to do a certain thing, not even God. That is called free will.

God created a world full of people who possess free will. He didn't want a world of robots that would only do what He said. He envisioned creatures that had the capacity to choose to enjoy and love Him. The starting place for defending our belief in an all-powerful and all-loving God in the face

> God created a world full of people who possess free will. He didn't want a world of robots that would only do what He said.

of so much evil and suffering in the world is the free will defense.

EXPLANATION #1: FREE WILL DEFENSE

God decided to create a world in which human beings were given the dignity of free will. Jesus clearly recognized this as He interacted with people in His public ministry. Listen to the following verse:

> O Jerusalem, Jerusalem, you who kill the prophets and stone those sent to you, how often I have longed to gather your children together, as a hen gathers her chicks under her wings, but you were not willing.
> Matthew 23:37

Jesus actually longed for the citizens of Jerusalem to respond to His message. However, there was something that even Jesus couldn't do. Jesus could not make someone act against that person's own choice. The nation willfully refused to turn to the Lord. This passage is absolutely clear—Jesus chose to honor the dignity of free will.

Think about the implications. In a world where God has granted people the dignity of free will we should expect that some people will choose to do evil. Obviously, we would like for everyone to choose good and to choose virtue. However, the simple reality is that if we truly believe that

> In a world where God has granted people the dignity of free will we should expect that some people will choose to do evil.

every single person in the history of mankind is a free, autonomous being, we must acknowledge that within that capacity is the freedom to choose evil, to choose a path that differs from God's ideal for humanity. ⬅

God does not tamper with our free will. He doesn't play mind-tricks with us. He doesn't hypnotize us. He gives us the dignity of free choice. ⬅

It's important to realize that for over a century secular philosophers and thinkers at major universities have made Christians squirm by using the following logical argument: If God is all-powerful He should be able to prevent evil and if God is all-loving He should be willing to prevent evil, but since He didn't then God doesn't exist. What?

Fortunately, Alvin Plantinga, a Christian thinker at Notre Dame has championed the free will defense so effectively that most secular philosophers admit that he's proven the point. Listen to his words:

> To create creatures capable of moral good, therefore, He must create creatures capable of moral evil; and He can't give these creatures the freedom to perform evil and at the same time prevent them from doing so. . . . The fact that free creatures sometimes go

wrong, however, counts neither against God's omnipotence nor against His goodness.[39]

> The simple reality is that if God grants people genuine freedom to choose as they like, it is impossible for Him to guarantee what their choices will be.

Before we go any further I believe it is really important to clarify a few things. I've presented these issues often enough to recognize that whenever free will is mentioned some Christians immediately begin to ask questions about God's sovereignty.

The Bible teaches a balance between human free will (Matt 23:37) and God's sovereignty (Acts 4:24, 28). Although we will never be able to perfectly explain that relationship I believe we should hold them in perfect balance.

Look at a moment in Jesus' public ministry when He affirmed the twin truths of God's sovereignty and man's responsibility within one single verse. Jesus was experiencing one of the most crucial and most stressful times of his ministry—the night of his betrayal. He was at the table with His disciples and he uttered these words:

> [21] But the hand of him who is going to betray me is with mine on the table. [22] The Son of Man will go as it has been decreed. But woe to that man who betrays him!
> Luke 22:21-22

Jesus recognized that His path to the cross was a part of God's pre-determined plan for the world. He affirmed that God's sovereign will had led Him to be crucified for the sins of the world. However, in the same breath, Jesus also pronounced personal judgment (woe) upon Judas for his actions. Judas was held personally responsible and culpable for his deceptive betrayal of Jesus.

---

[39] Alvin C. Plantinga, *God, Freedom, and Evil* (Grand Rapids: Eerdmans Publishing Company, 1977), 30.

Scripture clearly teaches that God holds free creatures morally responsible for their choices. Lucifer was condemned to hell for his rebellion (Rev. 20:10; 1 Tim.3:6). The angels who followed him were also held responsible (Rev 12:4, Jude 6-7). Adam and Eve were condemned for their actions (Gen. 3:1-19; Rom. 5:12), as are all humans since the fall (Rom. 3:19). Even depraved human beings have the power of free choice.

Theologian Norman Geisler, in his book *Chosen But Free* makes a compelling point that we can't afford to miss:

> It is not rational to hold someone responsible when he or she could not have responded, and God is not irrational . . . Reason also demands that all moral creatures are morally free; that is, they have the ability to respond one way or another. Whatever evil we do and are responsible for, we could have responded otherwise.[40]

Why eulogize people like Mother Theresa and Billy Graham if they had no free choice in the matter? Why vilify people like Adolf Hitler and Osama Bin Laden if they could not help doing what they did? Praise and blame make no real sense unless those praised or blamed were free to make those choices. Think about it this way—if you tell your child not to go out the front door but make it impossible for him or her to do anything other than go out the front door, why would you punish the child for their actions?

God determined that the betrayal must happen, but Judas was personally responsible for his act. Personal responsibility is built upon the bedrock truth of human free will. In other words, we are morally responsible for our free actions. John MacArthur puts it this way:

> Every detail of the crucifixion of Christ was under the sovereign control of God and in accord with His eternal purpose. The fact that Judas' betrayal was part of God's plan does not free him from the

---

[40] Norman L. Geisler, *Chosen But Free: A Balanced View of God's Sovereignty and Free Will* (Minneapolis: Bethany House Publishers, 2010), 41-42.

guilt of a crime he entered into willfully. God's sovereignty is never a legitimate excuse for human guilt.[41] *Say it again*

Within this one single verse Jesus revealed His belief in God's sovereignty and man's responsibility and made no attempt to resolve them. He left these twin truths in tension. Shouldn't we take the same approach? Gifted pastor and author, Timothy Keller expresses a similar insight in his book *Walking with God through Pain and Suffering*:

Wow

> The Bible teaches that God is completely in control of what happens in history and yet he exercises that control in such a way that human beings are responsible for their freely chosen actions and the results of those actions. Human freedom and God's direction of historical events are therefore completely compatible.[42]

Ultimately, we must embrace both God's sovereignty and man's responsibility knowing that this tension will only be fully resolved in the infinite mind of God. Distinguished Christian theologian J.I. Packer offers this perspective:

> Personal responsibility is built upon the bedrock truth of human free will. In other words, we are morally responsible for our free actions.

Wow?

> The whole point of an antinomy—in theology, at any rate—is that it is not a real contradiction, though it looks like one. It is an apparent incompatibility between two apparent truths. An antinomy exists when two principles stand side by side, seemingly irreconcilable, yet both undeniable. There are cogent reasons for believing each of them; each rests on clear and solid evidence; but it is a mystery to you how they can be squared with each other.[43]

---

[41] John MacArthur, *The MacArthur Bible Commentary* (Dallas: Thomas Nelson, 2005), 1326.

[42] Timothy Keller, *Walking with God through Pain and Suffering* (New York: Penguin Group, 2013), 140.

[43] J.I. Packer, *Evangelism and the Sovereignty of God* (Downers Grove: InterVarsity Press, 1977), 18-19.

WHY DOES GOD ALLOW EVIL & SUFFERING?

Ultimately, an antinomy (God's sovereignty and man's responsibility) can only be fully resolved in the infinite mind of God. Our defense of God in the presence of evil and suffering in the world must not eliminate man's free choice.

> God eternally determined that Christ would go to the cross, yet Jesus was absolutely clear that He gave His life freely. Jesus recognized the balance between sovereignty and free will.

EXPLANATION #2: THE GREATEST WAY DEFENSE

The free will defense is the first step of our defense, but sometimes we get tripped up on our way to the second step. People will ask, "Is this the best that God can do?" or, "Honestly, with so much of the world messed up, couldn't God have done a little better?"

Here's a tiny word of advice. Don't insult the intelligence of your skeptical friends or the greatness of God by suggesting that our present world is the very best that God can accomplish. It is more complicated than this. In fact, how we answer this question prepares us to build the second part of our defense.

The Christian does not claim that our present evil world is the best of all possible worlds. However, our present

> We believe that this world where God has decided to value the dignity of free will is the best path to get to the best possible world. *IN CLASS* *sited*

world is the best possible way to the best world. We believe that this world where God has decided to value the dignity of free will is the best path to get to the best possible world. ← *IN CLASS*

While honoring humanity's free will God also desires to maximize the amount of people who will freely choose to be with Him in heaven. This present world is the best way to accomplish this goal. Biblical expert Dr. Norman Geisler puts it this way:

> The greatest-way (defense) does not claim that this is the best of all possible worlds. On the contrary, it admits that the world is evil and is perhaps nearer to being the worst possible world than the best.

→ However, this view also holds that this evil world is the best possible way to the best world.[44]

Of course, people ask, many times with great sincerity, "Why couldn't God have immediately made this place called heaven and put all of us there?" In fact, people often get very, very mad at God because Earth is not heaven. I think it's time that we remember two fundamental truths about heaven.

WE ENTER HEAVEN BY CHOICE

Heaven is not the kind of place where God can simply place people. → Heaven must be chosen. The Apostle John makes this observation,

> Yet to all who received him, to those who believed in his name, he gave the right to become children of God.
> John 1:12

The message of the Bible is that God will not force people against their will to inhabit a place where He dwells. God has designed heaven to be a place for only those people who choose to be there. In a world where people have free will, entrance to the best possible world (heaven) must be gained through freedom of choice. It's the only way. C.S. Lewis eloquently expressed it this way:

> There are only two kinds of people in the end: those who say to God, 'Thy will be done,' and those to whom God says, in the end, 'Thy will be done.'[45]

WE ENTER HEAVEN PREPARED

✓ Heaven is a place where people have learned how to live in the presence of a perfect God. Matthew's Gospel records the unique request from the mother of the sons of Zebedee:

---

[44] Norman Geisler, *The Roots of Evil* (Grand Rapids: Zondervan, 1978), 45.
[45] C.S. Lewis, *The Great Divorce* (New York: Macmillan Publishing Co., 1946), 72.

She said, "Grant that one of these two sons of mine may sit at your right and the other at your left in your kingdom." 22 "You don't know what you are asking," Jesus said to them. "Can you drink the cup I am going to drink?" "We can," they answered. 23 Jesus said to them, "You will indeed drink from my cup, but to sit at my right or left is not for me to grant. These places belong to those for whom they have been prepared by my Father."
Matthew 20:22-23

Jesus' answer reveals a general principle. Our place of service in heaven will be determined in large measure by our faithfulness in our life on Earth. In a moral sense, we are learning on Earth how to live forever in heaven. We learn throughout our lives and through the witness of history that sin is horrific and that pursuing God is the only response that makes sense.

> We will eventually live in a suffering-free, evil-free world filled with redeemed human beings. However, this kind of world could not be entered into immediately. It can only be gained by choice and through the preparation of this world.

- This life prepares us to see the importance of faith.
- This life prepares us to see the awfulness of sin.
- This life prepares us to see that God can be trusted.
- This life prepares us to see the beauty of God's love.

We will eventually live in a suffering–free, evil-free world filled with redeemed human beings. However, that kind of world could not be entered into immediately. It can only be gained by choice and through the preparation of this present world.

EXPLANATION #3: SOUL MAKING DEFENSE

There's one final defense. Imagine for a moment that we have been asked to create a world where our child, grandchild, or niece/nephew is required to become the best human being possible. We've been given all the power. The only constraint is free will. What kind of world would have the best chance to produce the best human being?

Rerecd

97

Would you choose a world in which every pleasure can be experienced with no limitations, a world where the word "no" is never mentioned, and a world where there are absolutely no challenges? Or would you choose a world where people will ultimately face challenges, trials, and even difficulties and pain? The simple truth is that if your child or grandchild never faced any kind of difficulty, challenge, or struggle they would be ethically and morally disfigured.

This third defense is actually an explanation that we find within one of the most famous Scriptures:

> 28 And we know that in all things God works for the good of those who love him, who have been called according to his purpose. 29 For those God foreknew he also predestined to be conformed to the likeness of his Son
> Romans 8:28-29

Much of life is not good in and of itself. There are terrible, horrific, and painful things that happen all the time in our present evil world. However, Romans 8 reveals that God is able to use an imperfect world brought on by free will for a greater good. That ultimate good is to conform as many people as possible to the image of His Son.

If God's aim is to create people conformed to the likeness of His Son then it makes sense that we live in our present world. An idealistic playpen is simply not the kind of world that produces people who are in the process of being made like God and who wish to be with God. Think about what this means. Without an imperfect world, we lose:

- The chance to develop character.
- The chance to exhibit courage and faithfulness.
- The opportunity to trust and love God despite our circumstances.
- The chance to have faith.

We see this principle lived out every single day. Sometimes it is necessary to allow suffering in a person's life in order to bring about some greater good.

- Doctors often inflict painful procedures and treatments on people for the purpose of promoting better health and longer life. ✔
- Parents take away toys and privileges because they want their child to grow up with self-control.
- Contestants on *The Biggest Loser* go through incredible sacrifice because they know it's necessary for a greater good.
- All of us have had those moments when we look back on adversity and realize that we are a better person because of what we went through. ✔

Over the last three years I've personally found this to be true. My wife and I have faced the most difficult season in our lives. However, now that I am on the other side of those difficulties I can see the following things:

- He was preparing me on the inside.
- He was showing me the importance of utter dependence upon Him.
- He was giving me greater empathy toward people who face difficulties.
- He was preparing me for our apologetic ministry so that I can encourage the faith of others and expand His influence.

SUMMARY OF OUR DEFENSE

God decided to grant human beings the dignity of free will—an opportunity to enjoy Him. He knew that some would use this choice for evil. He realized that this was the only way for free moral beings to choose to live in a perfect place and choose to be like God. Finally, God has chosen to use the difficulties of this broken world to conform people to the likeness of His Son.

Once a Christian understands this threefold defense, it's vital that he or she understand how to answer some difficult questions that disturb people or are confusing.

WHY DID GOD CREATE EVIL?

Some critics faced with the reality of God as the creator and the reality of evil sincerely ask why God created evil. Let's try to answer this question both with the clear declaration of Scripture and with some practical wisdom.

First, God cannot and never did create evil. God is the ultimate source of good. He is perfect, good, and not capable of evil. In other words, God is not the direct author of evil. Scripture describes it this way:

> And this is the message we have heard from Him and announce to you, that God is light, and in Him there is no darkness at all.
> 1 John 1:5

The evil that exists is a corruption of a good thing—the power of free choice. Free choice is the cause of the corruption of the good world that God made. Think about the following examples that illustrate the corruption of things that are essentially good:

> God created something good and noble like the power of free choice; yet within the power of free choice came the potential corruption of evil.

- Blindness is a lack of sight.
- Absence of limbs results in the lack of normal physical mobility.
- Sickness is the lack of good health.

God created something good and noble like the power of free choice; yet within the power of free choice came the potential corruption of evil.

WHY COULDN'T GOD CREATE A WORLD WITHOUT EVIL?

If you were to take a poll of average people on the street and ask them to describe one quality about God, what do you think they would say? Many people might suggest that God is all-loving or all-powerful. Therefore, it's not surprising that whenever your typical unchurched family or friend thinks about the presence of evil, his or her mind naturally gravitates to the power of God:

- Why couldn't God create a world without evil?
- Why didn't He stop this guy from doing bad?
- Why did He allow this horrific act?

God's power is constrained in certain logical ways. In other words, there are certain things that God can't do, but not because He is somehow overwhelmed by the immensity of the task. It's simply a logical impossibility. Think of the following examples:

- He can't make a round object square.
- He can't make a rock so big that he can't move it.
- He can't act in a way that is inconsistent with His divine qualities.
- He can't prevent people with free will from doing evil.

C.S. Lewis described it this way:

> If you choose to say 'God can give a creature free-will and at the same time withhold free-will from it,' you have not succeeded in saying anything about God: meaningless combinations of words do not suddenly acquire a meaning because we prefix to them the two other words: 'God can.' . . . It is no more possible for God than for the weakest of his creatures to carry out both of two mutually exclusive alternatives, not because his power meets an obstacle, but because nonsense remains nonsense, even when we talk it about God.[46]

Before we address other difficult questions I would like to reflect upon a second insight that Jesus offered during His public ministry.

Jesus once encountered a woman with an incredibly diverse and sordid past. You couldn't find two more different people—the Samaritan woman and the Son of God. Think about this for a moment. Jesus had the moral high ground. He possessed absolute truth. He was smarter and more educated. But listen to what happens:

> [7] When a Samaritan woman came to draw water, Jesus said to her, "Will you give me a drink?" [8] (His disciples had gone into the town to buy food.) [9] The Samaritan woman said to him, "You are a Jew and I am a Samaritan woman. How can you ask me for a drink?" (For

---

[46] C.S. Lewis, *The Problem of Pain* (New York: Macmillan Publishing Co., 1976), 28.

Jews do not associate with Samaritans.) [10] Jesus answered her, "If you knew the gift of God and who it is that asks you for a drink, you would have asked him and he would have given you living water."
John 4:7-10

Jesus embarked on a series of questions and veiled statements so that the two of them could talk. Here's the insight that I believe we must glean from the example of Jesus:

INSIGHT: DON'T LECTURE, DIALOGUE

Most of our unchurched or unsaved friends don't want to hear a lecture, and most of us feel scared to even have a conversation. Why not just begin to ask questions?

- Asking questions is an effective way to start a conversation.
- Asking questions is an effective way to better understand why a person thinks the way they do.
- Asking questions is an effective way to gently challenge people to think outside their politically correct mindset.

There is a greater chance of us winning a hearing from someone if we ask the questions that we know will lead in the right direction rather than simply telling them that they are wrong. After all, no one likes to be told they're wrong. Sometimes it's easier if you find out yourself. Questions can help accomplish this. In fact, that's how Jesus affected the life of the Samaritan woman.

Let me illustrate this process as we tackle another related question.

WHY DOESN'T GOD STOP EVIL? CLASS site

People observe the most horrible of situations and ask out loud why God couldn't selectively intervene to stop evil.

- Why doesn't God stop the terrorist before he blows up something?
- Why doesn't God stop the murderer before he callously takes the innocent life of someone?

- Why doesn't God stop the drunk driver before he takes the life of another motorist?

Here's the basic answer to this question: God can't remove moral evil without contradicting human free will and the entire world that hinges on people's free choice. Of course, it's vitally important that we develop ways to communicate this truth in a fashion that is easy for people to understand. Think about the implications of the following scenarios.

> God can't remove moral evil without contradicting human free will and the entire world that hinges on people's free choice.

SCENARIO #1: IF HE DID, LIFE WOULD BE CHAOTIC

If God decided to intervene to stop evil, suffering, and pain, life as we know it would be chaotic. Imagine what it would actually look like if God felt compelled to intervene whenever someone was going to do something evil. I hope you'll see that with each scenario it gets more and more chaotic. Think of the following examples.

> If God was to stop evil, would He prevent the thought from coming into a person's head or simply freeze a person before they commit the act of evil?

First, if God was to stop evil, would He prevent the thought from coming into a person's head or simply freeze a person before he or she could commit the act of evil? The movie *Minority Report* starring Tom Cruise features three pre-cogs—mutated humans who have pre-cognitive ability. These mutants have the ability to see into the future to when a person is going to commit a crime. Before the crime is committed these pre-cogs notify the police, who intervene before the crime occurs. Would people embrace a world where God didn't allow the fullest expression of choice? Most people would not be willing to sacrifice our sense of choice if this meant that certain thoughts or desires could never be acted upon.

Second, if God had to freeze someone, how long would the person be paralyzed? When would he or she snap out of it? Would the person remember what he or she had been thinking about or would God wipe away the person's memory? Would those who watched this happen also be frozen? Furthermore, would it be possible for God to freeze time for one person while allowing time to continue for someone else?

Third, if God were to regularly intervene He couldn't keep it a secret. If God was to stop evil, isn't it possible that people would become even more empowered to attempt evil acts knowing that some divine force was going to reach down and attempt to stop it? This would create a world where all sorts of mad men would try to do things knowing or thinking that God might intervene. People might jump off buildings trying to kill themselves or seeking notoriety by getting their name in the newspaper. This environment would foster extreme cases of copy-cat evil.

SCENARIO #2: IF HE DID, LIFE WOULD BE SCARY

We must remember that one of the biggest causes of the pain and suffering that come into our world is also the source for most of the great satisfaction in our lives as humans. This satisfaction comes from the ability to freely choose how to live our lives.

In their hurt and pain a person may ask God to stop evil, but what if He decides to intervene in things in which you really don't want His involvement? What if God chose to selectively remove things that you don't like? If He did, life itself would become scary because God would be obligated to stop/intervene all acts of evil and not just certain acts of evil. Gifted Christian author Paul Little makes this observation:

> If God were to stamp out evil today, he would do a complete job. His action would have to include our lies and personal impurities, our lack of love, and our failure to do good. Suppose God were to decree that at midnight tonight all evil would be removed from the universe—who of us would still be here after midnight?[47]

---

[47] Paul Little, *Know Why You Believe* (Downers Grove: InterVarsity Press, 2008), 81.

WHAT ABOUT NATURAL DISASTERS AND OTHER TRAGEDIES?

The primary focus of this chapter has been moral evil. Moral evil is the kind of evil that human beings choose as a result of their own free will. But there is another kind of evil. Natural evil occurs as a consequence of nature. Examples of natural evil are earthquakes, tornadoes, floods, personal tragedies, and diseases.

A watching world is quick to believe God is morally responsible for these natural tragedies. When tragedies such as the 2005 earthquake in India and Pakistan that killed 80,000, or the tsunami that hit Sri Lanka, Thailand, and India that killed approximately 240,000, many observers struggle with God's inaction in our fallen world. As one newsman who was commenting on Hurricane Katrina, put it, "If this world is the product of intelligent design, then the designer has some explaining to do."[48]

> While some Scriptures indicate that God permitted events rather than ordaining them (Job 1), there are other cases, like the tragedy of the collapsed tower of Siloam, when Jesus Himself refused to speculate on God's direct role (Luke 13:1-5).

The challenge to the Christian faith that results from the presence of natural disasters and tragedies is for us to explain God's specific role. Of course, this is no easy task.

Some Christians believe God is powerless. They believe He can't prevent our world from being devastated by natural tragedies. Other Christians believe God has wound up the world and no longer interacts with the natural systems in place. However, as a person reads the Old Testament it becomes quite clear that God not only created the world but intervened at different times. The Bible provides many examples in which God was directly involved with natural disasters. The flood during Noah's time, the plagues of Egypt, and the great wind that hit Jonah's

[48] Erwin W. Lutzer, *Where Was God? Answers to Tough Questions About God and Natural Disasters* (Carol Stream: Tyndale House Publishers, 2006), xiii.

ship clearly show God's direct involvement in history. The Scriptures paint a picture of a truly sovereign God:

> [24] When they heard this, they raised their voices together in prayer to God. "Sovereign Lord," they said, "you made the heavens and the earth and the sea, and everything in them. . . . [28] They did what your power and will had decided beforehand should happen. "
> Acts 4:24-28

> [6]The LORD does whatever pleases him, in the heavens and on the earth, in the seas and all their depths. [7]He makes clouds rise from the ends of the earth; he sends lightning with the rain and brings out the wind from his storehouses.
> Psalm 135:6-7

In light of God's clear involvement in history, how is the Christian supposed to navigate these difficult issues? The following insights may be helpful:

INSIGHT #1: WE CANNOT UNDERSTAND ALL OF GOD'S SOVEREIGN PURPOSES.

Noted author John Piper says, "God had hundreds of thousands of purposes, most of which will remain hidden to us until we are able to grasp them at the end of the age."[49] Obviously, we will never know all of God's purposes and objectives for permitting the events that happen in our present evil world. It is clear that His purposes are more complex than merely keeping people alive on Earth as long as possible. God stands outside of time and therefore can see everything completely and perfectly—something we can never do.

---

[49] From John Piper, "Whence and Why?" World Magazine (September 4, 1999), quoted in Erwin Lutzer, *Where Was God?*, 38.

INSIGHT #2: WE CANNOT ALWAYS DISCERN WHETHER EVENTS ARE ORDAINED, PERMITTED, OR THE BY-PRODUCTS OF A FALLEN WORLD.

It is difficult, if not impossible to categorically state God's role in the events of our world. Sometimes He works directly while other times He works indirectly through secondary causes. The Scriptures gives us a very complex picture of God's working in the world:

- God ordains some events (Luke 22:22).
- God permits other events (Job 1).
- God uses tragic illness for His sovereign purposes (John 9:1-3).
- God allows the normal by-products of a fallen world (Luke 13:1-5).

INSIGHT #3: GOD'S MORAL CHARACTER IS WITHOUT BLAME.

In the midst of the moral quandary surrounding the destruction of the inhabitants of Sodom, Abraham proclaims that God is above reproach when he states:

> Far be it from you to do such a thing—to kill the righteous with the wicked, treating the righteous and the wicked alike. Far be it from you! Will not the Judge of all the earth do right?"
> Genesis 18:25

Lutzer affirms this same conclusion with the observation:

> Should God be blamed for destructive disasters that create unfathomable human suffering? Of course, the word blame implies wrongdoing and I don't believe such a word should ever be applied to the Almighty.[50]

---

[50] Erwin W. Lutzer, *Where Was God?*, 35-36.

INSIGHT #4: CERTAIN DISASTERS AND TRAGEDIES ARE BUILT INTO THE VERY FABRIC OF LIFE.

All of humanity lives in a fallen world. Scripture tells us "the creation was subjected to frustrations . . . We know that the whole creation has been groaning in the pains of childbirth right up to the present time (Romans 8:20, 22)." Lutzer draws the following implication:

> Natural disasters only catch our attention when they are of great magnitude with many simultaneous deaths and unbelievable devastations to property. These disasters are really only a dramatic acceleration of what is happening all the time.[51]

Although we will never be able to totally understand God's purposes for tragedies and disasters, the following explanations are helpful in explaining why God might not choose to intervene and stop natural disasters and tragedies.

> Although these natural processes produce natural evils, if God were to remove these natural evils He would also have to remove the natural processes themselves.

First, natural processes produce natural evil. The earth is the only planet in our solar system that maintains human life. Although these natural processes produce natural evils, if God were to remove these natural evils He would also have to remove the natural processes themselves.

Think about the following examples:

- There is rain; therefore there is flooding.
- There is too little rain; therefore there are droughts, fires, and famines.
- The earth's crust can move; therefore there are earthquakes.

---

[51] Ibid., 63.

- The earth's atmosphere produces conditions for rain and snow, but those same conditions produce hurricanes, typhoons, and tornadoes.

The amount of regular intervention necessary to remove all the natural evils would produce a world that we would not recognize and to which we would not be able to respond adequately. What would happen if God began to suspend the very natural laws that we count on every single day? What if we couldn't depend on gravity, on having the correct amount of oxygen in the air, and on many other life-sustaining properties? These fine-tuning factors give us order and understanding of our present world. I think God has done a pretty amazing job with our planet. After all, it is the only planet in the universe that can sustain intelligent life. God isn't obligated to intervene to forestall the negative or ultimate consequences of living in a fallen world where we will ultimately face disease and death.

Second, natural evil is intertwined with moral evil. Since God has granted people the dignity of free will, most, if not all, suffering is directly or indirectly related to free will. Here is a detailed list of five reasons that Dr. Geisler suggests might account for one hundred percent of physical evil and suffering in the world:

> Since God has granted people the dignity of free will, most, if not all, suffering is directly or indirectly related to free will.

- Some evil/suffering comes to us directly from our free choices—abuse of one's body, poor moral choices, and bad habits that may involve suffering later in life.
- Some evil/suffering comes to us indirectly from the exercise of our freedom. Suffering might come from choosing to do nothing, but poverty often results from laziness, and, consequently, the pain of being poor may be indirectly caused by one's own free choice to remain idle.
- Some physical evil comes to us directly from the free choices of others. In a free world, child abuse is possible, as are domestic violence and muggings. Given the nature of free choice and the

significant number of people and various relationships you might suspect that conflict and pain were inevitable.

- Some evil/suffering comes to us indirectly from the free choices of others. Parental laziness can cause child poverty. Ancestral choices have long-term consequences on generations to come.
- Some evil/suffering may be a necessary by-product of other good activities. In a world where people are free to enjoy boating and swimming, some people will drown. In a world where the natural laws that govern our universe work for the overall benefit of humanity, these laws, or the over-lapping of these laws, will result in natural evil. [52]

Third, natural evil is generated by certain biological, chemical, and genetic possibilities of humanity. It's absolutely devastating and heartbreaking to see what individuals and their families experience when they face a genetic malfunction or devastating disease. However, it is important to emphasize that genetic malfunction is not the norm. Our genetic makeup works on a remarkable scale of efficiency. Why would we request that God stop a process that is nothing short of an on-going miracle? Just think of the miracle of human birth and the DNA that is transmitted from two human beings to create a child.

> It is important to emphasize that genetic malfunction is not the norm. Our genetic makeup works on a remarkable scale of efficiency. Why would we request that God stop a process that is nothing short of an on-going miracle?

- Should God remove all micro-organisms that produce disease?
- Should He protect the human race against every malfunction or mutation of micro-organisms?
- Should He interact with and miraculously cure every person?
- Should God stop everyone from drinking contaminated water?

---

[52] Norman L. Geisler, *The Roots of Evil* (Grand Rapids: Zondervan, 1978), 71-72.

- Should God prevent human contact so disease is not transmitted from one person to another?

Of course, people are emotionally bothered whenever they watch children face horrific diseases. But here's the bigger question, should God insulate children from illness? If He did, how long should this insulation last? Would God insulate children until they are 12, 16, 18, or 21? Have you ever thought of what kind of world it would create if children believed they were immune from any kind of harm? How would they act? What would that do to normal parenting? Parenting is clearly a difficult task. Imagine how hard it would be if your children knew they were invincible. Imagine the harsh adjustment when children were no longer insulated from illness.

The reason I ask all these questions is because we are used to people sitting back and criticizing God for what He's not doing. However, no one ever bothers to point out all the things that would go wrong if God tried to step in.

> Should God insulate children from illness? If He did, how long should this insulation last? Would God insulate children until they are 16, 18, or 21?

Allow me to finish our discussion regarding evil and suffering by giving you one final timeless insight from Jesus of Nazareth. This may be the most important one because it's the part of evil and suffering that is most difficult for us to process.

INSIGHT #3: DON'T IGNORE THE EMOTIONAL PROBLEM OF EVIL

In one of the most poignant moments in Jesus' public ministry he came to his dear friends Mary and Martha in the aftermath of the death of their brother Lazarus. Listen to the account from John's gospel:

> 32 When Mary reached the place where Jesus was and saw him, she fell at his feet and said, "Lord, if you had been here, my brother would not have died."33 When Jesus saw her weeping, and the Jews who had come along with her also weeping, he was deeply moved in spirit and troubled. 34 "Where have you laid him?" he asked. "Come and see, Lord," they replied.35 Jesus wept.36 Then the Jews

said, "See how he loved him!"[37] But some of them said, "Could not he who opened the eyes of the blind man have kept this man from dying?"
John 11:32-37

Jesus understood something very important. There is a huge difference between the logical problem of evil and the emotional problem. Although Jesus had tried earlier to provide comfort to these two sisters by reminding them that He was the resurrection and the life, He knew the pain and hurt they were facing. Notice the observations that we glean from specific statements from John's Gospel,

- "When Jesus saw her weeping": He was deeply moved emotionally.
- "Where did you lay him?": He was sensitive to feelings of loss and the need for closure.
- "See how he loved him": He was deeply transparent.

Jesus understood the emotional hurt and trauma that came into the lives of His friends. Notice that Jesus doesn't stop to lecture Mary on God's bigger plan. He doesn't chide her lack of faith in the resurrection. He simply weeps with her! He stays connected with Mary in her emotional pain.

> We should not claim that we know the eternal reasons for why God specifically allowed someone to experience a tragedy. If we are too quick to claim that God has a reason, victims of loss usually transfer their hostility to God.

We should pattern our approach based upon the conversations of Jesus Himself. Logical arguments or incredible insights will not necessarily help a person come to grips with the reality of their loss, pain, or hurt. Here are some of the principles that we should emulate when speaking to family and friends in the wake of deep trauma and loss:

- Make sure a person understands that we feel their hurt and loss. Learn how to say the following, "I'm so very sorry for your loss. I can't begin to understand how you feel."
- Don't claim that we know the eternal reasons for why God specifically allowed someone to experience a tragedy. Sometime it is not even wise to say, "God has a reason for what you are going

through." People aren't necessarily ready for this absolute statement. If we are too quick to claim that God has a reason, victims of loss might transfer their hostility to God.

- Don't immediately rush to try to answer a question without seeing why it's asked.

CONCLUSION

The problem of evil and suffering is very complex. For many people this issue provides overwhelming evidence that God doesn't exist. Fortunately, the free will argument championed by Christian thinkers has supported our belief in an all-powerful and all-loving God.

At the beginning of this chapter I reminded all of us that our job is not to answer all the questions of why. We will never be able to do that. However, with the right attitude and with a series of well-thought-out and probing questions, we can give people a compelling reason to consider the existence of God and the Christian faith.

We must compassionately share truths. We must listen to the precise hurdles that stop people from embracing the truth of the Christian faith. We must be sympathetic to a person's feelings of loss and hurt. We must be willing to support family and friends emotionally while we prepare to give them tangible reasons for our belief that we can still believe in a powerful and loving God in a tragically broken world.

SUGGESTIONS FOR ADDITIONAL READING

Norman L. Geisler, *The Roots of Evil*

This is one of the shorter books (about one hundred pages) on the intellectual issues of evil and suffering. However, Dr. Geisler does a great job of making difficult issues understandable. I have returned to this book over and over again for a concise summary of the issues. It's a great place to start if you want to delve into these issues on a more intellectual level.

Erwin W. Lutzer, *Where Was God? Answers to Tough Questions About God and Natural Disasters*

In the aftermath of various worldwide and national disasters Erwin Lutzer, the gifted pastor of the famous Moody Memorial Church in Chicago provides practical answers to why God allows natural disasters. This short book (one hundred pages) is very helpful and easy to read.

Timothy Keller, *Walking with God through Pain and Suffering*

Tim Keller, the New York Times bestselling author, continues his legacy of writing wonderful books (*The Reason for God* and *The Prodigal God*) by addressing the issue of evil and suffering. Keller's book is longer (300+ pages) and he doesn't shy away from tough issues. Fortunately, his gift as an author allows the reader to comprehend the many difficult topics addressed in the book.

John S. Feinberg, *The Many Faces of Evil: Theological Systems and the Problems of Evil*

Feinberg's book is not for the faint of heart (500 pages). This book is geared toward a reader who has an interest and background in philosophical issues. *The Many Faces of Evil* provides one of the most thorough treatments of this issue from an evangelical perspective.

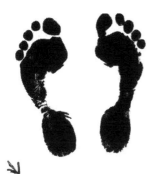

On August 7, 1961, Gherman Titov became the second Soviet cosmonaut to orbit the earth and return safely. Sometime later, when speaking at the World's Fair, he recounted his experience:

> Some say God is living here [in space]. I was looking around very attentively. But I did not see anyone there. I did not detect angels or gods. . . . I don't believe in God. I believe in man, his strength, his possibilities, and his reason.[53]

On Christmas Eve, 1968, three American astronauts (Apollo 8) were the first human beings to go around the dark side of the moon and away from the earth. On their return trip to earth they saw something that human eyes had never witnessed—the earth rising over the horizon of the moon draped in a glorious mixture of white and blue. In the midst of this awe-inspiring experience they opened the pages of the book of Genesis and read for the world to hear, "In the beginning God created the heavens and the earth (Genesis 1:1)."

We've just observed two similar experiences where people came to diametrically opposed conclusions about whether or not God exists. As you read this chapter you may fall into one of three categories:

- **You may be a devout follower of Jesus Christ.** Yet, you are still plagued from time to time with powerful doubts. Although you're

---

[53] Gherman Titov, quoted in Gerard Degroot, *Dark Side of the Moon: The Magnificent Madness of the American Lunar Quest* (New York: New York University Press, 2006), 133.

devoted to the Lord, you wonder whether or not your beliefs can stand the test of scrutiny. I hope this chapter will re-establish the foundation of the reasonableness of your faith.

- **You may simply be a very analytical thinker**. You've always felt a need to deliberately check things out before you've embraced them as true. You carefully weigh the merits of truth claims before you jump on board. I hope you'll be encouraged to continue to pursue truth in your spiritual journey.

- **You may be a religious skeptic.** You believe that life makes more sense without God in the world. You may simply feel more comfortable living as a skeptic. I hope you'll see compelling reasons for revisiting the truth claims of the Christian faith.

The simple reality is that we live within a culture that embraces a skeptical attitude toward truth and religion. Your thinking may be very similar to one of the great skeptics of the last century, Bertrand Russell, who was once asked what he would say if he died and God asked him why he didn't believe. His response was, "Not enough evidence, God, not enough evidence."[54]

The purpose of this chapter is to give five reasons why it's reasonable to believe in the existence of God. Each section will summarize a logical argument and provide tangible evidences for the reason.

REASON #1: THE UNIVERSE HAD A BEGINNING

If there was absolutely nothing prior to the existence of the universe—no God, no space, no time—how would the universe come into existence? I believe it's philosophically and scientifically reasonable to claim that this first event was caused by a transcendent and powerful being who operates outside the dimensions and limits of the universe.

William Lane Craig, who is one of the foremost Christian thinkers, regularly uses what is known as the Kalaam Argument to support his

---

[54] Bertrand Russell, quoted in Richard Dawkins, *The God Delusion* (New York: First Mariner Books, 2008), 131.

claim that belief in God is reasonable. The argument states the following:

- Whatever begins to exist has a cause.
- The universe began to exist.
- Therefore, the universe had a cause.

In essence, the argument is summarized with the beautiful words from *The Sound of Music*'s song, "Something Good:" "Nothing comes from nothing—nothing ever does!"[55]

Let's begin to evaluate the three-fold evidence for the claim that the universe had a beginning.

EVIDENCE #1: BIG BANG OF THE UNIVERSE ← Chapman

For the longest time, scientists and philosophers believed that the universe had always existed. Aristotle believed in an eternal universe. The great scientist Isaac Newtown believed in the uniform distribution of matter throughout the universe. Even Albert Einstein believed in an eternal universe for most of his academic career until he eventually changed his mind.

> The findings confirmed that the universe must have erupted from a single explosive event which by itself accounted for .99.97 percent of the radiant energy of the universe.

In the beginning of the 20th century scientific discoveries began to suggest that the universe was not infinite. Scientists and philosophers begin to see evidence that the universe had a beginning. Prior to the 1920s, scientists believed that the universe was stationary. However, in 1929 astronomer Edwin Hubble proved from his measurements of 40 different galaxies that the universe was indeed growing apart and expanding the same distance in all directions. Hubble ←

---

[55] "Something Good (Maria and the Captain)," *Metrolyrics*, accessed February 10, 2015, http://www.metrolyrics.com/something-good-maria-and-the-captain-lyrics-the-sound-of-music.html.

came to the remarkable conclusion that the entire known universe could be traced back to a single mathematical point where it began with a huge explosion. ⟵

However, nothing quite prepared the scientific community for the reports that surfaced on April 24, 1992. Newspapers around the world reported the historic findings from the Cosmic Background Explorer (COBE) satellite. The purpose of the COBE had been to measure the radiant energy at the outer reaches of the universe. The findings confirmed that the universe must have erupted from a single explosive event which by itself accounted for 99.97 percent of the radiant energy of the universe.

Here's the significance of the findings of the COBE. For the first time, scientists had indisputable proof that the universe came into existence at a distinct point in time. In other words, the universe literally sprang into existence as a result of an incredibly

> For the first time, scientists had indisputable proof that the universe came into existence at a distinct point in time.

hot explosion and continued to expand outward. The easiest way to envision this is to imagine inflating a balloon that has buttons on it. The more hot air that is blown into the balloon, the further the buttons expand away from one another.

This discovery made the front page headlines of *The London Times* for five consecutive days. Ted Koppel, on ABC's *Nightline*, interviewed George Smoot, a University of California at Berkeley astronomer and project leader for the COBE satellite, who made this assessment, "What we have found is evidence for the birth of the universe. . . . It's like looking at God."[56]

Science historian Frederic Burnham expressed the importance this way, "The community of scientists were prepared to consider the idea that

---

[56] George Smoot, quoted in Hugh Ross, *The Creator and the Cosmos: How the Greatest Scientific Discovery of the Century Reveals the Existence of God* (Colorado Springs: NavPress, 1993), 19.

God created the universe a more respectable hypothesis today than at any time in the last hundred years."[57]

Of course, the implication of a universe with a beginning was not lost on some scientists and philosophers. Sir Arthur Eddington expressed his deep concerns regarding a finite universe:

> Philosophically, the notion of a beginning of the present order of nature is repugnant. . . . I should like to find a genuine loophole. We must allow evolution an infinite time to get started.[58]

Eddington's response has been shared by many in the philosophical and scientific communities because it seems to open the door to the possibility of some kind of supernatural being that brought the universe into existence. Although many have tried to suggest various naturalistic explanations for the beginning of the universe there is no clear consensus on how this may have occurred.

EVIDENCE #2: ENERGY DEATH OF THE UNIVERSE

The Second Law of Thermodynamics is another piece of evidence that is often used to support the Christian belief that the universe was brought into existence by a transcendent being. This principle states that in a closed system, unless energy is constantly being added, that system will tend to run down and experience energy death.

Allow me to illustrate this important scientific principle with two practical examples. First, imagine that you live in Buffalo, New York during the coldest portion of the winter. The only way to keep your house warm is to have your thermostat set so that it regularly turns on your heater. Without continual bursts of heat from your heater your house will gradually grow colder and colder. In other words, in a closed system the

---

[57] Frederic Burnham, quoted in George Smoot and Hugh Ross, *The Creator and the Cosmos: How the Greatest Scientific Discovery of the Century Reveals the Existence of God* (Colorado Springs: NavPress, 1993), 19-20.
[58] Arthur Eddington, quoted in George Smoot and Hugh Ross, *The Creator and the Cosmos*, 51.

energy will gradually dissipate. Second, imagine that you run a really hot bath because your muscles are sore. Although it feels great, you can be assured that unless you continue to add hot water, the bath water will eventually go cold. There is no other option.

This same principle applies to the energy within our universe. The available energy within our universe is slowly yet surely decreasing. In other words, our universe is winding down. As a gigantic closed system, the universe and all its processes will eventually run down.

This is tremendously important as we determine whether or not the universe had a beginning. If the universe was eternal—if it has always existed—it should have already experienced energy death. In other words, our universe should have already run down. William Lane Craig puts it this way:

> If the universe was eternal—if it has always existed—it should have already experienced energy death.

If given enough time the universe will reach heat death, then why is it not in a state of heat death now, if it has existed forever, from eternity? If the universe did not begin to exist, then it should now be in a state of equilibrium. Its energy should be all used up. My wife and I have a very loud wind-up alarm clock. If I hear that the clock is ticking—which is no problem, believe me—then I know that at some point in the recent past it was wound up and has been running down since then. It's the same with the universe. Since it has not yet run down, this means, in the words of one baffled scientist, "In some way the universe must have been wound up."[59]

Our universe is an extremely large wind-up alarm clock. If it wasn't, then the energy contained within our closed-system universe would have already run out. The fact that our universe has not reached this point of

---

[59] William Lane Craig, *Reasonable Faith: Christian Truth and Apologetics* (Wheaton: Crossway Books, 1994), 115.

energy death indicates that our universe is still ticking. In other words, it had a beginning. ⟵

EVIDENCE #3: IMPOSSIBILITY OF AN INFINITE

I realize that many people are extremely uncomfortable with philosophical issues. Sometimes philosophy deals with complicated concepts and even more difficult terminology. However, it's important to realize that many philosophers support the Christian belief in the beginning of the universe.

Think for a moment about what it means when a person says, "The universe never had a beginning." If the universe never had a beginning, then an actual infinite number of past events exists within our universe. However, many philosophers don't believe in an actual infinite number of events.

> The logical reasoning goes something like this. If the universe didn't have a first event it would be like trying to climb a ladder out of a bottomless pit— no one could possibly get a foothold on the first step.

The logical reasoning goes something like this: if the universe didn't have a first event it would be like trying to climb a ladder out of a bottomless pit—no one could possibly get a foothold on the first step. Not only could a person never complete the journey, that person could never even get started because he or she would have to cross an infinite number of steps on the ladder before the person got to the first step. William Lane Craig describes the logical conclusion with these words:

> If the universe did not begin to exist a finite time ago, then the present moment would never arrive. But obviously it has arrived. Therefore, we know that the universe is finite in the past and began to exist.[60]

---

[60] William Lane Craig, *Reasonable Faith,* 100.

Of course, once a Christian lays a foundation for our belief that the universe had a beginning that was brought into existence by a divine being, most skeptics will ask the following question: "Where did God come from?" I would answer this question in the following fashion. God didn't come from anywhere. He didn't have to. God is eternal and has always existed. In other words, He is beyond the single dimension of time. As an all-powerful, self-existent being He doesn't need a cause (John 1:3; Col 1:16-17).

This evidence for the beginning of the universe clearly points to the existence of a supernatural being. The only way for a first event to arise spontaneously out of nothing is for the event to be caused by the free act of a person who is timeless and all-powerful. The following Scriptures seem to indicate this aspect of God's nature in relationship to time:

> This grace was given us in Christ Jesus before the beginning of time.
> 2 Timothy 1:9

> The hope of eternal life, which God, who does not lie, promised before the beginning of time.
> Titus 1:2

REASON #2: THE UNIVERSE HAS FINE-TUNING

In his book *Pale Blue Dot*, the immensely popular Carl Sagan made the following observation as he looked at an image of Earth as a pale blue dot in a sea of black taken by Voyager 1 (1990) from four billion miles away:

> Because of the reflection of sunlight . . . Earth seems to be sitting in a beam of light, as if there were some special significance to this small world. But it's just an accident of geometry and optics. . . . Our planet is a lonely speck in the great enveloping cosmic dark. In our

obscurity, in all this vastness, there is no hint that help will come from elsewhere to save us from ourselves.[61]

Most secular scientists believe that the earth, solar system, and sun are all ordinary. They believe that modern civilization is simply the by-product of chance, evolution, and naturalistic forces. However, with the increased technology of science and astronomy, we have developed a tremendous capacity to study the parameters of

> Scientists have discovered that our entire universe seems to have been extremely fine-tuned to make intelligent life here on Earth possible.

our physical world. In their book, *The Privileged Planet,* astronomer Guillermo Gonzalez and science philosopher Jay Wesley Richards make this powerful observation:

> It would take a star with highly unusual properties of our sun—the right mass, the right light, the right age, the right distance, the right orbit, the right galaxy, the right location—to nurture living organisms on a circling planet.[62]

In fact, scientists have discovered that our entire universe seems to have been extremely fine-tuned to make intelligent life here on Earth possible. In other words, there is an extraordinary combination of parameters and features that are absolutely necessary for any intelligent life to be possible. Christian astronomers have identified over one hundred fine-tuning factors for our universe. Here are some of these finely-tuned factors:

THE RIGHT KIND OF UNIVERSE
If the expansion rate caused by the Big Bang were any slower, gravity would have caused the universe to come breaking in on itself in something called the "Big Crush." If the expansion rate caused by the

---

[61] Carl Sagan, *Pale Blue Dot: A Vision of the Human Future in Space* (New York: Random House, 1997), 7.
[62] Lee Strobel, *The Case for a Creator: A Journalist Investigates Scientific Evidence That Points Toward God* (Grand Rapids: Zondervan, 2004), 281.

Big Bang were any faster, gravity would have been unable to attract material together in order to form planets.

THE RIGHT KIND OF GALAXY
Only certain types of galaxies will sustain intelligent life. Some galaxies are too close to each other or to other galaxies—some are too large and hot—which makes the occurrence of star systems very unlikely. Galaxies that are too elliptical or too irregular would have difficulty sustaining a stable star system. However, our galaxy is a nicely organized spiral galaxy. Even our planet is in the right location of our spiral galaxy—on the fringe of a spiral arm.

THE RIGHT KIND OF SUN
If the sun were larger it would burn its hydrogen up quicker and before planets were stable. It would also give off more deadly ultraviolet light. If the sun were smaller it would provide less energy for photosynthesis.

THE RIGHT DISTANCE FROM THE SUN
Our sun is ninety-three million miles from the earth. If we were closer, our planet would be too warm for liquid water and too hot to support life. If we were farther, our planet would be too cool for liquid water and we would freeze to death. The sun's current position is within the narrow band (between ninety to one hundred million miles) in which a planet must consistently orbit around a sun in order to sustain intelligent life. Astronomers call this the Habitable Zone.

THE RIGHT SIZE OF THE EARTH
If the gravity of the Earth was stronger the atmosphere would retain light gases like methane and ammonia. If the gravity of the Earth was weaker, water, oxygen, and nitrogen would not be retained. In other words, Earth would have the environment of Mars.

THE RIGHT SIZE OF THE MOON
If the moon were smaller the earth's orbit and tilt would be less stable. If the moon were larger tides would be too great and the earth's rotation would be slower.

THE RIGHT ROTATION RATE OF THE EARTH

If the earth rotated faster than it does, the wind velocities would be too great. The trade winds would create constant hurricanes. If it rotated slower than it does, there would be too much day and night temperature variation. In essence our planet would experience the rotisserie effect.

Harvard-educated astrophysicist John A. O'Keefe of NASA summarized the impact of this fine-tuning with this powerful conclusion:

> If the universe had not been made with the most exacting precision we could never have come into existence. It is my view that these circumstances indicate the universe was created for man to live in.[63]

The task facing the honest thinker is to determine whether or not the universe acquired these features by chance or by intelligent design. Think about it. How lucky does the universe have to be in order to exist? Astronomer Hugh Ross has calculated the odds at 1×10^{-42}. Oxford mathematician Roger Penrose calculated the precision necessary to create a universe with the various constants necessary for sustaining intelligent life—1 in 10 (10 to the power of 123). These odds are mathematically impossible as evidenced by the following detailed quotation:

> The eminent mathematical physicist Sir Roger Penrose calculated the chances of a life-supporting universe happening by chance to be 1 in $10^{10^{123}}$. Let me try to put that number into perspective: 10^{10^3} is a 1 followed by a thousand zeros, 10^{10^6} is a 1 followed by a million zeros and 10^{10^9} is a 1 followed by a billion zeros. These numbers are practically impossible to imagine, but $10^{10^{123}}$ is so big that it is totally inconceivable to the human mind. So with odds of only 1 in $10^{10^{123}}$ it can be said with absolute certainty that a life-supporting universe could never happen by chance.[64]

---

[63] John A. O'Keefe, quoted in Lee Strobel, *The Case for a Creator*, 281.
[64] Lee Bladon, *The Science of Spirituality: Integrating Science, Psychology, Philosophy, Spirituality & Religion* (Lulu.com, 2012),15.

All of us intuitively know the limitations of pure chance. Imagine that you participated in a poker game during which the dealer dealt himself four aces for twenty straight hands. Despite the dealer's insistence that it was logically possible for this to happen by chance, you would expect that someone or something was behind it. Or, consider the odds of winning the Mega Millions California Lottery. The odds are roughly one in 259 million. Imagine that your friend not only wins it once, but twice and three times. You might call this person lucky, but in reality we would all struggle to believe that this happened by pure chance.

The finely-tuned factors in our universe give a person the sense that our world was engineered to make it possible for us to exist and survive. A person who doesn't believe in the concept of God can always call it luck or chance. However, when the odds of this happening exceed the outer boundaries of what would be called possible, calling it luck or chance isn't much of an explanation.

The logical argument looks like this:

- Fine-tuning of the universe is due to logical necessity, chance, or design.
- It is not due to logical necessity or chance.
- Therefore, the fine-tuning of the universe is due to design.

> A person who doesn't believe in the concept of God can always call it luck or chance. However, when the odds of this happening exceed the outer boundaries of what would be called possible, calling it luck or chance isn't much of an explanation.

Did all this fine-tuning simply happen by chance or was there some kind of intelligence that ensured that the earth would be able to sustain intelligent life? Stephen Hawking—who is no friend of Christianity—puts it this way with two different observations:

> The discovery recently of the extreme fine-tuning of so many laws of nature could lead some to the idea that this grand design has a

Grand Designer. . . . True, the laws of the universe seem tailor made for humans.[65]

Many improbable occurrences conspire to create Earth's human friendly design. . . . We need liquid water to exist, and if the earth were too close (to the sun) it would all but boil off; if it is too far it would freeze . . . (or) even a small disturbance in gravity . . . would send the planet off its orbit and cause it to spiral into or away from the sun.[66]

REASON #3: THE UNIVERSE HAS MORAL VALUES

One of the darkest places in our world today is what remains of the concentration camp in Auschwitz. The Nazis committed horrific and inhumane acts of torture that resulted in countless deaths. Tragically, history will record the following haunting words of Adolf Hitler:

I freed Germany from the stupid and degrading fallacies of conscience and morality. . . . We will train young people before whom the world will tremble. I want young people capable of violence—imperious, relentless and cruel.[67]

Few people realize that the values and policies of Hitler were inspired by an atheist by the name of Frederick Nietzsche. Nietzsche believed that in a world without God there could be no moral values. Since God no longer existed, he believed this paved the way for the removal of the influence of Christian morality. Nietzsche wanted to view life with no God to obstruct his vision. Please don't misunderstand me. I am not blaming atheism for the atrocities of the Nazi regime. I am not suggesting that your atheistic family member or neighbor is devoid of moral virtue or principles. I'm not even saying that atheists can't be good without

---

[65] Stephen Hawking and Leonard Miodinow, *The Grand Design* (New York: Random House, 2010),161.
[66] Stephen Hawking and Leonard Miodinow, *The Grand Design*,161.
[67] Kelly Monroe Kullberg, *Finding God at Harvard: Spiritual Journeys of Thinking Christians* (Downers Grove: InterVarsity Press, 2007), 66.

believing in God. I am simply using this tragic chapter in history to remind us that if a person believes in a world without God there is no logical rationale to uphold one's belief in moral values. In other words, if people are simply the by-product of the physical processes of evolution, we can't answer the question, "Where do moral values come from?"

> If people are simply the by-product of the physical processes of evolution, we can't answer the question, "Where do moral values come from?"

Naturalistic evolution cannot explain the awareness of moral right. After all, if human beings are simply the by-product of naturalistic evolution, then we have no foundation for moral obligation. How could the awareness of a spiritual or moral reality be recognized in a purely naturalistic process? It is simply far too random.

Some would claim that moral values are merely personal preferences or feelings, but that is clearly not true. There are things that are clearly wrong. We don't have to prove they are wrong. We don't have to give a reason for why they are wrong because we know intuitively that they are wrong. Think about the following three examples of moral absolutes:

- Murder (an unjustified killing of an innocent person) is wrong.
- Torturing babies is wrong.
- Raping another person is wrong.

These actions are universally wrong by any definition or within any culture. Each of these events makes a person grimace in disgust. Everyone knows deep down inside that those actions are wrong. It's part of our moral intuition. We have basic moral instincts—the "yuck factor" at taking an innocent life or raping someone, or the "yes factor" at the self-sacrifice for the well-being of our children.

> Why are people outraged if there is no universal moral standard or absolute?

Further, it doesn't take much to be appalled at the defining atrocities of the 20th century. The extermination of Jews in World War II still haunts our world. The events that took place on the Killing Fields in Cambodia and the wholesale slaughter of one out of every ten persons in Rwanda has demonstrated the human race's tremendous capacity for evil. Civilized people look at the awful and stunning actions of ISIS in Iraq and Syria and their moral intuition clearly tells them that these actions are immoral and detrimental to everything good about society. However, if there is no universal moral standard why are people outraged at all of these atrocities?

> Moral values do not and could not have existed in a universe without a moral creator. In fact, in a world without God, there is no objective reason why a person should embrace moral virtue and value.

The late atheist philosopher J.L. Mackie said, "If there are objective values, they make the existence of a God more probable than it would have been without them." [68] In the same vein, philosopher Kai Nielsen, who is one of the sharpest atheistic minds in the 21st century, makes the following insightful comment:

> It is more reasonable to believe such elemental things [wife beating, child abuse] to be evil than to believe any skeptical theory that tells us we cannot know or reasonably believe any of these things to be evil. . . . I firmly believe that this is bedrock and right and that anyone who does not believe it cannot have probed deeply enough into the grounds of his moral beliefs.[69]

We live in a moral world where people recognize the presence of moral absolutes. In addition, we have compelling evidence that these moral principles could not exist in a naturalistic world but only in a world created by a moral lawgiver.

Logically, the argument looks like the following:

- If God does not exist, objective moral values do not exist.

---

[68] J.L. Mackie, *The Miracle of Theism: Arguments For and Against the Existence of God* (Oxford: Clarendon Press, 1983), 115-116.
[69] Kai Nielsen, *Ethics Without God* (Amherst, NY: Prometheus Books, 1990), 10-11.

- Objective moral values do exist.
- Therefore, God exists.

Moral values do not and could not exist in a universe without a moral creator. In fact, there is no objective reason why a person should embrace moral virtue and values. There is no explanation for why we embrace one action as a virtue and reject another action as a vice. Without a foundation in the moral creator of the universe, morality is simply a set of preferences. You may not like mine and I may not like yours, but no one is wrong.

Famous atheist Bertrand Russell once participated in a debate with philosopher Frederick Copleston in which he was asked to describe the basis on which he differentiated between right and wrong. Russell answered that he did so on the same basis that he differentiated between yellow and blue. Copleston challenged the analogy because difference in colors is based upon seeing. How does one differentiate between good and bad? Russell replied that he did so on the basis of feelings. Sensing an opportunity to blow his argument apart, Copleston made the following comment, "In some cultures people love their neighbors; in others they eat them, both on the basis of feeling. Do you have any preference?"[70]

REASON #4: THE UNIVERSE HAS NO MEANING WITHOUT GOD

In his powerful and haunting novel, *The Time Machine*, H.G. Wells' time traveler journeys far into the future to discover the destiny of man. What he finds in this future world is a dead Earth, except for a few lichens and moss, orbiting a gigantic red sun. The only sounds are the rush of the wind and the gentle ripple of the sea. He then writes:

> Beyond these lifeless sounds, the world was silent. Silent? It would be hard to convey the stillness of it. All the sounds of man, the

---

[70] Ravi Zacharias, *Can Man Live Without God?* (Dallas: Word Publishing, 1994), 182.

bleating of sheep, the cries of birds, the hum of insects, the stir that masks the background of our lives—all that was over.[71]

Ultimately, Wells' time traveler returned to an earlier point in the purposeless rush toward oblivion. Instinctively, a person wants to shout, "No, no . . . It can't end that way!" But if there is no God it will end that way. Without God, we are left with a desperate attempt to make believe there is a purpose in life. We are left trying to hide the reality of what we really know. We are left trying to fill our lives with experiences that mask the unpleasantness of what truly awaits us all. Life may be punctuated with tiny little purposes but no ultimate purpose.

> If we are simply the by-products of natural processes there is no objective purpose or meaning to our lives on Earth.

In a universe without God life becomes very similar to life on the Titanic. You may entertain yourself on the deck of the ship, or play a stimulating game of poker, or enjoy the last conversation with a family member or friend, but the boat will eventually go down.

Most of us would like to live in a world that offers better and brighter prospects. I think each of us would like to know that our very existence has been embodied by meaning by none other than the creator of the universe. If we are simply the by-products of natural processes there is no objective purpose or meaning to our lives on earth. The logical argument looks like this:

- If God does not exist then humanity is the by-product of blind chance.
- Something that is the by-product of blind chance has no objective purpose or meaning.
- Humanity has no objective purpose or meaning.

---

[71] H.G. Wells, quoted in William Lane Craig, *Reasonable Faith: Christian Truth and Apologetics* (Wheaton: Crossway Books, 1994), 62.

If the entire universe is an accident and each of our lives is simply a by-product of pure evolutionary chance, does this kind of universe have any objective meaning? I am not trying to say that people can't find subjective happiness in aspects of life. All of us obviously find great happiness with our family. We enjoy going to Disneyland, rooting for our sports teams, pursuing our passions, making a difference in our community, and spending time with family. However, what is the significance of living in a world where the universe is a great cosmic accident? It means that there is no overarching purpose behind it all. There can't be because it's all an accident. The great French philosopher Jean-Paul Sartre, who was one of the most influential atheists ever to dot the human landscape, made the following deathbed confession:

> I do not feel that I'm the product of chance, a speck of dust in the universe, but rather someone who is expected, prepared, prefigured, in short, a being whom only a creator God could have put there.[72]

He knew what so many secretly hope is true. They hope that God created our universe so that we might search and find Him. They also hope that God created our universe so that we'd experience ultimate happiness and fulfillment.

REASON #5: THE MIRACLE OF THE RESURRECTION

Christians look to the resurrection of Jesus Christ as one of the great validations of our belief in an almighty creator. Skeptics look to the resurrection of Jesus Christ as a clear example of an unreasonable belief that is not grounded in evidence but only in religious faith. Remember, a miracle by definition requires the action of a divine being who suspends the laws of nature. If Jesus of Nazareth died and was brought back to life through a physical resurrection this makes a strong argument for the reality of God. The argument looks like the following:

---

[72] J.P. Moreland and Kai Nielsen, *Does God Exist: The Debate Between Theists and Atheists* (Amherst, NY: Prometheus Books, 1993), 73.

- Miracles are acts of God.
- There are reasons to believe miracles have happened.
- Therefore, God exists.

William Lane Craig describes the significance of proving the resurrection of Jesus Christ:

> The miraculous act of God's raising Jesus from the dead is plausibly taken to be God's vindication of Jesus' radical personal claims for which He was crucified as a blasphemer. In light of God's raising Jesus, Jesus' personal claims to divinity take on a new credibility. The resurrection is God's imprimatur on those extraordinary claims.[73]

N.T. Wright, who is currently one of the great experts on the historical resurrection, makes this observation:

> Once you allow that something remarkable happened to the body that morning, all the other data fall into place with ease. Once you insist that nothing so outlandish happened, you are driven to ever more complex and fantastic hypotheses.[74]

Unfortunately, too many people within our secular culture have been trained to disbelieve certain historical facts. We will have the most influence on family and friends if we focus on facts that are clearer to understand. Gary Habermas, who is one of the greatest experts on the topic of Jesus' resurrection, adopts what he calls a minimal facts approach. This

A miracle by definition requires the action of a divine being who supersedes the laws of nature. If Jesus of Nazareth died and was brought back to life through a physical resurrection this makes a strong argument for the reality of God.

[73] William Lane Craig, *A Reasonable Response: Answers to Tough Questions on God, Christianity, and the Bible* (Chicago, IL: Moody Publisher, 2013), 309.
[74] N.T. Wright, quoted in Kenneth Boa & Robert Bowman Jr, *20 Compelling Evidences that God Exists* (Colorado Springs: Cook Communications Ministries, 2005), 139.

approach attempts to focus on events that are so strongly attested historically that they are embraced by nearly every scholar who studies the topic of the resurrection, believer and skeptic alike. Here are five facts that enjoy widespread acceptance in the academic world.

Fact #1: Jesus died by crucifixion.

The crucifixion of Jesus was recorded in all four of the Biblical gospel accounts. In addition, Roman historians like Tacitus and Jewish historians like Josephus also acknowledge the historical fact of the crucifixion of Jesus of Nazareth. In fact, one of the most vocal modern critics of the historical perspective of the life of Jesus actually endorses the historical nature of the crucifixion. John Dominic Crossan, who is a very liberal scholar and spokesperson for the Jesus Seminar, makes this assertion regarding the crucifixion of Jesus when he says, "That he was crucified is as sure as anything historical can ever be."[75]

Fact #2: Jesus' disciples believed that he rose and appeared to them.

There is a growing consensus among scholars that Jesus' disciples actually believed that He appeared to them after his death by crucifixion. This consensus is based upon a couple of clear pieces of evidence. First, the Apostle Paul claimed that he received an early church creed (I Corinthians 13:3-8) directly from the eyewitness accounts of Peter and James, who had seen Jesus alive.

Although tape recorders and DVRs were not available in the first century, creeds were a popular method of passing on important information for the next generation to memorize and retain. The early church creed mentioned in 1 Corinthians was given to Paul within three to five years after the crucifixion of Jesus Christ. Contained within the creed are repeated statements attesting to the fact that Jesus appeared

I corinthians 15:3-6

---

[75] John Dominic Crossan, quoted in Gary R. Habermas and Michael R. Licona, *The Case for the Resurrection of Jesus* (Grand Rapids: Kregel Publications, 2004), 49.

to his disciples and other followers. This creed was firmly established within the church before myth could obscure the facts of history.

Second, each of the gospel accounts attests to the fact that the disciples saw Jesus subsequent to his death. Contrary to skeptical claims, these accounts cannot be dismissed as legendary accounts. Habermas makes this powerful observation:

> Perhaps no fact is more widely recognized than that early Christian believers had real experiences that they thought were appearances of the risen Jesus. A critic may claim that what they saw were hallucinations or visions, but he does not deny that they actually experienced something.[76]

Fact #3: Paul the church persecutor was suddenly changed.

One of the most defining figures within the early history of the church was a Pharisee by the name of Saul of Tarsus. Saul was a devout follower of Judaism and was designated as a chief inquisitor against the fledgling Christian church. He was empowered to track down, imprison, and punish Christians for their role in opposing Judaism and supporting the teachings of Jesus of Nazareth. However, when Saul was converted on the Damascus road (Acts 9:1-19) by virtue of his experience with the risen Christ he became a devout follower of the Christian faith as well as one of the chief authors of most of the New Testament.

Many religious converts change their allegiance because they hear the message of that particular religion and believe it. Paul's experience was different. His conversion was based directly on the fact that he saw Jesus alive years after the Lord's death by crucifixion.

---

[76] Gary R. Habermas and Michael R. Licona, *The Case for the Resurrection of Jesus*, 60.

Fact #4: Jesus' skeptical brother James was suddenly changed.

The gospel accounts clearly portray the reality that Jesus had a family that was hesitant and skeptical of His claims to be the Son of God. Habermas and Licona conclude that James became a convert after the resurrection of Jesus. They make this conclusion based upon the following truths:

- The Gospels report that Jesus' brothers, including James, were unbelievers during his ministry (Mark 3:21, 31; 6:3-4; John 7:5).
- The aforementioned ancient creedal material in 1 Corinthians 15:3-8 lists an appearance of the risen Jesus to James: "then He appeared to James."
- Subsequent to the alleged event of Jesus' resurrection, James is identified as a leader of the Jerusalem church (Acts 15:12-21; Galatians 1:19).
- Not only did James convert to Christianity, his belief in Jesus and his resurrection was so strong that he died as a martyr because of it. His martyrdom is attested by both Christian and non-Christian sources.[77]

The case of James' conversion is equally as compelling as the story of Paul's conversion. It is one thing for a devout follower to affirm the resurrection of Jesus Christ. It is quite another thing for a life-long skeptic to convert based on what he believed was a personal appearance of the risen Jesus.

Fact #5: The tomb was empty.

Although this fact doesn't have the same universal support as the previous four facts, there is still strong evidence for it. Habermas cites the following, "75 percent of scholars on the subject accept the empty tomb as a historical fact." [78] These scholars cite a number of factors for believing the empty tomb as a historical fact. First, it seems unlikely that

---

[77] Ibid., 68.
[78] Ibid., 70.

the Christian faith could have survived in the face of Jewish and Roman critics if the body of Jesus had been still in the tomb. Remember, the Christian faith rises or falls on the resurrection of Jesus Christ. This was never a hidden fact. Supporters and enemies of Christianity always knew that the resurrection was the central truth.

Second, early critics tried to offer alternative explanations for the empty tomb. They accused Jesus' disciples of stealing the body (Matthew 28:12-13). This approach wouldn't be necessary if the body had still been accessible within the tomb. Even if Jesus' body had been decomposed and not available to modern scientific inquiries, the enemies of Jesus could easily have pointed out the apparent discrepancy between the claims of His followers and the facts on the ground.

> It seems unlikely that the Christian faith could have survived in the face of Jewish and Roman critics if the body of Jesus had still been in the tomb. Remember, the Christian faith rises or falls on the resurrection of Jesus Christ.

Third, the first century social hierarchy was not as fair and equitable as it is today. In both Jewish and Roman cultures, women were held in lower esteem than men and their testimony was not viewed as credible. It wouldn't make sense for the New Testament authors to invent a story about the resurrection of Jesus that featured a collection of women as the key witnesses.

Habermas concludes his explanation of the five minimal facts with this observation:

> These five facts that we have covered accomplish two things: (1) They provide compelling evidence for Jesus' resurrection and (2) they stand as data that must be accounted for by any opposing theory.[79]

---

[79] Ibid., 76.

CONCLUSION

Two thousand years ago the brilliant Apostle Paul made this timeless observation:

> For since the creation of the world God's invisible qualities—his eternal power and divine nature—have been clearly seen, being understood from what has been made [that is, his creation], so that men are without excuse.
> Romans 1:20

This passage informs us that there is evidence throughout our world that points to an innate knowledge of God. Our trust in God is not a leap of faith without any justification. Trust in God is fully warranted by the supporting evidence. Werner von Braun, the father of space science put it this way:

Reread → The vast mysteries of the universe should only confirm our belief in the certainty of its Creator. I find it as difficult to understand a scientist who does not acknowledge the presence of a superior rationality behind the existence of the universe as it is to comprehend a theologian who would deny the advances of science.[80]

This chapter has explained five compelling pieces of evidence for the reasonableness of believing in God. Hopefully, it will motivate the reader to a lifetime pursuit that confirms the reasons behind the existence of the God of the Bible. Fortunately, believing in the Christian faith is not intellectual suicide. Trust in God is reasonable because it conforms to evidence that is all around us.

---

[80] Werner von Braun, quoted in Lee Strobel, *The Case for a Creator: A Journalist Investigates Scientific Evidence That Points Toward God* (Grand Rapids: Zondervan, 2004), 273

SUGGESTIONS FOR ADDITIONAL READING

Kenneth D. Boa & Robert M Bowman Jr., *20 Compelling Evidences that God Exists*

Boa's and Bowman's book is a helpful overview of the various reasons that experts have provided for the existence of God.

Lee Strobel, *The Case for a Creator: A Journalist Investigates Scientific Evidence That Points Toward God*

Lee Strobel uses his approach in interviewing experts to provide multiple lines of evidence for the reliability of the existence of God. This book is the hardest to understand of Strobel's three books, but it is a great overview of evidence from the areas of cosmology, physics, astronomy, biochemistry, biology, and consciousness.

J.P. Moreland and Kai Nielsen, *Does God Exist? The Great Debate Between Theists and Atheists*

This is a very useful book featuring gifted Christian apologist J.P. Moreland in a debate with renowned atheist Kai Neilsen. The first part of this book consists of a transcript of a debate between Moreland and Nielsen. The debate transcript is then reviewed by theists William Lane Craig and Dallas Willard and atheists Antony Flew and Keith Parsons.

Antony Flew, *There is a God: How the World's Most Notorious Atheist Changed His Mind*

Antony Flew has a long and storied career as one of the world's preeminent atheists. This book tells his personal story of how his commitment to follow the truth led him to a belief in God as creator. The book also summarizes the evidence that led him to change his mind.

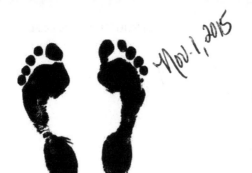

Nov. 1, 2015

FOOTPRINT SEVEN:
CAN YOU TRUST
THE BIBLE?

A 2014 Gallup Poll revealed that Americans hold the following views about the Bible:

> Twenty-eight percent of Americans believe the Bible is the actual word of God and that it should be taken literally. This is somewhat below the 38% to 40% seen in the late 1970s, and near the all-time low of 27% reached in 2001 and 2009. But about half of Americans continue to say the Bible is the *inspired* word of God, not to be taken literally—meaning a combined 75% believe the Bible is in some way connected to God. About one in five Americans view the Bible in purely secular terms—as ancient fables, legends, history, and precepts written by man—which is up from 13% in 1976.[81]

These statistics are alarming. Only a quarter of Americans believe the Bible is literally the word of God. Another quarter of Americans believe it is a purely legendary or mythical document. Unfortunately, the picture is actually much worse. A growing number of people have been convinced by vocal critics that the Bible simply can't be trusted as an accurate record of what the original authors of the New Testament wrote.

> A growing number of people have been convinced by vocal critics that the Bible simply can't be trusted as an accurate record of what the original authors of the New Testament wrote.

[81] Lydia Saad, "Three in Four in U.S. Still See the Bible as Word of God," *Gallup Poll*, last modified June 4, 2014, http://www.gallup.com/poll/170834/three-four-bible-word-god.aspx.

One of the most prominent of these vocal critics in America is a scholar by the name of Bart D. Ehrman. Ehrman has gained the attention of the public with his widely publicized claims against the reliability of the Bible. His book *Misquoting Jesus: The Story Behind Who Changed the Bible and Why* has emboldened those who question the authority of Scripture.

> They need to be ready for the barrage, because it is coming. The intentional dumbing down of the church for the sake of filling more pews will ultimately lead to defection from Christ.

His books have captured the imagination of secular critics and stunned devout Christians because of his evangelical pedigree. Ehrman graduated from two of the most historic evangelical institutions—Moody Bible Institute and Wheaton College. He was mentored by renowned conservative textual critic, Bruce Metzger. Notice one of his more controversial comments:

> Occasionally I see a bumper sticker that reads: "God said it, I believe it, and that settles it." My response is always, What if God didn't say it? What if the book you take as giving you God's words instead contains human words? . . . There are clear reasons for thinking that, in fact, the Bible is not this kind of inerrant guide to our lives: among other things, as I've been pointing out, in many places we (as scholars, or just regular readers) don't even know what the original words of the Bible actually were.[82]

Unfortunately, we live in an increasingly skeptical culture that questions Christian morality and criticizes the reliability of the Bible. Ehrman's claims are convincing to the typical secular thinker and are devastating to many Christians. Long held and cherished views about Scripture are being challenged in the public square. In this climate, it has never been more essential for Christians to understand the issues that relate to answering the question, "Can you trust the Bible?"

---

[82] Bart D. Ehrman, *Misquoting Jesus: The Story Behind Who Changed the Bible and Why* (New York: HarperCollins Publishers, 2005), 13-14.

As Christians we must possess the tools to respond to these claims. Unfortunately, the educational and intellectual climate of the church has prevented most Christians from even being aware of these issues. Daniel Wallace, professor at Dallas Theological Seminary and one of the premier evangelical textual criticism experts, effectively warns the church:

> Those in ministry must close the gap between the church and the academy. We have to educate believers. Instead of trying to isolate laypeople from critical scholarship, we need to insulate them. They need to be ready for the barrage, because it is coming. The intentional dumbing down of the church for the sake of filling more pews will ultimately lead to defection from Christ.[83]

In this spirit, the goal of this chapter is to provide Christians with some basic tools to help push back against the barrage of secular criticism of the Bible. Although it's unreasonable to think that this one chapter can answer every question that is raised by skeptics like Ehrman, it can begin to lay a helpful foundation for believing in the trustworthiness of the Bible. After all, far too many impressionable young Christians are at risk. Wallace eloquently cites the challenge facing the church:

> Sadly, tens of thousands of college students, raised in a Christian home, have abandoned the faith because of fear of embarrassment over these issues, especially due to *Misquoting Jesus*. In recent years, it has been estimated that over 60% of kids coming from Christian homes abandon the faith by the time they get done with college. It is time for pastors and other Christian leaders to educate the masses about the reality of the transmission of the Bible. If we don't, the fallout will only get worse.[84]

---

[83] Daniel B. Wallace, "The Gospel According to Bart: Review of '*Misquoting Jesus: The Story Behind Who Changed the Bible and Why*' by Bart D. Ehrman," *Journal of the Evangelical Theological Society 49*, no. 2 (2006) : 337.
[84] Daniel B. Wallace, "Can We Still Believe the Bible?," *Daniel B. Wallace*, last modified March 24, 2014, http://danielbwallace.com/2014/03/24/can-we-still-believe-the-bible/.

Although the issues involved with answering the question of whether we can trust the Bible are incredibly difficult and complex, I've found that providing evidence for two very specific observations is extremely helpful:

- Observation #1: The New Testament documents were eyewitness accounts.
- Observation #2: The New Testament documents were reliably transmitted.

OBSERVATION #1: THE NEW TESTAMENT DOCUMENTS WERE EYEWITNESS ACCOUNTS

Most skeptics believe that the Gospels were penned in the second century. They believe the Gospels were not eyewitness accounts of the life of Jesus Christ. The constant repetition of these claims has resulted in an intellectual climate in which people are convinced that the Bible is legendary. Consider the assertion by Bart Ehrman:

> Why was the tomb supposedly empty? I say supposedly because, frankly, I don't know that it was. Our very first reference to Jesus' tomb being empty is in the Gospel of Mark, written forty years later by someone living in a different country who had heard that it was empty. How would he know?[85]

Obviously, the New Testament Scriptures claim to be eyewitness accounts. Peter stated that he was an eyewitness in 1 Peter 5:1, "To the elders among you, I appeal as a fellow elder, a witness of Christ's sufferings and one who also will share in the glory to be revealed." Luke the historian went to great lengths to ensure that the Gospel According to Luke and the Acts of the Apostles were based upon eyewitness accounts. John the Apostle claimed to be an eyewitness as he began to write his epistle:

---

[85] Bart D. Ehrman, *Jesus, Interrupted: Revealing the Hidden Contradictions in the Bible (and Why We Don't Know About Them)* (New York: HarperCollins Publishers, (2010), 171.

> 1 That which was from the beginning, which we have heard, which we have seen with our eyes, which we have looked at and our hands have touched—this we proclaim concerning the Word of life. 2 The life appeared; we have seen it and testify to it, and we proclaim to you the eternal life, which was with the Father and has appeared to us. 3 We proclaim to you what we have seen and heard, so that you also may have fellowship with us.
>
> 1 John 1:1-3

Although these Scriptures are convincing and reassuring for the Christian, we can't merely cite the claims of Scripture when talking with our skeptical friends. We must be able to point to evidence that substantiates our belief that the gospel accounts were written by eyewitnesses. Think for a moment about the approach of police investigators who attempt to prove a crime. Many times investigators build a strong case simply by the collective weight of circumstantial evidence. Slowly yet surely, the investigators uncover one piece of evidence after another until it points to the most reasonable conclusion. We should take the same approach when showing the reliability of the Bible.

I believe there are many clues that lead a reasonable thinker to conclude that the New Testament documents were written by those who were eyewitnesses of the life and death of Jesus of Nazareth. Last year I had the opportunity to learn from J. Warner Wallace, former homicide detective and author of the ground-breaking book entitled *Cold-Case Christianity*. His book applies the techniques and principles of a cold-case detective and applies them to building a case for the reasonableness of the Christian faith. Much of the focus of *Cold-Case Christianity* revolves around displaying the circumstantial evidence that demonstrates that the New Testament documents were genuine eye-witness accounts.

Here are five of the insights that he provides in his book:

→ **Evidence #1: The New Testament fails to describe the destruction of the temple**. One of the most significant historical events in first century Palestine was the destruction of the temple in Jerusalem in AD 70 by the Roman army led by Titus. The destruction of the temple was

New testament written by eye witness. Nov. 1, 2015

Pg 140

DEFENDING
THE
FAITH
ELECTIVE SERIES

CAN YOU TRUST THE BIBLE?

DR. BRENT STRAWSBURG,

New testimont written B4 destruction of temple

The last foundation for any doubt that the Scriptures have come down to us substantially as they written has now been removed. Both the authenticity and the general integrity of the books of the New Testament may be regarded as finally established.
Sir Frederic Kenyon

OBSERVATION #1: THE N.T. DOCUMENTS WERE ___EYEWITNESS___ ACCOUNTS

1st John 1 : 1 - 3 won't win people to christ

Clue #1: The N.T. fails to describe the ___destruction___ of the temple.
Clue #2: Luke never mentions the deaths of ___James___, Paul, and Peter.
Clue #3: Luke's ___gospels___ predates Acts.
Clue #4: Archaeology and ___History___ points to ___Eyewitness___.
Clue #5: Early Pauline ___letters___ supported the claims of the gospels.

> [3] For what I received I passed on to you as of first importance: that
> Christ died for our sins according to the Scriptures, [4] that he was buried,
> that he was raised on the third day according to the Scriptures,
> 1 Corinthians 15:3-8 NIV   *written AD 53-57*

written AD 57 - AD 6 3

OBSERVATION #2: THE N.T. DOCUMENTS WERE RELIABLY *TRANSMITTED*

BASIC FACTS

- The original autographs of the New Testament no longer exist.
- Scribes were experts in making copies of ancient documents.
- Textual criticism is the science of affirming the original wording of ancient manuscripts.

INSIGHT #1: THE _Manuscript_ EVIDENCE FOR THE N.T. IS UNPARALLELED.

Pg 152 - 153

INSIGHT #2: ALL DIFFERENCES (VARIANTS) IN MANUSCRIPTS ARE NOT _Equal_

Pg 156

INSIGHT #3: DIFFERENCES (VARIANTS) IN MANUSCRIPTS ARE NOT _Fatal_

Pg 160

> 97-99% of the New Testament can be constructed beyond
> any reasonable doubt, and no Christian doctrine is founded
> solely or even primarily on textually disputed passages.
> Craig Blomberg, Author of *Can We Still Believe the Bible?*

KEY QUESTIONS

Pg 161

QUESTION #1: IF GOD INSPIRED THE ORIGINAL DOCUMENTS, WHY DIDN'T HE PRESERVE THE ORIGINAL DOCUMENTS?

QUESTION #2: ARE THERE VERSES OR PASSAGES THAT PROBABLY DON'T BELONG IN THE NEW TESTAMENT?

Experts say 97% Bible reliable
John 7:53 - 8:11

QUESTION #3: WHAT'S THE EARLIEST COPY (MANUSCRIPT) OR PORTION OF A COPY THAT WE POSSESS?

That was a stunning discovery. The reason: skeptical German theologians in the last century argued strenuously that the fourth gospel was not even composed until at least the year 160—too distant from the events of Jesus' life to be of much historical use. They were able to influence generations of scholars, who scoffed at this gospel's reliability. . . . This finding has literally rewritten popular views of history, pushing the composition of John's gospel much closer to the days when Jesus walked the earth.
Bruce Metzger, Legendary New Testament Manuscript Expert

not simply an important historical event. Jesus Himself predicted the fall of Jerusalem:

> ¹ Jesus left the temple and was walking away when his disciples came up to him to call his attention to its buildings. ² "Do you see all these things?" he asked. "I tell you the truth, not one stone here will be left on another; everyone will be thrown down." ³ As Jesus was sitting on the Mount of Olives, the disciples came to him privately. "Tell us," they said, "when will this happen, and what will be the sign of your coming and of the end of the age?"
> Matthew 24:1-3

Think about the implication of this piece of evidence. If the New Testament gospel accounts were actually written in the second century it would be quite unusual for the gospel authors to not mention the destruction of the temple. It would also be quite unusual for the authors to miss the opportunity to record the fulfillment of one of the great prophecies of Jesus of Nazareth. They didn't record this

> The clearest explanation for the omission of such an important historical fact is that the New Testament documents were written before the events of AD 70.

historical event because it hadn't yet happened. In other words, the New Testament documents were written before the events of AD 70. This fact points to an early authorship of the gospel accounts.

Evidence #2: Luke never mentions the deaths of James, Paul, and Peter. Years before the siege and destruction of Jerusalem the church had to bear witness to the martyrdom of the Apostle James (brother of Jesus and recognized leader of the church in Jerusalem) in AD 62, the Apostle Paul in AD 64, and the Apostle Peter in AD 65. What is powerful about this piece of evidence is that although Luke the historian wrote in depth about Paul and Peter in the book of Acts he never mentions their deaths. Why wouldn't Luke, the imminent historian, mention the historic death of the great Apostle Paul? Remember, Luke had previously mentioned the martyrdoms of Stephen (Acts 7:54-60) and James (Acts 12:1-2). The simplest explanation for the absence of these tragic deaths is that the Acts of the Apostles was written before the martyrdoms of James, Paul, and Peter. Luke concluded the book of Acts at a time

145

when Paul had not yet been martyred but was simply under house arrest in Rome.

➔ Evidence #3: Luke's gospel predates Acts. Luke the historian wrote the companion volumes of the Gospel According to Luke and the Acts of the Apostles. In his introduction to Acts, Luke clearly states (Acts 1:1-2) that his gospel account of Jesus was written prior to the book of Acts. This is significant because it provides evidence that the gospel accounts came before some of the previously mentioned landmark events that are written in the Acts of the Apostles.

➔ Evidence #4: Archaeology and history point to eyewitnesses.
Historians confirm the accuracy of the New Testament record when it is compared to extra-biblical records. This accuracy depends upon information that would have been recognized by eyewitness accounts.

> This is significant because it provides evidence that the gospel accounts came before some of the landmark events that are written in the Acts of the Apostles.

For example, the Jewish historian Josephus confirms the events reported by the historian Luke, including a famine in Judea during the reign of the Roman emperor Claudius (Acts 11:28) and the death of Herod Agrippa 1 (Acts 12:20-23). Luke also used the proper titles of various officials in the Roman Empire—information that only an eyewitness of that period would know. The historicity of the Pool of Bethesda in John 5 has been doubted by many skeptics who questioned the reality of five covered colonnades. However, archaeologists have discovered "two pools bordered by four covered colonnades in a rough trapezoid, with a fifth colonnade separating the two pools"[86] located near the Church of St. Anne in the Old City.

---

[86] Andreas Kostenberger, "John," in *The Holman Apologetics Commentary on the Bible: The Gospel and Acts,* ed. Jeremy Royal Howard (Nashville, TN: Holman Reference, 2013), 533.

Evidence #5: Early Pauline letters supported the claims of the gospels. The earliest letters of the Apostle Paul affirmed the historical facts of the gospel eyewitnesses. A mere three to five years after the crucifixion, Paul met two eyewitnesses to the crucifixion of Jesus Christ. In his meeting with Apostles Peter and James he was given an early church creed. This creed, which appears in First Corinthians 15:3-8, was a clear statement of the beliefs of the

> Paul not only saw the risen Jesus but heard first-hand testimony from the Apostles a mere five years after the crucifixion.

Christian church and directly reflected eyewitness accounts:

> 3 For what I received I passed on to you as of first importance: that Christ died for our sins according to the Scriptures, 4 that he was buried, that he was raised on the third day according to the Scriptures, 5 and that he appeared to Peter, and then to the Twelve. 6 After that, he appeared to more than five hundred of the brothers at the same time, most of whom are still living, though some have fallen asleep. 7 Then he appeared to James, then to all the apostles, 8 and last of all he appeared to me also, as to one abnormally born.
> 1 Corinthians 15:3-8

This creed describes the accounts of eyewitnesses, not myth or legend that arose in the second century. Paul's account in Galatians does something very similar as he describes the timeline of significant meetings between himself and eyewitnesses to the resurrection. Paul was converted from AD 33 to AD 36, and according to Galatians 1:19 he visited Peter and James within three years of his conversion.

This meeting with Peter and James occurred fourteen years before he wrote the letter to the Galatians (written between AD 53 to AD 57). Think about the significance of this timeline. Paul had firsthand information from eyewitness accounts to the life of Jesus of Nazareth. Paul not only saw the risen Jesus but heard firsthand testimony from the apostles a mere five years after the crucifixion.

The evidence that has been cited leaves us with several very clear conclusions. Key events were missing from the Acts of the Apostles because they hadn't yet happened at the time that Luke wrote the Acts of the Apostles. The absence of a handful of huge historical events (destruction of the temple and the martyrdom of James, Paul, and Peter) can best be explained if the book of Acts was written prior to AD 61 to AD 62. Furthermore, Luke's gospel clearly pre-dates the Acts of the Apostles. Paul's tendency to quote from Luke's gospel in both 1 Timothy and 1 Corinthians clearly points to the existence of Luke's gospel before AD 53 to AD 57.

Finally, Luke tells us that he borrowed information from "those who from the beginning were eyewitnesses and servants of the word (Luke 1:2)." The fact that Luke refers to or quotes from nearly five hundred verses found in Mark's gospel and Matthew's gospel would seem to imply that these accounts were in existence before the historical investigation of Luke. The evidence seems to point to the early dating of Mark in either the late 40s or very early 50s.

J. Warner Wallace summarizes the evidence:

> The reasonable inference from the circumstantial evidence is that the Gospels were written very early in history, at a time when the original eyewitnesses and gospel writers were still alive and could testify to what they had seen. . . . The circumstantial evidence supports an early dating for the Gospels. The gospel writers appear in history right where we would expect them to appear if they were, in fact, eyewitnesses. This early placement alone does not ensure that the Gospels are reliable accounts, but it keeps them "in the running" and becomes an important piece of circumstantial evidence, in and of itself, as we determine the reliability of the gospel writers.[87]

---

[87] J. Warner Wallace, *Cold-Case Christianity: A Homicide Detective Investigates the Claims of the Gospels* (Colorado Springs: David C. Cook, 2013), 171.

OBSERVATION #2: THE NEW TESTAMENT DOCUMENTS WERE RELIABLY TRANSMITTED

Once we determine that the gospel accounts were the by-product of eyewitness accounts we must determine whether or not the New Testament documents we have today were reliably transmitted from those original ancient documents. In other words, are we looking at a reasonable facsimile of what the apostles wrote nearly 2,000 years ago?

To be honest, this might be the most difficult issue for Christians to fully understand. However, it's an issue that must be explored and explained. Before we jump into the deep end of the pool, there are three basic facts

> The original parchments that the apostles used to write the gospels and the epistles were either destroyed or worn out due to age and extensive use.

that lay a foundation for Christians to better understand the issue of the reliability of the New Testament.

BASIC FACT #1: THE ORIGINAL AUTOGRAPHS OF THE NEW TESTAMENT NO LONGER EXIST

Some Christians are more than a little troubled when they discover for the first time that there are no surviving originals of the New Testament. Scholars call the actual documents written by the apostles the original autographs. The parchments that the apostles used to write the gospels and the epistles were either destroyed or worn out due to age and extensive use. As a result, it was necessary for the early church to make copies of these hallowed Scriptures. Unfortunately, this basic fact can be disturbing for Christians because they wonder, if everything is a copy of a copy, how can we have any confidence that the New Testament we read today is the same as the document that was originally written? It seems that Bart Ehrman began to slip away from the Christian faith when he was unable to resolve his doubts on this issue:

> I kept reverting to my basic question: how does it help us to say that the Bible is the inerrant word of God if in fact we don't have the

149

words that God inerrantly inspired, but the only words copied by the scribes—sometimes correctly and sometimes (many times!) incorrectly.[88]

BASIC FACT #2: SCRIBES WERE PROFESSIONAL EXPERTS IN MAKING COPIES OF ANCIENT DOCUMENTS

The ancient world lacked so many of the wonderful conveniences of the modern world. No one had a personal printer in their home office or down the hallway at their work. No one had a scanner or access to a business like Fed-Ex Kinkos to take care of all copying needs. Instead, the ancient world depended upon the professionalism of the scribe to produce copies of valued written records.

> Instead, the ancient world depended upon the professionalism of the scribe to produce copies of valued written records.

Within the Jewish community, the concern for holy documents was incredibly high. As a result, scribes were professionally trained to be exceptionally careful in copying the Scriptures. The scribes and copyists were meticulous. They took extraordinary steps to avoid copying mistakes (counting the number of letters per page, detailed notes on the texts, etc.). As a result, they produced remarkably reliable copies of the original documents.

History has demonstrated the remarkable accuracy of ancient Jewish scribes who believed that the documents they were copying were indeed the words of God. As a result, the level of accuracy in the Old Testament was extremely high. The story of the Dead Sea Scrolls

> "A comparison of the Qumran manuscripts of Isaiah proved to be word for word identical with our standard Hebrew Bible in more than 95 percent of the text."

---

[88] Bart D. Ehrman, *Misquoting Jesus: The Story Behind Who Changed the Bible and Why* (New York: HarperCollins Publishers, 2005), 7.

clearly illustrates this truth. In 1947, a Bedouin herdsman found clay jars that held a number of scrolls. These scrolls contained fragments of almost every Old Testament book of the Bible. Of particular interest was a complete copy of the book of Isaiah that was dated to approximately 100 BC; it was 1,000 years older than any previous copy of Isaiah maintained by the ancient Masoretes.

As scholars analyzed the Dead Sea Scrolls they discovered something truly amazing. J. Warner Wallace reveals their discovery:

> A comparison of the Qumran manuscripts of Isaiah proved to be word for word identical with our standard Hebrew Bible in more than 95 percent of the text. Some of the 5 percent differences were simply a matter of spelling (like you might experience when using the word favor instead of favour). Some were grammatical differences (like the presence of the word and to connect two ideas or objects within a sentence). Finally, some were the addition of a word for the sake of clarity (like the addition of the Hebrew word for "light" to the end of 53:11, following "they shall see"). None of these grammatical variations changed the meaning of the text in any way.[89]

The New Testament authors were keenly aware of the tradition of the scribes who cared for the transmission of the Old Testament scrolls which contained the Scriptures. Similarly, the followers of Jesus elevated the transmission of the Scriptures ensuring:

> that the documents would be honored and cared for in a manner befitting the Masoretic tradition. The first-century Christian scribes didn't have access to photocopiers, microfiche, or digital imaging like modern police-department records divisions do, but they understood the importance of divine record keeping, and they used the first-century equivalent in technology (the meticulous tradition of their predecessors) to carefully guarantee the accuracy of the texts.[90]

---

[89] J. Warner Wallace, *Cold-Case Christianity: A Homicide Detective Investigates the Claims of the Gospels* (Colorado Springs: David C. Cook, 2013), 233.
[90] J. Warner Wallace, *Cold-Case Christianity*, 233.

→ Basic Fact #3: Textual Criticism is the Science of Recovering the Original Wording of Ancient Manuscripts

In a world where we no longer have the original documents of the New Testament it is essential that we have experts who can recover the original wording of ancient manuscripts. These experts are called textual critics. Although the ancient scribes were incredibly professional and competent, sometimes they made errors or alterations when copying manuscripts by hand. The ultimate job of the textual critic is to provide evidence that the New Testament

> Textual criticism refers to the process of recovering the original wording of ancient manuscripts. The textual critic uses all the available manuscript copies to reconstruct the original text as closely as possible.

documents were reliably transmitted. They examine all the existing manuscripts and attempt to determine the wording of the original documents. We look to textual critics to give us a reasonable assurance that the Bible we possess is a reliable representation of the books authored by the apostles.

These basic facts help Christians better understand the issue of the reliability of the New Testament. However, in light of the scathing attacks of critics like Bart Ehrman it is crucial for us to understand four essential insights—each of these insights helps us defend our belief in the reliability of the Bible.

→ Insight #1: The Manuscript Evidence for the New Testament is Unparalleled

> In summary, we have over 20,000 handwritten manuscripts of the New Testament. The New Testament manuscript evidence is head and shoulders above any ancient classic work.

The dictionary defines the word "unparalleled" as having no parallel or equal; exceptional. There is no better word in the English language to describe the manuscript evidence for the New Testament documents.

→ Currently, we have 5,795 manuscripts in the Greek language. In addition, we have 10,000 manuscripts in Latin and another 5,000 in a variety of languages. In summary, we have over 20,000 handwritten manuscripts of the New Testament. *comparing ancient documen.*

The New Testament manuscript evidence is head and shoulders above any ancient classic work. It is not even close. *Caesar's Gallic War* only has 251 existing manuscripts and the oldest is 950 years after the event. The Roman *History of Livy* is survived by 150 manuscripts, the earliest of which is from the fifth century. *The Histories* and *Annals* of Tacitus depend primarily on two surviving manuscripts that date from between 750 to 950 years after it was written. The *History* of Thucydides, written in fifth century BC, is survived by 96 manuscripts and most of the manuscripts date 1,350 years later. The work of antiquity that has the greatest amount of manuscript evidence, other than the Bible, is Homer's *Iliad*. There are 1,757 Greek manuscripts, but the earliest copies are from 400 years after Homer wrote his epic in 800 BC.

New Testament textual scholars enjoy a wealth of evidence as it relates to the distance of time that separates the earliest copies from the original autographs. Here are the facts:

> From 10 to 15 NT manuscripts were written within the first 100 years of the completion of the NT. To be sure, they are all fragmentary, but some of them are fairly sizable fragments, covering large portions of the Gospels or Paul's letters. . . . Within two centuries, the numbers increase to at least four dozen manuscripts. Of manuscripts produced before AD 400, an astounding 99 still exist—including the oldest complete NT, Codex Sinaiticus.[91]

Noted evangelical textual expert, Craig L. Blomberg, describes the evidence this way:

---

[91] *The ESV Study Bible, English Standard Version* (Wheaton: Crossway Bibles, 2008), 2587.

A full 102 copies of individual New Testament books or portions of them have been recovered from the second and third centuries. And every single one of them is written with the very careful handwriting of an experienced scribe, not with the more careless scrawls of less literate individuals whom Ehrman postulates would have introduced many more errors in these earliest centuries.[92]

Manuscript evidence for the New Testament is important for a simple and powerful reason. It provides us a more detailed snapshot of our Bible. The greater the number of manuscripts and the shorter interval between the copy and original provide us a more detailed snapshot of our Bible. This is similar to when you are trying to create a photo album for a special family gathering. In order to recreate all the moments of the event you want to gather as many pictures from as many people as possible—this insures that you are able to recreate every moment of the actual event. Collecting a lot of manuscripts does the same thing—you get the most complete and accurate picture of the New Testament.

> The greater the number of manuscripts and the shorter interval between the copy and original provide us a more detailed snapshot of our Bible.

One of the great scholars in the 20th century, F.F. Bruce summarizes the comparison this way:

> The evidence for our New Testament writings is ever so much greater than the evidence for many writings of classical authors, the authenticity of which no-one dreams of questioning. And if the New Testament were a collection of secular writings, their authenticity would generally be regarded as beyond all doubt. It is a curious fact that historians have often been much readier to trust the New Testament records than have many theologians.[93]

---

[92] Craig L. Blomberg, *Can We Still Believe the Bible?: An Evangelical Engagement with Contemporary Questions* (Grand Rapids: Brazos Press, 2014), 27.

[93] F.F. Bruce, *The New Testament Documents: Are They Reliable?* (Downers Grove: InterVarsity Press, 1981), 15.

Sir Frederic Kenyon, former director of the British Museum and one of the greatest authorities on the history of New Testament textual criticism makes this authoritative claim, "in no other case is the interval of time between the composition of the book and the date of the earliest manuscripts so short as in that of the New Testament."[94] Kenyon continues to make his point:

> "In no other case is the interval of time between the composition of the book and the date of the earliest manuscripts so short as in that of the New Testament."

> The number of manuscripts of the New Testament, of early translations from it, and of quotations from it in the oldest writers of the Church, is so large that it is practically certain that the true reading of every doubtful passage is preserved in one or other of these ancient authorities. This can be said of no other ancient book in the world.[95]

Daniel Wallace describes it in these glowing terms:

> In terms of extant manuscripts, the New Testament textual critic is confronted with an embarrassment of riches. If we have doubts about what the original New Testament said, those doubts would have to be multiplied a hundred-fold for the average classical author. And when we compare the New Testament manuscripts with the very best that the classical world has to offer, it still stands head and shoulders above the rest. The New Testament is far and away the best-attested work of Greek or Latin literature from the ancient world.[96]

---

[94] Sir Frederic Kenyon, quoted in Lee Strobel, *The Case for Faith: A Journalist's Personal Investigation of the Evidence for Jesus* (Grand Rapids: Zondervan, 1998), 82.
[95] Sir Frederic Kenyon, *Our Bible and the Ancient Manuscripts* (New York: Harper Row, 1958), 23.
[96] Bart D. Ehrman and Daniel B. Wallace, *The Reliability of the New Testament: Bart D. Ehrman and Daniel B. Wallace in Dialogue* (Minneapolis: Fortress Press, 2011), 34.

Kenyon makes a similar convincing statement:

> The last foundation for any doubt that the Scriptures have come down to us substantially as they written has now been removed. Both the authenticity and the general integrity of the books of the New Testament may be regarded as finally established.[97]

→ INSIGHT #2: ALL DIFFERENCES (VARIANTS) IN MANUSCRIPTS ARE NOT EQUAL

In understanding this observation it's helpful to make sure we define a very important term. The term variant refers to "any place among the manuscripts in which there is variation in wording, including word order, omission or addition of words, even spelling differences."[98]

This definition is crucial since Ehrman regularly questions the reliability of the Bible by asserting that there are between 200,000 and 400,000 variants in the New Testament manuscripts. Furthermore, he claims that there are more variants among our manuscripts than there are words in the New Testament. He draws the following implications:

> All scribes did this [i.e., made mistakes and/or intentionally changed the text of Scripture when copying]. So rather than actually having the inspired words of the autographs (i.e., the originals) of the Bible, what we have are error-ridden copies of the autographs.[99]

Ehrman gives the impression that there are so many variants in our manuscripts that we could never know what the New Testament authors originally wrote. He claims that the Bible's picture of Jesus has totally lost contact with the actual Jesus of the first century.

---

[97] Sir Frederic Kenyon, quoted in F.F. Bruce, *The New Testament Documents: Are They Reliable?* (Downers Grove: InterVarsity Press, 1981), 20.
[98] Bart D. Ehrman and Daniel B. Wallace, *The Reliability of the New Testament: Bart D. Ehrman and Daniel B. Wallace in Dialogue* (Minneapolis: Fortress Press, 2011), 32.
[99] Bart D. Ehrman, *Misquoting Jesus: The Story Behind Who Changed the Bible and Why* (New York: HarperCollins Publishers, 2005), 5.

It's important to remember that the sheer number of variants is directly related to the incredibly high number of manuscripts in comparison to manuscripts of other ancient works of antiquity. The English Standard Version Study Bible expresses it this way:

> If this were the only piece of data available, it might discourage anyone from attempting to recover the wording of the original. But the large number of variants is due to the large number of manuscripts. Hundreds of thousands of differences among the Greek manuscripts, ancient translations, and patristic commentaries exist only because tens of thousands of such documents exist.[100]

It's also helpful to note that these variants are clustered around a small grouping of verses or passages. Craig Blomberg describes it this way:

> Less than three percent of them are significant enough to be presented in one of the two standard critical editions of the Greek New Testament. Only about a tenth of one percent are interesting enough to make their way into footnotes in most English translations. It cannot be emphasized strongly enough that no orthodox doctrine or ethical practice of Christianity depends solely on any disputed wording.[101]

Blomberg clarifies it even further:

> Those 400,000 variants, if there are that many, are spread across more than 25,000 manuscripts in Greek or other ancient languages. Suddenly the picture begins to look quite different. This is an average of only 16 variants per manuscript, and only 8 if the estimate of 200,000 variants is the more accurate one. Nor are the variants spread evenly across a given text; instead, they tend to cluster in places where some kind of ambiguity has stimulated them.

---

[100] *The ESV Study Bible, English Standard Version* (Wheaton: Crossway Bibles, 2008), 2588.
[101] Craig L. Blomberg, *Can We Still Believe the Bible?: An Evangelical Engagement with Contemporary Questions* (Grand Rapids: Brazos Press, 2014), 27.

. . . Only 6 percent of the New Testament and 10 percent of the Old Testament contain the vast majority of these clusters.[102]

Although the ancient scribes were incredibly meticulous, errors were inevitable. However, most of these errors were minor—simple one-character spelling errors or an occasional omission of a word.

Textual expert Daniel Wallace helps us better understand these variants:

> Once it is revealed that the great majority of these variants are inconsequential—involving spelling differences that cannot even be translated, articles with proper nouns, changes in word order, and the like—and that only a very small minority of the variants alter the meaning of the text, the whole picture begins to come into focus. Indeed only about one percent of the textual variants are both meaningful and viable.[103]

Consider the example provided by gifted apologist and author Francis Beckwith:

> George Bush was a Prosident of the United States.
> George Busl was a President of the United States.
> George Bush was a President of the Onited States.
> George Bush was a President of the United Stetes.
> Geroge Bush was a President of the United States.
> George Bush was a President of the United.

---

[102] Craig L. Blomberg, *Can We Still Believe the Bible?*, 16-17.
[103] Daniel B. Wallace, "The Gospel According to Bart: Review of '*Misquoting Jesus: The Story Behind Who Changed the Bible and Why,*'" by Bart D. Ehrman, 330.

In comparing the six examples above, it is quite easy to recognize that the original sentence read; "George Bush was a President of the United States." Although each of the six example sentences has a minor error, the original sentence can be reconstructed with a very high degree of certainty.[104]

70 percent of the 400,000 differences are simple things like spelling errors. Wallace concludes that "70 to 80 percent of all textual variants are spelling differences that can't even be translated into English and have zero impact on meaning."[105]

> "70 to 80 percent of all textual variants are spelling differences that can't even be translated into English and have zero impact on meaning."

The beauty of the modern Bible is that those gifted textual experts have attempted to identify those textual variants that might have some significance on the meaning of the Scripture. The English Standard Version (ESV) notes:

> Textual variants are noted in the ESV with a footnote that begins, "Some manuscripts . . . " The absence of any such footnote (which is the case with far more than 99 percent of the words in the English NT) indicates that these translation teams have a high degree of confidence that the words in their English translation accurately represent the words of the NT as they were originally written.[106]

---

[104] Francis Beckwith, quoted in "Reliability of Scripture," *Reliable Truth*, accessed November 5, 2014, http://radicaltruth.net/index.php/learn/radical-truth-christianity/29-reliability-of-scripture.
[105] Daniel Wallace, quoted in Lee Strobel, *The Case for the Real Jesus: A Journalist Investigates Current Attacks on the Identity of Christ* (Grand Rapids: Zondervan, 2007), 86.
[106] *The ESV Study Bible, English Standard Version* (Wheaton: Crossway Bibles, 2008), 2589.

INSIGHT #3: DIFFERENCES (VARIANTS) IN MANUSCRIPTS ARE NOT FATAL

Although critics like Ehrman enjoy sensationalizing the number of variants, these differences are not fatal. These differences do not place the reliability of the New Testament in doubt. Actually, we have discovered that ninety-seven to ninety-nine percent of the content of the New Testament manuscripts are beyond question. Furthermore, of the differences or variants that cause textual criticism scholars significant concern, it is important to recognize that none of them impact or change a central doctrine of the Christian faith. Listen to the assurances of great textual experts who emphasize that no manuscript variant has changed a single central doctrine. Historian Philip Schaff makes this observation:

> Of the differences or variants that cause textual criticism scholars significant concern, it is important to recognize that none of them impact or change a central doctrine of the Christian faith.

> Only 400 of the so-called 100,000 or 150,000 variations materially affect the sense. Of these, again, not more than about fifty are really important for some reason or other; and even of these fifty not one affects an article of faith or a precept of duty which is not abundantly sustained by other and undoubted passages, or by the whole tenor of Scriptures.[107]

Sir Frederic Kenyon makes this authoritative claim:

> One word of warning, already referred to, must be emphasized in conclusion. No fundamental doctrine of the Christian faith rests on a disputed reading. . . . It cannot be too strongly asserted that in substance the text of the Bible is certain.[108]

---

[107] Phillip Schaff, *A Companion to the Greek Testament and the English Version* (New York: Harper & Brothers, 2012), 177.
[108] Sir Frederic Kenyon, *Our Bible and the Ancient Manuscripts* (New York: Harper Row, 1958), 23

Blomberg puts it this way:

> 97-99% of the New Testament can be constructed beyond any reasonable doubt, and no Christian doctrine is founded solely or even primarily on textually disputed passages.[109]   *CLASS*

Kenyon uses the strongest terms to reassure the Christian:

> The Christian can take the whole Bible in his hand and say without fear or hesitation that he holds in it the true Word of God, handed down without essential loss from generation to generation throughout the centuries.[110]

Even Biblical critic Bart Ehrman concedes in the appendix of his book, "essential Christian beliefs are not affected by textual variants in the manuscript tradition of the New Testament."[111]

It's reassuring to realize that textual criticism experts hold the New Testament documents with such tremendous reliability. Although the Christian can have great confidence in the reliability of the Bible, there are still several questions that Christians naturally ask when thinking about these issues.

QUESTION #1: IF GOD INSPIRED THE ORIGINAL DOCUMENTS, WHY DIDN'T HE PRESERVE THE ORIGINAL DOCUMENTS? *No LAMINATOR MACHINE*

Christians believe in the inspiration of Scripture. Divine inspiration teaches that God superintended the human authors in such a way that they wrote without error. This is why we believe that Scripture is "God-breathed." God so directed the writers that the sixty-six books they

---

[109] Craig Blomberg, "The Historical Reliability of the New Testament," quoted in William Lane Craig, *Reasonable Faith: Christian Truth and Apologetics* (Wheaton: Crossway Books, 1994), 194.

[110] Sir Frederic Kenyon, *Our Bible and the Ancient Manuscripts (New York: Harper Row, 1958)*, 23.

[111] Bart Ehrman, quoted in Craig L. Blomberg, *Can We Still Believe the Bible?: An Evangelical Engagement with Contemporary Questions* (Grand Rapids: Brazos Press, 2014), 28.

produced were free of error and exactly what God revealed to the human authors of Scripture:

> [16] All Scripture is God-breathed and is useful for teaching, rebuking, correcting and training in righteousness, [17] so that the man of God may be thoroughly equipped for every good work.
> 2 Timothy 3:16-17

> [20] Above all, you must understand that no prophecy of Scripture came about by the prophet's own interpretation. [21] For prophecy never had its origin in the will of man, but men spoke from God as they were carried along by the Holy Spirit.
> 2 Peter 1:20-21

However, when we speak of divine inspiration we are referring only to the process by which the original documents were composed. Technically speaking, when someone asks the question, "Are the translations of the Bible inspired and inerrant?" The answer is no, they are not. While many of the translations available today are superb in quality, they are not absolutely free of error. Of course, this doesn't mean that we can't trust the Bibles that we read in the morning or at church. Due to the dedicated efforts of textual critics and Christian translators the translations available today are superb and trustworthy.

> Due to the dedicated efforts of textual critics and Christian translators the translations available today are superb and trustworthy.

The natural question arises, "If God inspired the text perfectly, why didn't He preserve the text perfectly?"

Allow me to begin with a personal illustration from my 90-year-old father who is a proud World War II veteran. He served on the U.S.S. Barrier and the U.S.S. Black for over two years toward the end of the war. Of course, he's equally proud and eager to receive senior citizen and military discounts at restaurants and stores like Lowes. Obviously, at ninety my dad doesn't need to show proof that he is a senior citizen, although he looks great for his age. However, when he's not wearing his World War II cap he needs to prove his veteran status. He decided to shrink his official discharge certificate to the size of a credit card and laminate it. However, imagine if my dad had folded his original discharge papers and placed them in his wallet. Over time, they would have faded and torn apart.

Here's the simple truth—the New Testament authors did not have a laminating machine that would protect the documents from normal wear and tear. Repeatedly handling and sharing the original New Testament documents would have eventually caused them to fade and disintegrate. As they began to fall apart copies had to be made so that the Bible was available to each and every generation across the world.

> As they begin to fall apart copies had to be made so that the Bible was available to each and every generation across the world. God wasn't surprised by this development.

God wasn't surprised by this development. He knew it was coming. It's part of living in a world where thoughts get written down on documents that can ultimately fall apart. Although the Scriptures claim that the original autographs are inspired by God (2 Timothy 3:16; 2 Peter 1:20,21) it was clear that natural processes, due to the writing materials and extensive handling, would eventually cause these valuable documents to deteriorate.

Although it might have solved some trust issues if God had promised to preserve the original documents this was clearly not God's design. Fortunately, we have more New Testament documents than for any other ancient document in antiquity.

However, before we leave the issue of the original autographs, listen to the perspective from Craig Blomberg:

> Most laypeople and scholars alike have usually assumed that a heavily used manuscript would wear out after a decade or two so that there might be dozens of copies (of copies of copies . . .) having to be produced over just a few centuries (exactly the model Ehrman depends on for his theories). In fact, the original copy of a biblical book would most likely have been used to make countless

new copies over a period of several centuries, leading to still more favorable conditions for careful preservation of its contents. This is precisely what we see at Qumran, with scrolls of Old Testament books being preserved for 200-300 years. So when Bart Ehrman writes 'We don't even have . . . copies of the copies of the copies of the originals,' he is almost certainly wrong. Second- and third-century New Testament manuscripts may well be copies of the very autographs, or at least copies of those copies.[112]

QUESTION #2: CAN WE TRUST THE SELECTION OF THE BOOKS OF THE CANON?

In addition to questioning the accuracy of the existing New Testament manuscripts some modern-day thinkers question how the books were selected to be part of the official canon of Scripture. Ehrman expresses it this way:

> For the most part they were suppressed, forgotten, or destroyed—in one way or another lost, except insofar as they were mentioned by those who opposed them, who quoted them precisely in order to show how wrong they were.[113]

In order to answer this scathing critique there are a series of observations that are extremely helpful. First, the New Testament provides helpful insight into the early process of the church's recognition of letters as Scripture. 1 Timothy 5:18 and 2 Peter 3:15-16 both seem to imply that the Apostle Paul and the Apostle Peter recognized that widely circulated letters in their day were already viewed as Scripture.

Second, the early church recognized three universal tests which enabled them to determine whether or not a book was Scriptural. The three criteria were apostolicity, catholicity, and orthodoxy. Apostolicity refers to whether or not the books were written during the apostolic

---

[112] Craig L. Blomberg, *Can We Still Believe the Bible?*, 34.
[113] Bart Ehrman, quoted in Craig L. Blomberg, *Can We Still Believe the Bible?*, 44.

age. Put another way, the early church was looking for books that were written by first-century eyewitnesses. Catholicity refers to whether or not believers from around the world were in agreement on the importance and use of these books. Orthodoxy refers to whether or not the books were faithful to the historic teaching of Jesus and the apostles. The twenty-seven books of the New Testament passed these three tests while other books failed. Craig Blomberg describes it this way:

> There is very little chance that the books not included in the New Testament canon, at any significant point in which they differ from those that were included . . . came to be recognized as orthodoxy.[114]

Third, although the claims of critics make a splash on social media it's important to realize that in reality there are very few books that were seriously considered to be included as part of the New Testament canon. Blomberg cites a study by Lee McDonald that details the thirty earliest known "Lists and Catalogues of New Testament Collections from the second through sixth centuries." He makes this observation:

> Exactly fourteen writings outside of the standard twenty-seven-book New Testament are commended at least once, though sometimes in separate categories that indicate the writer's or compiler's doubts about them. Ten of these fourteen documents appear on only one of the thirty lists.[115]

This doesn't paint a picture of books that barely missed the cut to be included into the New Testament canon. The belief that the church suppressed or excluded books from the canon is a myth created by critics to suggest that the church mishandled the process. Nothing could be further from the truth.

---

[114] Ibid., 59.
[115] Ibid., 56-57.

Furthermore, in the early centuries of the church including these writings into the recognized New Testament canon was not seriously considered. Once again, Blomberg cites the evidence:

> In the late second century, the Muratorian Canon listed the twenty undisputed books of the New Testament mentioned above plus Hebrews, making twenty-one. Irenaeus acknowledges twenty-two by including 2 John. . . . Tertullian, at the beginning of the third century, mentions twenty-three books for a New Testament, including James and Revelation but not 2 John.[116]

It's important to recognize that although some of the twenty-seven books were doubted because of their size or uncertainty regarding apostle authorship, other books like the Didache, the Epistle of Barnabas, The Shepherd of Hermas, the Preaching of Peter, and the Acts of Paul were always considered dubious.

During the Council of Nicea in AD 325 Constantine commissioned Eusebius to have fifty new Bibles copied, yet there was never any record of a debate considering which New Testament books to include—an indication that the issue of the canon was already settled. Blomberg summarizes the facts regarding the official recognition of the canon:

> The first official promulgation of a list with the twenty-seven books of our New Testament canon occurred a generation later, in AD 367, when Athanasius, bishop of Alexandrea, wrote his Easter encyclical (papal letter) to the rest of the church and listed precisely the books that Christians still acknowledge today. The Councils of Hippo (393) and Carthage (397), both in North Africa, more formally ratified the recognition of these twenty-seven books.[117]

---

[116] Ibid., 67.
[117] Ibid., 68.

QUESTION #3: ARE THERE VERSES OR PASSAGES THAT PROBABLY DON'T BELONG IN THE NEW TESTAMENT?

Experts in the study of textual criticism have repeatedly affirmed that the Bible is reliable to a tremendously high degree—ninety-seven to ninety-nine percent. However, there have been a handful of questionable verses and/or passages that have bothered evangelical scholars for quite a long time.

Although this entire issue may be disconcerting for the reader I think pastors, leaders, and scholars have an ethical obligation not only to raise these issues but to provide Christians with answers so that their faith can withstand the criticism from skeptics and scholars.

> Although there are no textual differences (variants) that impact a central doctrine of the church there are a handful of passages (1 John 5:7; John 7:33-8:1; Mark 16:9-20, etc.) that the manuscript evidence seems to indicate were probably not part of the original autographs.

As I've previously mentioned, Christians have every reason to believe in the reliability of the Bible. However, we must be willing to make some tough admissions. Although there are no textual differences (variants) that impact a central doctrine of the church there are a handful of passages (1 John 5:7; John 7:53-8:1; Mark 16:9-20, etc.) that the manuscript evidence seems to indicate were probably not part of the original autographs. Fortunately, Mark 16:9-20 and John 7:53-8:1 are the only disputed passages involving more than two verses in length. Devout evangelical Daniel Wallace summarizes it this way:

> Three of these passages have been considered inauthentic by most NT scholars—including most evangelical NT scholars—for well over a century (Mark 16:9-20; John 7:53-8:11; and 1 John 5:7-8).[118]

---

[118] Daniel B. Wallace, "The Gospel According to Bart: Review of 'Misquoting Jesus: The Story Behind Who Changed the Bible and Why,'" by Bart D. Ehrman, 335.

Textual experts are highly trained to use both external and internal evidence in evaluating those rare passages that are considered inauthentic. External evidence refers to the amount and quality of the manuscripts that support the different variant readings. Internal evidence refers to the kinds of changes a scribe was most likely to make as well as determining the original intent of the author.

A quick glance at virtually any contemporary English Bible still shows these passages (with the exception of 1 John 5:7-8) in their traditional places within the text. Most of these passages are enclosed in brackets and are accompanied by a very clear footnote that indicates some of the difficulties that academic scholars have with these sections. The reason for this concern is that the oldest and best manuscripts simply don't mention these portions of Scripture.

Although the evidence is clear, translators seem quite hesitant to clearly indicate that certain passages were not part of the original autographs. Wallace puts it this way:

> Translations follow *a tradition of timidity*. My own examination of over 75 translations in a dozen different languages reveals the same monotonous story: Translators keep these passages in the text of their Bibles because to do otherwise might upset some uninformed Christians. But Ehrman has let the cat out of the bag. . . . It is time for us to relegate these likely inauthentic texts to the footnotes. Otherwise, we will continue to placate uninformed believers, setting them up for a Chicken Little experience when they read books like *Misquoting Jesus*.[119]

Blomberg suggests something similar:

> The answer is that some people take serious offense at anything being left out of a given Bible translation that previous translations

---

[119] Daniel B. Wallace, "Can We Still Believe the Bible?," *Daniel B. Wallace*, last modified March 24, 2014, http://danielbwallace.com/2014/03/24/can-we-still-believe-the-bible/.

have typically included, and Bible translators and publishers want to avoid unnecessary hostility against them.[120]

In the spirit of providing Christians with the tools to be better prepared to answer questions I've included brief explanations of these three questionable passages. These explanations appear in readily accessible books such as the *English Standard Version Study Bible* (ESV), the widely popular *Bible Knowledge Commentary*, and Craig Blomberg's helpful book *Can We Still Believe the Bible?*

EXAMPLE #1: LAST TWELVE VERSES OF MARK (MARK 16:9-20)

The *English Standard Version* (ESV) places a bracket around this section and writes that "some of the earliest manuscripts do not include 16:9-20." The footnote at the bottom of the page indicates the following:

> This longer ending is missing from various old and reliable Greek manuscripts (esp. Sinaiticus and Vaticanus), as well as numerous early Latin, Syriac, Armenian, and Georgian manuscripts. . . . On the other hand, some early and many later manuscripts (such as the manuscripts known as A, C, and D) contain vv. 9-20. As for the verses themselves, they contain various Greek words and expressions uncommon to Mark, and there are stylistic differences as well. Many think this shows vv. 9-20 to be a later addition. In summary, vv. 9-20 should be read with caution. As in many translations, the editors of the ESV have placed the section within brackets, showing their doubts as to whether it was originally part of what Mark wrote, but also recognizing its long history of acceptance by many in the church.[121]

Many Christians have asked, "Where did the last twelve verses come from if they aren't considered authentic?" If Mark chose to finish his gospel account at verse eight he would have concluded it with the angel informing the women of Jesus' resurrection. It's possible that some

---

[120] Craig L. Blomberg, *Can We Still Believe the Bible?*, 23.
[121] *The ESV Study Bible, English Standard Version* ,1933.

ancient scribes might have doubted whether this was a legitimate way to end a Gospel. This might have led some to include a section similar to the ending of other gospel accounts.

Some evangelical scholars believe that Mark wrote his account to emphasize the fear of all the disciples. It's possible that he ended the way he did not because he was hiding the resurrection but simply to reaffirm the fear and confusion that was experienced by the disciples even as they realized that Jesus is risen.

The *Bible Knowledge Commentary* uses two whole pages describing its official position on this disputed passage:

> The two earliest manuscripts (Sinaiticus and Vaticanus) omit the verses though their respective scribes left some blank space after verse 8, suggesting that they knew of a longer ending but did not have it in the manuscript they were copying. Most all other manuscripts (fifth century on) as well as early versions support the inclusion of verses 9-20. . . . A view which seems to account for the relevant evidence and to raise the least number of objections is that (a) Mark purposely ended his Gospel with verse 8 and (b) Verses 9-20, though written or compiled by an anonymous Christian writer, are historically authentic and are part of the New Testament canon. In this view, very early in the transmission of Mark's Gospel (perhaps shortly after AD 100) verse 9-20 were added to verse 8 without any attempt to match Mark's vocabulary. . . . The material was included early enough in the transmission process to gain recognition and acceptance by the church as part of canonical Scripture.[122]

After evaluating the manuscript evidence, the obvious difference in the style of writing in the disputed portion and the troubling inclusion of snake-handling in verse 18 cause Craig Blomberg to doubt the authenticity of the last twelve verses of Mark when he concludes, "All

---

[122] John D. Grassmick, "Mark," in *Bible Knowledge Commentary, New Testament Edition,* ed. John F. Walvoord and Roy B. Zuck (Wheaton: Victor Books, 1983), 193-194.

this makes it overwhelmingly likely that Mark did not originally contain these verses."[123]

EXAMPLE #2: THE STORY OF THE ADULTERESS WOMAN (JOHN 7:53-8:11)

John's story of Jesus dealing with the adulteress woman is a beloved portion of the Bible. It contains a lot of emotional meaning for most Christians. Unlike the questionable portion in Mark's Gospel there is no objectionable content such as handling snakes or drinking their venom. What's troubling is that the story actually appears in multiple places in various manuscripts. Although this story is a favorite of pastors and Christians, the manuscript evidence for this story is very weak. The *English Standard Version* (ESV) places a bracket around this section and in the footnote section makes this comment:

There is considerable doubt that this story is part of John's original Gospel, for it is absent from all of the oldest manuscripts. But there is nothing in it unworthy of sound doctrine. It seems best to view the story as something that probably happened during Jesus' ministry but that was not originally part of what John wrote in his Gospel. Therefore it should not be considered as part of Scripture and should not be used as the basis for building any point of doctrine unless confirmed in Scripture.[124]

The *Bible Knowledge Commentary* makes a similar conclusion:

Almost all textual scholars agree that these verses were not part of the original manuscript of the Gospel of John. The NIV states in brackets that "The earliest and most reliable manuscripts do not have John 7:53-8:11." The style and vocabulary of this passage differ from the rest of the Gospel, and that passage interrupts the

---

[123] Craig L. Blomberg, *Can We Still Believe the Bible?: An Evangelical Engagement with Contemporary Questions* (Grand Rapids: Brazos Press, 2014), 19.
[124] *The ESV Study Bible, English Standard Version*, 2039.

sequence from 7:52-8:12. It is probably a part of true oral tradition which was added to later Greek manuscripts by copyists.[125]

EXAMPLE #3: THE TRINITARIAN FORMULA (1 JOHN 5:7)

The King James Version contains what scholars call the "Trinitarian Formula" in 1 John 5:7-8:

> For there are three that bear record in heaven, the Father, the Word, and the Holy Ghost: and these three are one. And there are three that bear witness in earth, the Spirit, and the water, and the blood: and these three agree in one.

The first sentence in verse seven is only found in seven or eight copies written in the fifteenth and sixteenth century. The evidence is so weak that most current translations have actually corrected the King James Version to the following (NIV):

> For there are three that testify: the Spirit, the water and the blood; and the three are in agreement.

This verse is one of the clearest examples of a verse that no textual scholar and no modern Bible translation believes is part of the original text of the New Testament. Apparently, a scribe in the Reformation period attempted to make the doctrine of the Trinity absolutely clear by including a verse that spelled it out in theological terms. Daniel Wallace observes:

> Finally, regarding 1 John 5:7-8, virtually no modern translation of the Bible includes the "Trinitarian formula," since scholars for centuries have recognized it as added later. Only a few very late manuscripts have the verses. . . . The passage made its way into our Bible through political pressure, appearing for the first time in 1522, even though scholars then and now knew that it was not authentic. The

---

[125] Edwin A. Blum, "John," in *Bible Knowledge Commentary, New Testament Edition*, ed. John F. Walvoord and Roy B. Zuck (Wheaton: Victor Books, 1983), 302-303.

early church did not know of this text, yet the Council of Constantinople in AD 381 explicitly affirmed the Trinity![126]

QUESTION #4: WHAT'S THE EARLIEST COPY (MANUSCRIPT) OR PORTION OF A COPY THAT WE POSSESS?

For well over a century an overwhelming number of liberal skeptics and scholars have claimed that the gospels and other New Testament letters were not written until AD 160. Because of this dating they taught that these documents could not have been written by eyewitnesses. Fortunately, a discovery was made in the 1930s that changed the landscape of how people look at the New Testament. The following background will help us appreciate this discovery:

> Fortunately, a discovery was made in the 1930s that changed the landscape of how people look at the New Testament.

- The earliest manuscripts discovered of the New Testament were made of fragments of the papyrus plant that grew in the Nile Delta in Egypt. Scholars have ninety-nine papyrus fragments that contain portions of passages or books of the New Testament.
- The Chester Beatty Biblical Papyri include portions of the four gospels and various letters from the apostles. They date as early as AD 200.

However, one of the most exciting discoveries was made in 1934 when C.H. Roberts of Saint John's College discovered a very significant scrap of papyrus that contained five verses (John 18:31–33, 37-38) from the Gospel of John. Roberts dated it to between AD 100 and AD 150. Other prominent researchers have concluded that it goes back to the reign of Emperor Hadrian (AD 117-138) or Emperor Trajan (AD 98-117). Lee Strobel in his interview with legendary New

---

[126] Daniel B. Wallace "The Gospel According to Bart: Review of 'Misquoting Jesus: The Story Behind Who Changed the Bible and Why,' " by Bart D. Ehrman, (New York: HarperCollins, 2005), 348.

Testament manuscript expert Bruce Metzger puts the discovery of this scrap of papyrus in historic perspective:

> That was a stunning discovery. The reason: skeptical German theologians in the last century argued strenuously that the fourth gospel was not even composed until at least the year 160—too distant from the events of Jesus' life to be of much historical use. They were able to influence generations of scholars, who scoffed at this gospel's reliability. . . . This finding has literally rewritten popular views of history, pushing the composition of John's gospel much closer to the days when Jesus walked the earth.[127]

CONCLUSION

The modern church is fighting an up-hill battle against our secular culture. The built-in bias against the biblical record has been an integral part of the academic mindset for close to 200 years. It is all too common for skeptics to make the following comments:

- The New Testament is comprised of legend and myth.
- The Gospels were not written until the second century.
- The New Testament is full of mistakes that make it unreliable.

Fortunately, the church has gifted scholars who provide Christians with the necessary tools to defend the Bible in the face of critics. This chapter has established a brief yet systematic approach that gives believers the confidence to believe in the reliability of the Bible.

Personally, whenever I feel fatigued by the non-stop criticism of the reliability of the Bible, I am reminded of Norman Geisler and William Nix's powerful assertion:

> The New Testament, then, has not only survived in more manuscripts than any other book from antiquity, but it has survived

---

[127] Lee Strobel, *The Case for Faith: A Journalist Investigates the Toughest Objections to Christianity* (Grand Rapids: Zondervan, 2000), 80.

? New test B4 AD 160

in a purer form that any other great book—a form that is 99.5 percent pure.[128]

SUGGESTIONS FOR ADDITIONAL READING

Lee Strobel, *The Case for Christ: A Journalist's Personal Investigation of the Evidence for Jesus*
Lee Strobel has perfected the art of interviewing Christian experts in his best-selling series of books (*The Case for Faith*, *The Case for a Creator*, and *The Case for Christ*). Strobel spends the first section of *The Case for Christ* focused on the trustworthiness of the Biblical record related to Jesus Christ. The last half of the book focuses on the evidence for the resurrection of Jesus Christ. Strobel's book is very helpful and easy to understand. He interviews the absolute best experts on these topics. A student interested in delving into this topic should start here.

J. Warner Wallace, *Cold-Case Christianity: A Homicide Detective Investigates the Claims of the Gospels*
J. Warner Wallace is a former homicide detective in Los Angeles County. He uses his extensive experience in working on cold cases to investigate the evidence related to many of the thorny issues facing the Christian faith. Wallace's use of real-life cold-case stories and straightforward conversation makes this a compelling read. Although he addresses issues of the existence of God, most of the content of this book surrounds evidence for the reliability of the gospel accounts. This book is a very helpful resource for the believer who wants to have greater confidence in the reliability of the New Testament gospel accounts.

---

[128] Norman L. Geisler and William E. Nix, *A General Introduction to the Bible*, quoted in Lee Strobel, *The Case for Christ*, 85.

Daniel B. Wallace and Bart D. Ehrman, *The Reliability of the New Testament: Bart D. Ehrman and Daniel B. Wallace in Dialogue*

This book records the dialogue between two scholars—a Christian and a self-described skeptic who walked away from the Christian faith. Daniel B. Wallace is a prolific Christian scholar and expert in the New Testament manuscripts. Bart D. Ehrman is a prolific New York Times best-selling author who is world famous for questioning the reliability of the New Testament. This book provides the Christian with insight into the very technical field of New Testament textual criticism. It's important to read a book that directly addresses many of the damaging comments made by Bart Ehrman, and Wallace is a trusted academic and evangelical who can answer Ehrman's claims.

Craig Blomberg, *Can We Still Believe the Bible?: An Evangelical Engagement with Contemporary Questions*

This book is a scholarly treatment of the issues facing the trustworthiness and reliability of the Bible. This is probably one of the more technical and detailed books that I recommend. Despite the technical nature of the material, Blomberg provides Christians with the tools to navigate this complex issue. This book is a superb resource and guide regarding the implication of the Bible's trustworthiness.

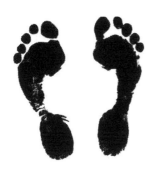

FOOTPRINT EIGHT:
THE RESURRECTION OF
JESUS CHRIST:
MYTH OR MIRACLE?

On a crisp autumn afternoon, candy heiress Helen Brach flew into the world's busiest airport, stepped into a crowd, and promptly disappeared without a trace. For close to forty years the mystery of what happened to this red-haired, animal-loving, philanthropist has baffled police and journalists alike. Police have been unable to determine the specific circumstances surrounding her disappearance. They have never found the body. Brach's disappearance remains a mystery in the most tragic sense of the word.

If mystery surrounded the disappearance of a candy heiress, it shouldn't surprise any of us that after 2,000 years there is mystery and intrigue surrounding the death and resurrection of Jesus Christ. Over 200 years ago, a Scottish scholar by the name of David Hume, who was a contemporary of Benjamin Franklin, weighed in on this very topic:

> When anyone tells me, that he saw a dead man restored to life, I immediately consider with myself, whether it be more probable, that this person should either deceive or be deceived, or that the fact, which he relates, should really have happened.[129]

In the same way that Charles Darwin gave people intellectual permission to disbelieve in God, David Hume gave people permission to disbelieve in miracles. In his groundbreaking work entitled *A Treatise of Human Nature*, Hume established the intellectual reasoning against both the possibility and probability of miracles. One of the most famous portions of Hume's argument goes like this:

---

[129] David Hume, quoted in R. Douglas Geivett and Gary R. Habermas, *In Defense of Miracles: A Comprehensive Case for God's Action in History* (Downers Grove: InterVarsity Press, 1997), 64-65.

A miracle is a violation of the laws of nature; and as a firm and unalterable experience has established these laws, the proof against a miracle, from the very nature of the fact, is as entire as any argument from experience can possibly be imagined.[130]

Natural laws are clearly the normal or regular ways that our world operates. However, miracles don't violate the regular laws of cause and effect; they simply have a supernatural cause that transcends nature. A miracle occurs as a unique and specific act of God, who stands outside the universe. Famous physicist Sir George Stokes described it this way:

> In the same way that Charles Darwin gave people intellectual permission to disbelieve in God, David Hume gave people permission to disbelieve in miracles.

It may be that the event which we call a miracle was brought on not by a suspension of the laws in ordinary operation, but by the super addition of something not ordinarily in operation.[131]

As Christians we must help people who struggle with the reality of the resurrection by figuring out whether they believe miracles are strictly impossible or simply improbable. The following is a brief approach for how to respond to our skeptical friends when they question the possibility or probability of miracles.

MIRACLES ARE IMPOSSIBLE

We live with a skeptical culture that believes that miracles are simply not possible. There is no need to evaluate any evidence or look into the issue—miracles simply don't happen.

---

130 David Hume, quoted in R. Douglas Geivett and Gary R. Habermas, *In Defense of Miracles: A Comprehensive Case for God's Action in History, 33*
131 Sir George Stokes, quoted in Norman L. Geisler and Ronald M. Brooks, *When Skeptics Ask: A Handbook on Christian Evidences* (Grand Rapids: Baker Books, 1990), 76.

Some skeptics assume that all experience is against miracles before they even look at the available evidence. Unfortunately, this is a crucial error in logic. Philosophers and thinkers call this circular reasoning. Great Christian thinker C.S. Lewis expresses the weakness of this thinking:

> Now of course we must agree with Hume that if there is absolutely "uniform experience" against miracles, if in other words they have never happened, why then they never have. Unfortunately we know the experience against them to be uniform only if we know that all the reports of them are false. And we can know all the reports to be false only if we know already that miracles have never occurred. In fact, we are arguing in a circle.[132]

MIRACLES ARE IMPROBABLE

Some skeptics don't automatically dismiss miracles as impossible, but they strenuously argue for the lack of evidence in supporting miracles. David Hume didn't believe there was enough evidence to support claims of a divine miracle such as a man being raised from the dead. It's not too hard to see how many of our family and friends

> They legitimately ask whether the available proof is sufficient to support something as amazing as bringing a person back from the dead.

might struggle with miracles based on the issue of evidence. They legitimately ask whether the available proof is sufficient to support something as amazing as a person coming back from the dead.

As we begin to have conversations with people who struggle with the evidence that surrounds miracles I would like to suggest several talking points:

---

[132] C.S. Lewis, *Miracles: A Preliminary Study* (New York: Macmillan Publishing Co., 1947), 105.

Talking Point #1: History can be trusted as an eyewitness to miracles. Although many skeptics routinely doubt our ability to know various truths, there are a number of clear pieces of evidence that show that history can be trusted to tell us facts. Although we can't determine everything in history there is a common core of undeniable historical facts which everyone can embrace. For example, we can objectively believe "in the assassination of Abraham Lincoln, the date of the Declaration of Independence, the selling of indulgences in 1517, and Caesar's crossing of the Rubicon."[133]

In addition, we frequently appeal to history in an effort to protect our culture from "made up" history. There are anti-Semitics who doubt the reality of the holocaust. Therefore, we appeal to the clear facts and evidence within history that point to the reality of the extermination of six million Jews during World War II.

> History has to be objective in order to protect us from bad history. We frequently appeal to history in an effort to protect our culture from "made up" history.

Finally, history has the ability to provide evidence for miracles because skeptics try to disprove a miracle by pointing out possible historical inconsistencies. Think of the following helpful illustration by gifted apologist and philosopher Francis Beckwith:

> For example, suppose archaeologists discover conclusive proof that the tomb of Jesus of Nazareth was not empty after his burial, that he did not consider himself to be the Son of God, and that his followers never claimed to have seen him alive after he died. Opponents of miracles would rightfully conclude that such evidence counts against the claim that Jesus was resurrected from the dead by God. But this implies that historians can investigate miraculous claims.[134]

---

[133] Francis Beckwith "History and Miracles," quoted in R. Douglas Geivett and Gary R. Habermas, *In Defense of Miracles: A Comprehensive Case for God's Action in History* (Downers Grove: InterVarsity Press, 1997), 91.
[134] Francis Beckwith "History and Miracles," quoted in R. Douglas Beivett and Gary R. Habermas, *In Defense of Miracles*, 88.

Talking Point #2: The weight of evidence is not the same as the amount of evidence. If one thing is clear it's this—more people die than come back to life. However, just because death occurs over and over again and a physical resurrection occurs only on rare occasions, this does not eliminate or minimize the evidence for the rare supernatural event. Here's the idea—evidence must be weighed. Just because the amount of deaths outweighs the number of resurrections, it does not automatically disprove the rare event. Remember, a truly wise individual does not make a decision merely on the probabilities but on the precise evidence for the occurrence of a specific event.

> Just because death occurs over and over again and a physical resurrection occurs only on rare occasions, this does not eliminate or minimize the evidence for the rare supernatural event.

Talking Point #3: Rare and unrepeatable events can be trusted. Hume seemed to think that repeated events have the greatest probability of occurring. Of course, it is important to remember that not everything in our experience is repeatable. What if scientific evidence can point to the supernatural cause of the beginning of our universe through a singular, non-repeatable event called the Big Bang? Gifted theologian and apologist Norman Geisler describes the significance this way:

> Indeed, if the scientist, based on observation of regular causal conjunctions in the present, can conclude that the weight of the evidence points to a big bang singularity in which the material, space-time universe exploded into being out of nothing some billions of geological years ago, then not only are miracles possible, but the big one has already been confirmed![135]

---

[135] Norman L. Geisler, "Miracles and the Modern Mind," quoted in R. Douglas Geivett and Gary R. Habermas, *In Defense of Miracles*, 82.

We live in a culture where there is a widespread anti-supernatural bias. As Christians we need good reasons to believe that miracles have happened. Remember, there is a lot at stake. The New Testament authors used miracles in order to provide compelling reasons to believe in Jesus. John's gospel concludes with this powerful argument:

> [30] Jesus did many other miraculous signs in the presence of his disciples, which are not recorded in this book. [31] But these are written that you may believe that Jesus is the Christ, the Son of God, and that by believing you may have life in his name.
> John 20:30-31

In our increasingly secular culture there are many people who view the events of history with a tremendous deal of skepticism. Although many applaud Jesus of Nazareth as a person of noble virtue, they believe it is too difficult to reach back into history to determine the validity of the resurrection of Jesus Christ. However, it is also very clear that if we systematically remove the possibility of the miracle of the resurrection, then we are left to try to explain clear historical events with a handful of naturalistic theories. N.T. Wright, who is one of the great current historical experts on the resurrection, makes this observation:

> Once you allow that something remarkable happened to the body that morning, all the other data fall into place with ease. Once you insist that nothing so outlandish happened, you are driven to ever more complex and fantastic hypotheses.[136]

In an attempt to address the growing skepticism of modern thinkers, this chapter will attempt to accomplish two things. First, it will outline several clear facts that support the contention that Jesus of Nazareth rose from the dead. Second, it will use the framework of these basic facts to challenge several naturalistic explanations for the empty tomb. Although it is not within the scope of this chapter to address every naturalistic explanation for the resurrection, it will attempt to briefly address three

---

[136] N.T. Wright, quoted in Kenneth Boa & Robert Bowman Jr, *20 Compelling Evidences that God Exists* (Colorado Springs: Cook Communications Ministries, 2005), 139.

naturalistic myths (Apparent Death Theory, Wrong Tomb Theory, and Hallucination Theory) that are common in normal conversations.

Many people who are reading these words are intimidated by the thought of broaching this concept with a skeptical family member or friend. I would like to make this process as easy as possible. I'm not going to quote a whole bunch of obscure facts or give you facts that your non-churched friends will struggle to believe. Instead I am going to use an approach that gifted resurrection experts like Gary Habermas and Michael Licona use effectively across the country. I'd like to briefly address four facts that the overwhelming majority of historians—secular or religious—agree are true. Each of these facts meets two criteria. They are supported by clear historical evidence and nearly every scholar accepts them.

> I'd like to briefly address four facts that the overwhelming majority of historians—secular or religious—agree are true. Each of these facts meets two criteria. They are supported by clear historical evidence and nearly every scholar accepts them.

FACT #1: JESUS CHRIST DIED BY CRUCIFIXION

The first step in developing a case for the resurrection is to establish the basic fact that Jesus of Nazareth died as a result of his public crucifixion. From the moment Jesus of Nazareth was put on public trial in front of Jewish and Roman authorities he was placed on an excruciating path toward death. There is much evidence that clearly points to the historical reality of the crucifixion of Jesus of Nazareth.

EARLY CHRISTIAN WITNESS

All four gospel accounts acknowledge the crucifixion and death of Jesus Christ. First Corinthians, which is one of the earliest and most attested New Testament books, records the following church creed:

> ³ For what I received I passed on to you as of first importance: that Christ died for our sins according to the Scriptures, ⁴ that he was buried, that he was raised on the third day according to the Scriptures, ⁵ and that he appeared to Peter, and then to the Twelve. ⁶ After that, he appeared to more than five hundred of the brothers at the same time, most of whom are still living, though some have fallen asleep.
> I Corinthians 15:3-6

Reading these verses is like stepping into a time machine. Don't miss the importance of what I am about to say. A mere three to five years after the crucifixion, Paul met two eyewitnesses to the crucifixion of Jesus Christ. In his meeting with Apostles Peter and James he was given an early church creed. This creed was a clear statement of the beliefs of the Christian church. This belief was not

> A mere three to eight years after the crucifixion, Paul met two eyewitnesses to the crucifixion of Jesus Christ. In his meeting with Apostles Peter and James he was given an early church creed.

gradually developed as a legend nor did it arise as myth. Listen to the observation of William Lane Craig: "The Christian saying quoted by Paul must have been in circulation prior to his visit in AD 36 and thus must have been formulated within the first five years after Jesus' death."[137]

NON-BIBLICAL HISTORIANS

Tacitus, one of the four Roman historians who covered the reign of Tiberius, records the death of Jesus as a known historical fact:

> Nero fastened the guilt and inflicted the most exquisite tortures on a class hated for their abominations, called Christians by the populace. Christus, from whom the name had its origin, suffered the extreme penalty during the reign of Tiberius at the hands of one of

---

[137] William Lane Craig, *Reasonable Faith: Christian Truth and Apologetics* (Wheaton: Crossway Books, 1994), 273.

our procurators, Pontius Pilatus, and a most mischievous superstition thus checked for the moment, again broke out not only in Judaea, the first source of the evil, but even in Rome . . . [138]

Josephus the Jewish historian made this statement about Jesus of Nazareth:

About this time there lived Jesus, a wise man. . . . For he was one who wrought surprising feats and was a teacher of such people as accept the truth gladly. He won over many Jews and many of the Greeks. . . . When Pilate, upon hearing him accused by men of the highest standing amongst us, had condemned him to be crucified, those who had in the first place come to love him did not give up their affection for him. . . . And the tribe of the Christians, so called after him, has still to this day not disappeared.[139]

The evidence provided by the early church and non-Biblical historians makes it difficult for skeptics to doubt the reality of the crucifixion of Jesus of Nazareth. For years the representatives of the Jesus Seminar have questioned many of the Biblical statements concerning Jesus. However, John Dominic Crossan, the leader of the Jesus Seminar, makes this remarkable admission related to the crucifixion:

I take it absolutely for granted that Jesus was crucified under Pontius Pilate. Security about the fact of the Crucifixion derives not only from the unlikelihood that Christians would have invented it but also from the existence of two early and independent non-Christian witnesses to it, a Jewish one from 93-94 C.E. and a Roman one from the 110s or 120s C.E.[140]

---

[138] Cornelius Tacitus, *The Annals 15.44*, quoted in Gary Habermas and Michael Licona, *The Case for the Resurrection of Jesus* (Grand Rapids: Kregel Publications, 2004), 49.

[139] Josephus, *Antiquities 18.64. vol. 9 Josephus in Ten Volumes*, trans. Louis H. Feldman (Cambridge, MA: Harvard University Press, 1981), quoted in Gary Habermas and Michael Licona, *The Case for the Resurrection of Jesus* (Grand Rapids: Kregel Publications, 2004), 49.

[140] John Dominic Crossan, *The Historical Jesus: The Life of a Mediterranean Jewish Peasant* (New York: HarperCollins, 1993), 372.

MYTH #1: APPARENT DEATH THEORY

Although the academic world is nearly unanimous regarding the certainty of Jesus' death by crucifixion, the ill-informed skeptic might resort to claiming that Jesus never really died but only appeared to die. They often ask, "Were the soldiers bribed to make sure He didn't die? Was there a plot? How can we really know Jesus was dead?"

> It is simply not feasible to believe that Jesus survived the crucifixion. Crucifixion victims experienced the most brutal of conditions including trauma, loss of blood, and shock.

There are several reasons to deny the apparent death theory. First, it is simply not feasible to believe that Jesus survived the crucifixion. Crucifixion victims experienced the most brutal of conditions including trauma, loss of blood, and shock. However, a crucifixion victim did not usually die of blood loss or excruciating pain. Habermas and Licona observe:

> The many physicians who have studied crucifixion over the years have invariable concluded that the major problem faced by victims of crucifixion was breathing, or more precisely—asphyxiation.[141]

Although it was brutal, the common practice of breaking the legs of crucified victims was a merciful act intended to bring death quickly to a victim who could no longer push up to breathe. In Jesus' case, the gospel accounts reveal that the Roman soldiers did not need to break his legs because the soldiers had already determined that he was dead. The Roman soldier pierced Jesus' side with a spear to ensure that he was dead. The spear entered through the rib cage and pierced the lung, the sack around the heart, and the heart itself and released blood and pleural fluids. Unquestionably, the crucifixion caused the death of Jesus

---

[141] William D. Edwards, Wesley J. Gabel, and Floyd E. Hosmer, "On the Physical Death of Jesus Christ," *Journal of the American Medical Association*, 255.11 (1986) : 1457, quoted in Gary Habermas and Michael Licona, *The Case for the Resurrection of Jesus*, 101.

of Nazareth. In a 1986 article in *The Journal of the American Medical Association*, Dr. William Edwards concluded:

> Clearly, the weight of the historical and medical evidence indicates that Jesus was dead before the wound to his side was inflicted. . . . Accordingly, interpretations based on the assumption that Jesus did not die on the cross appear to be at odds with modern medical knowledge.[142]

The second reason to deny the apparent death theory is that it is improbable that a deeply injured Jesus could have recuperated over the short span from the beginning of Passover to Sunday morning. More importantly, it would have been implausible for Jesus to have convinced His followers that he was the conquering Messiah resurrected from the dead. The German scholar D.F. Strauss wrote:

> It was not plausible that, having been scourged and crucified, Jesus pushed the heavy stone away from the tomb with pierced hands and walked blocks on pierced and wounded feet. Even if such a ridiculous scenario were possible, when he appeared to his disciples in his pathetic and mutilated state, would this convince them that he was the risen Prince of life?[143]

FACT #2: JESUS CHRIST WAS BURIED

The historic reliability of the burial of Jesus is the second key fact in building a case for the validity of the resurrection. In fact, as Craig observes, "If the burial account is historically credible, the fact of the empty tomb is nearly proved."[144]

---

[142] Edwards, Gabel, and Hosmer, "On the Physical Death of Jesus Christ," 1463, quoted in Habermas and Licona, *The Case for the Resurrection of Jesus*, 102
[143] David Strauss, *A New Life of Jesus*, 2 Vols. (Edinburg: Williams and Norgate, 1879), 1:412, quoted in Gary Habermas and Michael Licona, *The Case for the Resurrection of Jesus* , 102.
[144] William Lane Craig, *The Son Rises: The Historical Evidence for the Resurrection of Jesus* (Eugene: Wipf and Stock Publishers, 2000), 49.

The historic reliability of Jesus' burial has three significant implications. First, if the burial story is true the disciples could not have believed in the resurrection if a body still lay in the grave. Second, if the burial story is true the Jews wouldn't have believed in the disciples' message regarding the resurrection because they would have known where Jesus was buried. Third, if the burial story is true the Jewish authorities would have exposed the falsity of the resurrection by simply pointing to the tomb where the body of Jesus lay.

> One of the most historically convincing pieces of evidence is that Jesus of Nazareth was buried in the tomb of a known benefactor, Joseph of Arimathea.

In fact, one of the most historically convincing pieces of evidence is that Jesus of Nazareth was buried in the tomb of a known benefactor, Joseph of Arimathea. Joseph was a member of the Sanhedrin, which was the ruling party of the Jewish faith in the first century. Craig observes:

Even the most skeptical scholars acknowledge that Joseph was probably the genuine, historical individual who buried Jesus, since it is unlikely that early Christian believers would invent an individual, give him a name and nearby town of origin, and place that fictional character on the historical council of the Sanhedrin, whose members were well known.[145]

In the ancient world, the tomb of a prophet or holy man was typically preserved and venerated. When Jesus was crucified and buried, the disciples had no idea that He would rise from the dead. They would have been eager to learn exactly where Jesus had been entombed. William Lane Craig confirms the following ancient practiceDuring Jesus' day, there was an extraordinary interest in the graves of Jewish martyrs and holy men, and these were scrupulously cared for and honored. This suggests that the grave of Jesus would have also been noted. The disciples had no inkling of any resurrection prior to the general

---

[145] William Lane Craig, *The Son Rises*, 53.

resurrection at the end of the world, and they would therefore not have allowed the burial site of the Teacher to go unnoticed.[146]

The observation of the burial by the women as indicated by the gospel accounts also appears to have all the earmarks of a historical event. Habermas notes, "In the Mediterranean world in general, female testimony was normally avoided wherever possible in courts of law. . . . It was often disbelieved."[147]

> The majority of New Testament scholars agree with John A.T. Robinson that the honorable burial of Jesus is "one of the earliest and best-attested facts about Jesus."

If the early church was trying to promote a myth or legend they would not have used the testimony of women as the first and most important witnesses to the empty tomb and appearance of Jesus. As Habermas and Licona observe, "Given the low first-century view of women . . . it seems highly unlikely that the Gospel authors would either invent or adjust such testimonies."[148]

Finally, the early testimony by the Apostle Paul is evidence for the genuineness of the burial account of Jesus of Nazareth. In 1 Corinthians 15 Paul cites an early church creed that contains the recorded belief of the church regarding the burial of Christ. The majority of New Testament scholars agree with John A.T. Robinson that the honorable burial of Jesus is "one of the earliest and best-attested facts about Jesus."[149]

---

[146] William Lane Craig, "Did Jesus Rise from the Dead?," quoted in *Jesus Under Fire: Modern Scholarship Reinvents the Historical Jesus*, ed. Michael J. Wilkins and J.P. Moreland (Grand Rapids: Zondervan, 1995), 148-149.

[147] Gary R. Habermas, Antony Flew, and David J. Baggett, *Did the Resurrection Happen? A Conversation with Gary Habermas and Antony Flew* (Downers Grove: Intervarsity Press, 2009), 29.

[148] Gary Habermas and Michael Licona, *The Case for the Resurrection of Jesus*, 73.

[149] John A.T. Robinson, *The Human Face of God* (Philadelphia, PA: Westminster, 1979), 131.

Myth #2: Wrong Tomb Theory

Some critics attempt to explain away the evidence for the empty tomb by speculating that the women and the disciples simply went to the wrong tomb. When they discovered that it was empty they falsely believed that Jesus had risen from the dead. Richard C. Carrier clearly articulates the wrong tomb theory by claiming:

> Was Christianity begun by mistake? It is a distinct possibility. The surviving evidence, legal and historical, suggests the body of Jesus was not formally buried Friday night when it was placed in a tomb by Joseph of Arimathea, that instead it had to have been placed Saturday night in a special public graveyard reserved for convicts. On this theory the women who visited the tomb Sunday morning mistook its vacancy.[150]

A couple of things become clear from the historical account as it pertains to this naturalistic explanation for the empty tomb. First, the evidence clearly indicates that the tomb's location was known because a very prestigious man within the Jewish community (Joseph of Aramathea) buried Jesus in his own tomb. Second, according to the gospel accounts, the women noted precisely where the body of Jesus had been laid (Luke 23:55). It is improbable that the women would have gone to the wrong tomb after such a short span of time. If the disciples had gone to the wrong tomb:

> All that the Roman and Jewish authorities would have had to do would have been to go the right tomb, exhume the body, publicly display it, and clear up the misunderstanding. Yet, not a single critic is recorded to have even thought of this explanation for the Resurrection [sic] during the first few centuries of Christianity.[151]

---

[150] Richard C. Carrier, "The Burial of Jesus in Light of Jewish Law," quoted in Robert M. Price and Jeffery Jay Lowder, *The Empty Tomb: Jesus Beyond the Grave* (Amherst, NY: Prometheus, 2005), 369.
[151] Gary Habermas and Michael Licona, *The Case for the Resurrection of Jesus*, 98.

FACT #3: THE DISCIPLES SAW POST-CRUCIFIXION APPEARANCES OF CHRIST

The New Testament clearly indicates that the disciples saw what they believed were the post-crucifixion appearances of Jesus of Nazareth. Habermas and Licona make the following stunning statement:

> There is a virtual consensus among scholars who study Jesus' resurrection that subsequent to Jesus' death by crucifixion, his disciples really believed that he appeared to them risen from the dead.[152]

Evidence provides sufficient proof that these appearances were historically validated well before legends would have developed. First, each of the gospel accounts attests to the fact that the disciples saw Jesus subsequent to his death. Contrary to skeptical claims, these accounts cannot be dismissed as legendary accounts. Habermas and Licona observe:

> It is well-accepted that all the four gospels were written during the first century. Each gospel attests to the resurrection of Jesus, and Acts is the sequel to the third gospel, Luke. This means that four accounts were written within seventy years of Jesus at the latest, reporting the disciples' claims that Jesus rose from the dead.[153]

Furthermore, William Lane Craig observes:

> Legends do not rise significantly until the generation of eyewitnesses dies off. Hence, legends are given no ground for growth as long as witnesses are alive who remember the facts. In the case of the resurrection narratives, the continued presence of the 12 disciples, the women and the others who saw Jesus alive from the dead would prevent legend from significantly accruing.[154]

---

[152] Gary Habermas and Michael Licona, *The Case for the Resurrection of Jesus*, 49.
[153] Ibid., 53.
[154] William Lane Craig, *The Son Rises*, 107.

Second, the Apostle Paul claims that the early disciples had seen Christ subsequent to his death by crucifixion. The former persecutor of the church travelled to Jerusalem just three years after his conversion and five years after the crucifixion of Jesus to meet with Peter and James the brother of Jesus. Paul spent two weeks with Peter (Galatians 1:18) and spoke to James; both of these men claimed to have seen Jesus alive after death.

During this meeting Paul received the aforementioned church creed that outlined the historic facts of the death, burial, and resurrection of Jesus Christ. Habermas says, "The Christian saying quoted by Paul must have been in circulation prior to his visit and thus must have been formulated within the first five years after Jesus' death."[155]

MYTH #3: HALLUCINATION THEORY

In light of the evidence that the disciples of Jesus believed that they actually saw resurrection appearances of Jesus, some skeptics hypothesize that the disciples merely imagined or hallucinated the post-crucifixion appearances of Jesus Christ. Skeptics theorize that the disciples must have wanted for Jesus to come back from the dead so badly that they imagined it.

In his debate with William Lane Craig, Gerd Ludemann stated the hallucination theory in the following argument:

> Paul is the main source of the thesis that a vision is the origin of the belief in the resurrection. . . . When we talk about visions, we must include something we experience every night when we dream. That's our subconscious way of dealing with reality. A vision of that sort was at the heart of the Christian religion; and that vision, reinforced by enthusiasm, was contagious and led to many more

---

[155] Gary R. Habermas, Antony Flew, and David J. Baggett, *Did the Resurrection Happen? A Conversation with Gary Habermas and Antony Flew* (Downers Grove: Intervarsity Press, 2009), 48.

visions, until we have an 'appearance' to more than five hundred people.[156]

Several observations suggest the weakness of the hallucination theory. First, the disciples had not anticipated Jesus coming back from the dead after His crucifixion. They were not the likeliest candidates for a hallucination since they weren't sitting around hoping beyond hope that Jesus would come to life. In addition, it's important to remember that hallucinations are a projection of the mind. If the disciples were to project hallucinations of Jesus, they would have projected him in Paradise, where the righteous dead went and awaited the resurrection at the end of the world.

> The disciples had not anticipated Jesus coming back from the dead after His crucifixion. They were not the likeliest candidates for a hallucination since they weren't sitting around hoping beyond hope that Jesus would come to life.

Secondly, hallucinations are not group experiences; they are individual experiences. Habermas and Licona quote clinical psychologist Gary R. Collins, who observes that:

> Hallucinations are individual occurrences. By their very nature only one person can see any given hallucination at a time. They certainly are not something which can be seen by a group of people. Neither is it possible that one person could somehow induce a hallucination in somebody else. Since a hallucination exists only in this subjective, personal sense, it is obvious that others cannot witness it.[157]

Collins's observations demonstrate that the belief that hallucinations are contagious does not square with the reality of the psychological world. Finally, hallucinations can't explain the empty tomb. If the disciples had actually hallucinated, a person could have visited the tomb and seen that

---

[156] *Jesus' Resurrection: Fact or Figment? A Debate Between William Lane Craig & Gerd Ludemann*, ed. Paul Copan and Ronald K. Tacelli (Downers Grovelinois: Intervarsity Press, 2000), 45.

[157] Gary Habermas and Michael Licona, *The Case for the Resurrection of Jesus*, 303.

it was not empty. Although hallucinations might account for the appearance to individual disciples, how do we account for the Christ's appearance to the Apostle Paul? Habermas and Licona observe:

> He did not appear to have been in the frame of mind to experience a hallucination, since it seems he hated both Jesus and his followers and believed it was God's will to stop them. He was far from grieving over Jesus' death.[158]

Hallucinations also don't account for the testimony of James, who during Jesus' life did not believe that his brother was the Christ. Habermas and Licona observe, "It is unlikely that a pious Jewish unbeliever . . . was in the frame of mind to experience a life-changing hallucination with the risen Jesus."[159]

Fact #4: The Dramatic Change in the Disciples

The personal change and transformation in the lives of the disciples of Jesus Christ is documented beyond doubt. The disciples were shocked, devastated, and hopeless in the aftermath of Jesus' death (Luke 24:19-21). At one stage in their journey they were full of doubt, cowering in fear, and feeling hopeless about the future. At another stage they were bold, unafraid, and ultimately willing to die a martyr's death. Only the resurrection of Jesus Christ would have elicited this kind of transformation. Harbermas and Licona make the observation that:

> Shortly after Jesus' crucifixion, their lives were radically transformed to the point that they were willing to endure imprisonment, sufferings, and even martyrdom. This indicates that their claim of seeing the risen Jesus was the result of a strong and sincere belief that they truly had seen him.[160]

---

[158] Gary Habermas and Michael Licona, *The Case for the Resurrection of Jesus*, 107.
[159] Ibid., 107.
[160] Ibid., 93.

Skeptics claim that people will die for their religious beliefs if they sincerely believe they are true, but this misses the point. Contemporary martyrs die for what they believe to be true. The disciples of Jesus died knowing whether the resurrection was true or false. If Jesus did not rise from the dead then it is clear that the disciples knew they were dying for a lie. However, the early disciples knew without a doubt whether or not Jesus had risen from the dead. They claimed that they actually saw him, talked with him, and ate with him. If they weren't absolutely certain, would they have allowed themselves to be tortured to death for believing and teaching that the resurrection might have happened?

> The early disciples knew without a doubt whether or not Jesus had risen from the dead. If they weren't absolutely certain, would they have allowed themselves to be tortured to death for believing and teaching that the resurrection might have happened?

N. T. Wright concludes his comprehensive research on the resurrection by issuing this statement:

> The historian, of whatever persuasion, has no option but to affirm both the empty tomb and the 'meetings' with Jesus as 'historical events.' . . . We cannot account for early Christianity without them.[161]

The disciples were eyewitnesses to a miracle—the resurrection of Jesus Christ from the dead. William Paley states the following:

> Would men in such circumstances pretend to have seen what they

---

[161] N.T. Wright, *The Resurrection of the Son of God*, vol. 3, *Christian Origins and the Question of God* (Minneapolis: Fortress Press, 2003), 709.

never saw; assert facts which they had not knowledge of; go about lying to teach virtue, and, though not only convinced of Christ's being an imposter, but having seen the success of his imposture in his crucifixion, yet persist in carrying on; and so persist, as to bring upon themselves, for nothing, and with full knowledge of the consequence, enmity and hatred, danger and death?[162]

CONCLUSION

Modern man has fully embraced the talking point that, "The universe is all there is, all there was, and all there ever will be." They believe that humanity is an accident of nature and that man is no more significant than any other beast of the field. Unfortunately, without God, modern

> Is it so difficult to believe that Jesus Christ would do something so noble, good, and powerful that it would change the course of human history?

man will face the final challenge of death as a cosmic orphan—all alone and with no hope. The resurrection of Jesus Christ holds the ultimate proof that God has a future for humanity beyond the grave. If the resurrection is true:

> Then the Cosmic Orphan has found his home; for the resurrection of Jesus gives him both God and the immortality at once. . . . Therefore, the paramount question that we must now address is: Did Jesus of Nazareth really rise from the dead?[163]

I have often wondered why it is so very difficult for people to believe that God entered human history. Is it so difficult to believe that Jesus Christ would do something so noble, good, and powerful that it would change the course of human history? After all, history is full of stories of

---

[162] William Paley, *A View of the Evidences of Christianity*. 2 vols. 5th ed. (London: R. Faulder, 1796. Reprint. Westmead, England: Gregg, 1970), 1:327-328, quoted in William Lane Craig, *Apologetics an Introduction* (Chicago, Il; Moody Press, 1984), 176-77.

[163] William Lane Craig, *The Son Rises: The Historical Evidence for the Resurrection of Jesus* (Eugene: Wipf and Stock Publishers, 2000), 22.

remarkable, heroic, and brave people who have selflessly given of themselves for a greater good.

Maximilian Kolbe was a Catholic priest in Poland during World War II. The Nazis arrested Kolbe in February 1941 for publishing unapproved materials. By May, he was serving his sentence at Auschwitz. Life expectancy there for a priest was about a month. After guards beat him and left him for dead, fellow prisoners nursed him so that he survived, and he was transferred to Barracks 14.

In July, a single prisoner escaped from Barracks 14. Commandant Fritsch punished the remaining prisoners by sentencing ten prisoners to die in the starvation bunker. One of the ten cried out, "My poor wife! My poor children! What will they do?" Father Kolbe then broke rank and pleaded with the Commandant, "I would like to die in place of that man." Father Kolbe chose to die for prisoner 5659. After his confession, Father Kolbe was stripped of his clothes and marched with the other nine to their grave.

The basement was dark and hot. No food or water was provided because they were there to die. As days passed by, people heard their screams less frequently. To the contrary, faint sounds of singing arose from the basement. By August 14, all but four prisoners were dead. The living skeleton of Father Kolbe was one of those still alive. He was propped against the wall with a ghost of a smile on his lips. His eyes were wide open as though fixed on a faraway vision. He, like the other three, was given a lethal injection, and death relieved his pain. Father Kolbe's life is a compelling story of sacrifice for another human being.

Two thousand years ago Jesus of Nazareth died for all of humanity at the hands of the Roman Empire. His manner of death was so remarkable that a hardened and callous Roman Centurion said, "Surely this was the Son of God." Jesus of Nazareth was willing to be crucified for the sake of the prisoner inside all of us. He was willing to experience the unthinkable so that we could know and enjoy life with God. His resurrection from the dead validates the importance of His sacrifice. It stands as a testimony in history of God's concern for humanity.

SUGGESTIONS FOR
ADDITIONAL READING

William Lane Craig, *Did Jesus Rise from the Dead?*
Although many of Craig's books are profound and philosophically difficult to understand, this one hundred page book covers all of the evidence related to the resurrection of Jesus Christ.

Gary R. Habermas and Michael R. Licona, *The Case for the Resurrection of Jesus*
This book provides the greatest collection of positive arguments for the resurrection of Jesus Christ. Habermas and Licona are two of the greatest scholars in the field of evidence for the resurrection. The authors follow the minimal facts approach, which makes it easier for the reader to digest the fundamental issues. This book is a must for the Christian who wishes to master and defend the Christian position of the resurrection of Jesus.

Gary R. Habermas and Antony Flew, *Did Jesus Rise From the Dead?*
This debate featured the foremost Christian expert on the resurrection and one of the most influential atheists in the 21st century. The interaction between the two scholars is friendly yet insightful. If you wish to better understand the mindset of the skeptic this book will help.

IS MORMONISM CHRISTIAN?

Several years ago, *USA Today* printed the following headline,

> Christian but Different: Members of the Church of Jesus Christ of
> Latter-day Saints say they are Christian but neither
> Protestant nor Catholic.

In one moment the debate over the response to Mormonism took a dramatic step in a new direction. More than other groups, Mormons claim to be Christian. They cite their official name as the Church of Jesus Christ of Latter-day Saints. They believe Jesus Christ is the Savior of the world (although not in the Biblical sense of salvation by grace alone and faith alone). They insist that their devotion to Christ makes them authentically Christian. Gordon B. Hinckley, who served as president of The Church of Jesus Christ of Latter-day Saints from 1995 to 2008, makes this powerful statement on the official Mormon website:

> We are Christians in a very real sense and that is coming to be more and more widely recognized. Once upon a time people everywhere said we are not Christians. They have come to recognize that we are, and that we have a very vital and dynamic religion based on the teachings of Jesus Christ. We, of course, accept Jesus Christ as our Leader, our King, our Savior . . . the dominant figure in the history of the world, the only perfect Man who ever walked the earth, the living Son of the living God. He is our Savior and our Redeemer through whose atoning sacrifice has come the opportunity of eternal life. Members of The Church of Jesus Christ of Latter-day Saints pray and worship in the name of Jesus Christ. He is the center of our faith and the head of our Church. The Book of Mormon is another

Testament of Jesus Christ and witnesses of His divinity, His life, and His Atonement.[164]

The movement to legitimize Mormonism was highlighted on a national stage when Mitt Romney, a practicing Mormon, ran for President of the United States in 2012. His Mormon faith was presented as part of the religious mainstream of America. It's within this political and religious environment that Christians must ask two essential and overarching questions,

- Is Mormonism uniquely Christian?
- Is Mormonism uniquely true?

Both of these are valid questions because Mormonism makes some extraordinary claims. Mormons claim that the Church of Jesus Christ of Latter-day Saints is the one true representation of Christianity. They claim that their views are not only true but best represent the views of Jesus Christ when He stepped foot on this planet.

Mormons believe that about 180 years ago, a young man by the name of Joseph Smith was faced with the dilemma of which church to join. Having decided that only God could tell him which church was right, he recorded the following interaction with two divine beings:

> My object in going to inquire of the Lord was to know which of all the sects was right, that I might know which to join. . . . I asked the Personages who stood above me in the light, which of all the sects was right (for at this time it had never entered in my heart that all were wrong)—and which I should join. I was answered that I must join none of them, for they were all wrong; and the Personage who addressed me said that all their creeds were an abomination in his sight; that those professors were all corrupt.[165]

---

[164] Gordon B. Hinckley, "Are Mormons Christians?," *Mormon.org*, accessed on January 20, 201, http://www.mormon.org/faq/mormon-christian.
[165]Joseph Smith, *Pearl of Great Price*, quoted in R. Philip Roberts, *Mormonism Unmasked: Confronting the Contradictions Between Mormon Beliefs and True Christianity* (Nashville, TN: Broadman and Holman Publishers, 1998), 28.

Because of these extraordinary claims, it is the obligation of the Christian to test or evaluate whether the Mormon claim is genuinely Christian and whether it is genuinely true:

> [1] Dear friends, do not believe every spirit, but test the spirits to see whether they are from God, because many false prophets have gone out into the world. [2] This is how you can recognize the Spirit of God: Every spirit that acknowledges that Jesus Christ has come in the flesh is from God, [3] but every spirit that does not acknowledge Jesus is not from God. This is the spirit of the antichrist, which you have heard is coming and even now is already in the world.
> 1 John 4:1-3

Is Mormonism Uniquely Christian?

The Mormon Church claims that Mormonism is the one true representation of Christianity. In addition, Mormons repeatedly use standard Christian terms to explain their understanding about God and salvation. However, despite their attempts to depict Mormonism as Christian, a number of individuals and groups have suggested that Mormonism is not uniquely Christian.

> The Mormon Church claims that Mormonism is the one true representation of Christianity. In addition, Mormons repeatedly use standard Christian terms to explain their understanding about God and salvation.

Time Magazine reported the following:

> In 1995 the Presbyterian Church (U.S.A.) issued national guidelines stating that the Mormons were not "within the historic apostolic tradition of the Christian Church." A more sharply edged report by the Presbyterians' Utah subunit concluded that the Latter-day Saints "must be regarded as heretical." [166]

---

[166] David Van Beame, "Kingdom Come," *Time Magazine*, last modified June 24, 2001, http://content.time.com/time/magazine/article/0,9171,138108,00.html.

The predominately Catholic intellectual magazine *First Things* wrote a powerful article entitled, "Is Mormonism Christian?" in which they conclusively answered, "No."

In his lecture on Mormonism at Biola University, Carl Mosser, a respected evangelical authority on Mormonism, described the Mormon faith as being outside the bounds of orthodox Christianity in its basic beliefs. In their book entitled *The New Mormon Challenge*, Mosser and fellow editors Francis Beckwith and Paul Owen summarize their concerns about Mormon doctrine:

> There are other areas where we would like to see Mormon theology change: the doctrine of the materiality of spirit, the doctrine of divine embodiment, and the LDS form of the doctrine of the Trinity. But the three issues outlined above are absolutely fundamental and nonnegotiable. We do not feel that the status of Mormonism in relation to Christianity can ever change unless there is a willingness within the structures of the LDS Church to reconsider those issues. [167]

Although it is important for an alleged Christian movement to demonstrate devotion to Christ, it is not enough. Consider the insightful observations of Mosser:

> Devotion to Christ is obviously necessary for a religious movement to be considered Christian. But is it in itself sufficient? The New Testament and early Christian writers recognized that it is not— one's understanding of Jesus must be informed by a biblical understanding of reality. They also recognized that unbiblical worldviews can undermine one's understanding of Jesus in ways that inhibit true knowledge of God, thereby imperiling salvation.

---

[167] Francis Beckwith, Carl Mosser, Paul Owen, *The New Mormon Challenge: Responding to the Latest Defenses of a Fast-Growing Movement* (Grand Rapids: Zondervan, 2002), 400.

Erroneous worldviews are expressions of the idolatry that the gospel calls upon everyone to abandon.[168]

We live within a secular culture and a Christian climate that is too easily satisfied with sound bites and shallow theological answers. It is absolutely necessary that we explore beyond the simple Mormon claims of devotion to Christ to determine whether or not their understanding of Jesus is genuinely informed by a Biblical understanding of reality. After all, what we believe about God is far more important than what we call ourselves in public.

Noted religion expert Dr. James Beverley states that three tests—the God test, the salvation test, and the Bible test—are quite useful in evaluating whether or not Mormonism is uniquely Christian or whether a person must conclude that Mormonism is sub-Christian or non-Christian.

THE GOD TEST: Does the Mormon Church recognize the one God of the Bible as the true God, the God who is the Almighty Creator of heaven and earth?

Orthodox Christianity claims that God is an eternal being. God did not come into existence but has always existed as God. He is a self-existent being who has no prior cause or end. In addition, He is outside the normal time constraints of a finite being. As the unique Supreme Being of the universe, God knows all things and sustains the universe. Orthodox Christianity also claims that God is a spirit, not a physical being. The following Scriptures describe the orthodox Christian position:

> Before the mountains were born or you brought forth the earth and the world, from everlasting to everlasting you are God.
> Psalm 90:2

---

[168] Carl Mosser and Paul Owen, "Mormonism," in *To Everyone an Answer,* ed. Francis J. Beckwith, William Lane Craig, and J.P. Moreland (Downers Grove: InterVarsity Press, 2004), 330.

Now to the King eternal, immortal, invisible, the only God, be honor and glory forever and ever. Amen.
1 Timothy 1:17

No one has ever seen God, but God the One and Only, who is at the Father's side, has made him known.
John 1:18

Mormonism presents a very different picture of God. Their view of God is clearly different than the historic and orthodox Christian viewpoint. Mormonism claims that God the Father was once a mortal man who continually progressed to become a god. The following quotation from a Mormon training manual explains their view:

> Mormonism presents a very different worldview as it relates to God. The Mormon view of God is clearly different than the historic and orthodox Christian viewpoint.

The Prophet Joseph Smith said: 'If the veil were rent today, and the great God who holds this world in its orbit, and who upholds all worlds and all things by his power, was to make himself visible—I say, if you were to see him today, you would see him like a man in form . . .' God is a glorified and perfected man, a personage of flesh and bones.[169]

Mormonism teaches that humans are literally the younger siblings of Jesus since we are all born in preexistence. In other words, Mormons believe that every human existed in another world before they were born on Earth. As stated by Mormon expert James Beverley, "All humans lived in a prior state before life on Earth and are, like Jesus, the literal creations of heavenly parents."[170] Beverley continues his observations of the Mormon view of God:

---

[169] Gordon B. Hinckley, *Truth Restored - Gospel Principles* (Salt Lake City, UT: Deseret Book Company, 1990), 6.
[170] James Beverley, *Mormon Crisis: Anatomy of a Failing Religion* (Pickering, Ontario, Canada: Castle Quay Book, 2013), 116.

Mormons believe that there are many gods and that these gods formed and organized the universe. Mormons believe that gods used to be men and grew up to become gods. Mormons believe that worthy Mormon males can become gods someday. Mormons believe that Elohim is the one God of planet Earth. Elohim, the Father of Jesus, has a god over him.[171]

LDS apostle Bruce R. McConkie's comments confirm that Mormonism teaches this concept:

Three separate personages—Father, Son, and Holy Ghost—comprise the Godhead. As each of these persons is a God, it is evident, from this standpoint alone, that a plurality of Gods exists. To us, speaking in the proper finite sense, these three are the only Gods we worship. But in addition there is an infinite number of holy personages, drawn from worlds without number, who passed on to exaltation and are thus Gods.[172]

It's clear that Mormonism is not in keeping with orthodox views related to the nature of God. Although Mormons love to use the same Christian verbiage, their views about God appear to blend polytheism and New Age beliefs. Beverley makes this observation:

The Mormon view that there is more than one God is contradicted by clear biblical teaching in Deuteronomy 4:35, Isaiah 44:6-8, and John 17:3, among hundreds of other verses in the Bible that teach that only one God exists. . . . Further, the Mormon notion that God used to be a man is a stunning aberration from the mind of Joseph Smith. . . . That God is not a man is taught in Malachi 3:6 and Isaiah 44:6. Likewise, the Mormon view that God has a body of flesh and

---

[171] James A. Beverley, *Nelson's Illustrated Guide to Religions* (Nashville, TN: Thomas Nelson, 2009), 364.
[172] Bruce R. McConkie, *Mormon Doctrine* (Salt Lake City, UT: Bookcraft, 1958), 576-77.

bones is contrary to Psalm 139:7-10, Jeremiah 23:24, and John 4:24.[173]

THE SALVATION TEST: Does the Mormon Church recognize the central gospel message that salvation, rather than being merit-based, is by grace alone and faith alone in the sacrificial work of Christ on the cross?

According to the Christian faith, the human race is sinful and corrupt. Although we were all created by God, we are in a state of rebellion. All humanity has sinned (Romans 3:23) by virtue of their fallen nature and their flawed actions. Mankind's sin has created a spiritually bankrupt relationship between humanity and a perfect God (Romans 6:23).

The tremendous message of the gospel is that the death and resurrection of Jesus afford human beings the opportunity to be forgiven for their sins. Orthodox Christianity claims that salvation is by grace alone and faith alone (Ephesians 2:8, 9). The singular message of the Bible is that man is unable to atone for his sinful condition by his own meritorious actions or adherence to Biblical commands.

Mormon teaching differs from the Biblical teaching of salvation. Mormonism presents a view on salvation that alludes to similar Biblical terms but with a very clear difference. In the Articles of Faith, which express the central tenets of Mormon doctrine,

> Mormonism presents a view on salvation that alludes to similar Biblical terms but with a very clear difference.

the following statement is made, "We believe that through the Atonement of Christ, all mankind may be saved, by obedience to the laws and ordinances of the Gospel."[174] Consider the statement from former Mormon president, Spencer Kimball:

---

[173] James A. Beverley, *Nelson's Illustrated Guide to Religions* (Nashville, TN: Thomas Nelson, 2009), 375.

[174] James A. Beverley, *Nelson's Illustrated Guide to Religions*, 359.

One of the most fallacious doctrines originated by Satan and propounded by man is that man is saved alone by the grace of God; that belief in Jesus Christ alone is all that is needed for salvation.[175]

Dr. Beverley confirms the false teaching of Mormonism,"The Mormon understanding of eternal life is not rooted in an emphasis on grace alone through faith alone. Rather, eternal life is linked to following the rules and procedures of the Mormon Church."[176]

In fact, while Christians view salvation as a gift, Mormons view it as a loan. In other words, Jesus pays for our sins up front (and thus they call him "Savior"), but we have to pay him back for what he did with our good works. Listen to the description by President Spencer Kimball:

However good a person's works, he could not be saved had Jesus not died for his and everyone else's sins. And however powerful the saving grace of Christ, it brings exaltation to no man who does not comply with the works of the gospel.[177]

The Mormon version of salvation is taught using an analogy involving a benefactor who relieves a debtor from a huge debt. In exchange for keeping him from prison and paying his debts, the debtor must now keep the terms of the contract. In the Mormon worldview this analogy means that the person must repent and keep God's commandments if he or she is going to live with God.

The message of Mormonism continues to stray from the Bible's teaching on sin and salvation. Listen to this scary observation of Mormonism:

---

[175] Spencer W. Kimball, *The Miracle of Forgiveness* (Salt Lake City, UT: Bookcraft Inc., 1969), 206.

[176] James A. Beverley, *Nelson's Illustrated Guide to Religions*, (Nashville, TN: Thomas Nelson, 2009), 363.

[177] *The Teachings of Spencer W. Kimball, Twelfth President of the Church of Jesus Christ of Latter-day Saints* (Salt Lake City, UT: Bookcraft Inc., 1995), 71.

The fundamental problem for human beings is not sin but the fact that they exist in an unexalted state. That is, humans are divine beings in embryonic form who have not yet fulfilled their potential. . . . God and human beings share the same divine nature. The chief difference between us is that God has actualized far more of his divine potential than we have. In our current state we are but gods in embryo. On the more traditional reading of Mormon theology, God has not always existed as God. Rather, at one time he was like we are now. By obeying the laws of eternal progression he was exalted to the status of a God by the God above him.[178]

The ultimate goal is best expressed by former Mormon President Lorenzo Snow who stated, "As man is God once was; as God is, man may be."[179]

THE BIBLE TEST: Does the Mormon Church really follow the Bible? Are the clear and dominant teachings of Scripture believed? Does Mormonism add to, take away from, or ignore God's Word?

Orthodox Christianity claims that the Bible is the inspired Word of God in the original autographs. Christianity believes that the inspired record is absolutely inerrant (without error) as it was originally written by the authors. In addition, orthodox Christianity believes that the Bible is by far the most reliable ancient document of antiquity. However, Mormonism teaches that the Bible became corrupted over the years and must be corrected today by the Book of Mormon, the Doctrine and Covenants, the Pearl of Great Price, and the words of the living prophets—the presidents of the church. On their official website the Mormon Church details the official Articles of Faith, of which Article 8 states the following:

---

[178] Carl Mosser and Paul Owen, "Mormonism," in *To Everyone an Answer,* ed. Francis J. Beckwith, William Lane Craig, and J.P. Moreland (Downers Grove: InterVarsity Press, 2004), 334.
[179] R. Philip Roberts, *Mormonism Unmasked: Confronting the Contradictions Between Mormon Beliefs and True Christianity* (Nashville, TN: Broadman and Holman Publishers, 1998), 46-47.

We believe the Bible to be the word of God as far as it is translated correctly; we also believe the Book of Mormon to be the word of God.[180]

The Book of Mormon likewise alludes to this corruption of the Bible in 1 Nephi 13:26 which states:

And after they go forth by the hand of the twelve apostles of the Lamb, from the Jews unto the Gentiles, thou seest the formation of that great and abominable church, which is most abominable above all other churches; for behold, they have taken away from the gospel of the Lamb many parts which are plain and most precious; and also many covenants of the Lord have they taken away.[181]

Despite the all too common claims from Mormons about the unreliability of the Bible, it is important to point out that Mormons should be careful about casting aspersions on the historic reliability of the Bible. Modern anthropology has found little or no evidence for any of the cities and peoples listed in Mormon writings.

> Unfortunately, Mormonism's mistrust of the Bible has gained increasing notoriety because of the popularity of noted biblical skeptic, Bart Ehrman.

Unfortunately, Mormonism's mistrust of the Bible has gained increasing notoriety because of the popularity of biblical skeptic Bart Ehrman, whose books and public skepticism have stirred up much controversy and empowered groups like the Mormons to question the reliability of the Bible. Ehrman claims that the number of variants or differences that are found in various existing New Testament manuscripts total between 200,000 and 400,000. He makes the following statement:

---

180 Joseph Smith, *Pearl of Great Price, LDS.org*, accessed on February 10, 2015, https://www.lds.org/scriptures/pgp/a-of-f/1.8?lang=eng.
181 Ryan Turner, "Mormonism and the Corruption of the Bible," *CARM.org*, accessed on February 10, 2015, https://carm.org/mormonism-and-the-corruption-of-the-bible.

How does it help us to say that the Bible is the inerrant word of God if in fact we don't have the words that God inerrantly inspired, but only the words copied by the scribes—sometimes correctly but sometimes (many times!) incorrectly. . . . We don't have the originals! We have only error-ridden copies, and the vast majority of these are centuries removed from the originals and different from them, evidently, in thousands of ways.[182]

In contrast to Ehrman, evangelical experts in the science of textual criticism have made a couple of important observations. First, the discovery of the Dead Sea Scrolls solidified the claim that the Old Testament Scriptures are reliable records. The Dead Sea Scrolls contained fragments of almost every Old Testament book. Most importantly, they contained a complete copy of the Book of Isaiah dated approximately

> The New Testament Scriptures are the most reliable documents of ancient antiquity.

100 BC—almost one thousand years before any previous existing copy of Isaiah. Listen to the following observation regarding the significance of this discovery:

The Dead Sea Scroll version of Isaiah allowed scholars to compare the text over this period of time to see if copyists had been conscientious. Scholars were amazed by what they discovered. A comparison of the Qumran manuscripts of Isaiah proved to be word for word identical with our standard Hebrew Bible in more than 95 percent of the text. [183]

Some of the differences were simply matters of spelling or grammar. None of these differences changed the meaning of the passage in any way.

---

[182] Bart Ehrman in Lee Strobel, *The Case for the Real Jesus: A Journalist Investigates Current Attacks on the Identity of Christ* (Grand Rapids: Zondervan, 2007), 67.
[183] J. Warner Wallace, *Cold-Case Christianity: A Homicide Detective Investigates the Claims of the Gospels* (Colorado Springs: David C. Cook, 2013), 232-233.

Second, the New Testament Scriptures are the most reliable documents of ancient antiquity. The number of existing manuscripts, along with the short distance in time between the writing of the original and the earliest copies, places the Bible in a category of reliability unlike any other ancient document. Biblical textual expert Daniel Wallace observes:

> The quantity and quality of the New Testament manuscripts are unequalled in the ancient Greco-Roman world. The average Greek author has fewer than twenty copies of his works still in existence, and they come from no sooner than five hundred to a thousand years later. . . . We've got 25,000 to 30,000 handwritten copies of the New Testament.[184]

In contrast to Ehrman's skeptical view of the New Testament, Wallace makes an impressive case for the supreme reliability of the New Testament documents:

> Ehrman didn't prove that any doctrine is jeopardized. Let me repeat the basic thesis that has been argued since 1707: No cardinal or essential doctrine is altered by any textual variant that has plausibility of going back to the original. The evidence for that has not changed to this day.[185]

Dr. Geisler makes a similar observation:

> When a comparison of the variant readings of the New Testament is made with those of other books which have survived from antiquity, the results are little short of astounding. . . . The evidence for the integrity of the New Testament is beyond question.[186]

---

[184] Daniel Wallace, quoted in Lee Strobel, *The Case for the Real Jesus: A Journalist Investigates Current Attacks on the Identity of Christ* (Grand Rapids: Zondervan, 2007), 83.
[185] Daniel Wallace, quoted in Lee Strobel, *The Case for the Real Jesus*, 88-89.
[186] Norman Geisler and William Nix, *From God to Us: How We Got Our Bible* (Chicago, IL: Moody, 1974), 180.

IS MORMONISM UNIQUELY TRUE?

The second vital question that we must help people answer is whether or not Mormonism is uniquely true. The following section will address two questions—was Joseph Smith a true prophet and is the Book of Mormon true?

WAS JOSEPH SMITH A TRUE PROPHET?

When considering the truthfulness of Mormonism a person must consider the unique background and history concerning Joseph Smith. Is it more reasonable to believe that Joseph Smith had a genuine encounter with God or is it more reasonable to believe that it was a hoax of monumental proportions? In other words, is it more reasonable that the events surrounding Smith's vision from God were a genuine prophetic revelation or that Smith used his personal experiences and outside resources to create the master storyline contained within the Book of Mormon?

> Is it more reasonable to believe that Joseph Smith had a genuine encounter with God or is it more reasonable to believe that it was a hoax of monumental proportions?

EVIDENCE #1: JOSEPH SMITH'S FLAWED CHARACTER

Although the average Mormon holds Joseph Smith in incredibly high regard, there is mounting evidence that the moral fiber of his character was not consistent with an alleged prophet of God. For example, the Mormon Church publically acknowledged for the first time in November of 2014 that its founder participated in polygamous relationships. *The Salt Lake Tribune* publicized the admission of the Mormon Church:

> Mormon founder Joseph Smith took his first "plural wife," Fanny Alger, in the mid-1830s. He later married many additional women—including young teens and some who already were wed to other men—and introduced the practice of polygamy to select members in the 1840s. But Smith and his church distinguished between bonds for this life, which included full matrimonial relations, and

partnerships that would exist only in eternity—though it was not always clear which type of marriage the LDS prophet was practicing in every case.[187]

In response to the revelation by *The Salt Lake Tribune*, the official website of the Mormon Church admitted the following:

> In biblical times, the Lord commanded some of His people to practice plural marriage—the marriage of one man and more than one woman. Some early members of The Church of Jesus Christ of Latter-day Saints also received and obeyed this commandment given through God's prophets. After receiving a revelation commanding him to practice plural marriage, Joseph Smith married multiple wives and introduced the practice to close associates.[188]

Dr. Beverley describes the troubling aspect of Smith's behavior with this observation:

> The issue with Joseph Smith is not about polygamy per se or whether polygamy is ever right. It is about the lying, stealing, adultery, manipulation, coercion, spousal abuse and criminal behavior that Joseph engaged in while he practiced his particular brand of polygamy. It is about a so-called prophet of God using his alleged divine mantle to bed young women, including two under his own guardianship. Mormons who can defend all this can defend anything.[189]

In addition, Joseph Smith had a clear history of fraud and deception during the formative years of Mormonism. Researcher Fawn Brodie in her book *No Man Knows My History* details discovered documents that implicate Joseph Smith in criminal activity—using psychic means to find buried treasure, which was also called money-digging. This is very

---

[187] Salt Lake Tribune, November 11, 2014

[188] "Plural Marriage in Kirtland and Nauvoo," *LDS.org*, accessed February 10, 2015, https://www.lds.org/topics/plural-marriage-in-kirtland-and-nauvoo.

[189] James Beverley, *Mormon Crisis: Anatomy of a Failing Religion* (Pickering, Ontario, Canada: Castle Quay Book, 2013), 48.

troubling since Smith's account of translating the golden plates of the book of Mormon included the continued use of the same seer stone that he employed in his various illegal money-digging episodes. Smith's procedure was to place the stone in a white stovepipe hat, put his face over the hat to block the light, and then "see" the necessary information in the stone's reflections.

Mormon scholars have had to acknowledge the authenticity of various court records and the profile of Joseph Smith as a money digger. Mormon authority James Beverley states the implications of these findings:

> Researcher Fawn Brodie in her book *No Man Knows My History* details discovered documents that implicate Joseph Smith in criminal activity— using psychic means to find buried treasure, which was also called money-digging.

> As strange as it may seem, the Book of Mormon was birthed via an occult practice, one that earned Mormonism's founding prophet a criminal sentence. This is not a very inspiring start to a group that claims to be the only true Church of Jesus Christ.[190]

Further, Mormons cite the unlikelihood of the unschooled and Biblically illiterate Joseph Smith single-handedly writing the Book of Mormon as evidence for the supernatural origin for the book. However, several things make the human production of the Book of Mormon plausible. Smith was known to have told stories about American Indians that seemed similar to those contained in the Book of Mormon. Smith could have been creative enough to incorporate the theological issues of his day into the storyline of the Book of Mormon. Historians have noticed the similarity between Ethan Smith's *View of the Hebrews* written in 1823 and the Book of Mormon, which wasn't completed until 1830.

Former Mormon historian B. H. Roberts cites the following thirteen similarities between the two books:

---

[190] James Beverley, *Mormon Crisis*, 41.

- Both books set forth the Hebrew origin of the American Indian.
- Both talk of an ancient book hidden and buried in the ground.
- Both speak of prophets and seers.
- Both mention the Urim and Thummim and a breastplate.
- Both speak of ancient Egyptian inscriptions.
- Both talk of a civilized and barbaric element in the population.
- Both have references to the destruction of Jerusalem.
- Both talk of the gathering of Israel "in the last days."
- Both quote extensively from Isaiah.
- Both speak of a great Gentile nation rising up in America in the last days to save Israel.
- Both speak of the practice of polygamy among the early people.
- Both speak of widespread ancient civilizations on the American continent.
- Both speak of an appearance of a white god on the American continent.[191]

In light of his research, B. H. Roberts "found the possible connections between *View of the Hebrews* and the Book of Mormon very troubling."[192] Researcher Harry L. Ropp makes a similar observation, "Joseph Smith could have used his own natural genius and both the Spaulding manuscript and View of Hebrews, as well as other materials, to produce the Book of Mormon."[193]

EVIDENCE #2: JOSEPH SMITH'S FLAWED PROPHETIC ROLE

Joseph Smith has failed in his role as a prophet of God in several key instances. Many of Joseph Smith's prophecies have been inaccurate:

---

[191] B.H. Roberts in R. Philips Roberts, *Mormonism Unmasked: Confronting the Contradictions Between Mormon Beliefs and True Christianity* (Nashville, TN: Broadman and Holman Publishers, 1998), 107-108.
[192] James A. Beverley, *Mormon Crisis: Anatomy of a Failing Religion* (Pickering, Ontario, Canada: Castle Quay Book, 2013), 73.
[193] Harry L. Ropp, quoted in R. Philips Roberts, *Mormonism Unmasked: Confronting the Contradictions Between Mormon Beliefs and True Christianity* (Nashville, TN: Broadman and Holman Publishers, 1998), 108.

- The New Jerusalem would be built in Missouri.
- Jesus Christ would return by about 1890.
- People who were one thousand years old and dressed like Quakers actually lived on the moon.

In addition to these failed prophecies, Joseph Smith will forever be linked to erroneous claims of the Book of Abraham. In 1835, a traveling merchant presented mummies and papyri from ancient Egypt to the Mormon community in Kirtland, Ohio. Joseph Smith announced that these antiquities contained the actual writings of Abraham the patriarch. In addition, LDS leaders eventually ratified the Book of Abraham as part of the canon of the Mormon Church.

> There is nothing about the Book of Abraham that confirms that Joseph Smith was an authentic prophet and spokesman for God's revelation. Rather, the evidence continues to point to the Book of Abraham as a fraudulent representation of the life of Abraham.

This action might have been one of the most significant errors in LDS history. The evidence clearly points to the Book of Abraham as a fraudulent representation of the life of Abraham. As Beverley points out:

> Egyptologists over the last century and a half have all agreed that Joseph's handling of the facsimiles is evidence of his utter failure to understand Egyptian language and culture. They have also agreed that the papyrus is from a time period long after Abraham lived. So, there is a failure by Joseph Smith in relation to both the nature and dating of the material purchased by the Church in 1835.[194]

IS THE BOOK OF MORMON TRUE?

The Book of Mormon tells the story of God's alleged dealings with the ancient inhabitants of the American Continent, including a visit by the risen Jesus to the people of the New World. Mormon was an ancient

---

[194] James Beverley, *Mormon Crisis: Anatomy of a Failing Religion* (Pickering, Ontario, Canada: Castle Quay Book, 2013), 102.

American prophet who compiled the history of the ancient civilization from old records. The document was inscribed on plates of gold, which Mormon's son Moroni buried for safety in what is now New York State. Moroni returned in 1823 as an angel and showed Joseph Smith (founder of the church) where the plates were hidden. Smith translated the plates into the Book of Mormon, which was first published in 1830.

Here is a brief sample of evidences that demonstrate that the Book of Mormon lacks the credibility of a document that is uniquely true.

EVIDENCE #1: QUESTIONABLE ORIGIN OF THE BOOK OF MORMON

Joseph Smith declared the absolute correctness of the Book of Mormon in the following assessment:

> The Book of Mormon is the most correct of any book on earth, and the keystone of our religion, and a man would get nearer to God by abiding its precepts, than by any other book.[195]

The method Joseph Smith used to translate the Book of Mormon should have eliminated the possibility of error. Smith used a seer stone through which he would see one character at a time. After each character would disappear another would appear in its place. In theory this allowed for no possibility of error. However, thousands of changes have been introduced into the Book of Mormon since it was originally published. Many of the additions made since 1830 cleaned up glaring problems of grammar that reflected Joseph Smith's lack of education. Yet those shouldn't have been problems since Joseph was allegedly receiving ancient words by the power and grace of God. In addition, Mormons play a dangerous game when they accuse the Bible of being inaccurate when the Book of Mormon has been edited and changed many times.[196]

---

[195] Joseph Smith, *The Book of Mormon,* LDS.org, accessed February 10, 2015, https://www.lds.org/manual/teachings-joseph-smith/chapter-4?.
[196] Jerald and Sandra Tanner, "Changing the Revelations," *Utah Lighthouse Ministry,* accessed January 20, 2015, http://www.utlm.org/onlinebooks/changingtherevelations.htm.

As previously noted, there is clear evidence that Joseph Smith was regularly involved in money-digging and occult practices. Both of these practices were used in the translation of the Book of Mormon. Although it was denied for years, researchers have finally found actual court records in New York documenting the arrest of Joseph Smith in 1826 on the charge of disorderly conduct. During this arrest they charged Smith as a "glass looker," or a person who used a seer stone.

In addition to the money-digging and occult practices, some of the top Mormon critics have cited the following questionable activities related to the origin of the Book of Mormon:

- No one was allowed to examine the plates up close.
- The plates were carried around in a box or sat on a table covered by a cloth.
- The plates do not seem to have been necessary to the translation process. Instead the interpreters or (more often) a seer stone was used. Smith would usually place the seer stone in a hat, cover his face with it and dictate the text to a scribe.
- Joseph Smith often had a cloth erected to separate him from his scribe.
- Suggestions by the Three and Eight Witnesses that they saw the plates in visionary experiences.
- 116 pages were lost in the original translation and were never reproduced.[197]

EVIDENCE #2: NUMEROUS PLAGIARISMS FROM THE KING JAMES VERSION

Plagiarism occurs everywhere. All incoming freshmen in college are instructed concerning the dangers and unethical character inherent in plagiarism. In 2013, Actor Shia LaBeouf released a short film online called *HowardCantour.com*. However, almost immediately after LaBeouf posted the film, allegations began to rise that it was a plagiarism of 2007 graphic novel *Justin M. Damiano*, which was written by Daniel Clowes. LaBeouf took down the film and apologized for the plagiarism.

---

[197] Dr. Carl Mosser, "The Changing World of Mormonism," (seminar, Biola University, La Mirada, CA, 2013).

Regrettably, it appears that acts of plagiarism account for major portions of the Book of Mormon. The Book of Mormon contains extensive and verbatim quotations from the King James Version Bible (2 Nephi 12 through 24 contain verbatim quotations from Isaiah 2 through 14). This plagiarism is very troubling for the following reasons. First, if the Book of Mormon was first penned between 600 BC and AD 421, how is it possible that this alleged ancient document would reflect the writing style of a document that was written in the 1600s? Second, why would a document allegedly translated from Reformed Egyptian hieroglyphics look exactly like the language used in the King James Bible? Third, why would expressions like "it came to pass" and "behold, it came to pass" (expressions which are unique to the King James Bible) be found in this ancient language?

> One of the more unusual qualities of the Book of Mormon is that it contains extensive and verbatim quotations from the King James Version Bible (2 Nephi 12 through 24 contain verbatim quotations from Isaiah 2 through 14). This plagiarism is very troubling.

Dr. Beverley expresses the problem facing the Mormon Church:

> Some who have left the Mormon faith cite the exact parallels between the Book of Mormon text and the King James Version as a reason for departure from the church. One study notes that the Book of Mormon contains twenty-six full chapters from a 1769 edition of the King James. Why does the Book of Mormon allegedly from the fifth century quote the Bible in the words of a version over one thousand years later?[198]

For a religious movement that believes that the Book of Mormon is its greatest proof that Joseph Smith is a prophet of God, the presence of this evidence is particularly damaging.

---

[198] James A. Beverley, *Mormon Crisis: Anatomy of a Failing Religion* (Pickering, Ontario, Canada: Castle Quay Book, 2013), 73.

EVIDENCE #3: NO ARCHAEOLOGICAL EVIDENCE

The Book of Mormon faces enormous archaeological difficulties. These difficulties provide a clear circumstantial case against the reliability of the Book of Mormon. Mormons believe that three ancient Jewish groups migrated to the America before the time of Christ. Despite this claim, scientists have clearly demonstrated that Native American Indians possess no genetic similarity to the Semitic peoples of Palestine. Scientific data indicates that Native Americans have very distinctive

> The issue of anachronisms in the Book of Mormon (things that wouldn't have been known at the time the events occurred between 600 BC to AD 400) is a significant indicator that the truth-claims concerning the Book of Mormon cannot reasonably be true.

DNA markers. These markers are most similar to the DNA of people anciently associated with the Altay Mountains area of central Asia, not from ancient Jews. Beverley asserts, "Anthropologists repudiate the common Mormon view that American Natives are descendants of ancient Jews who migrated to the Western hemisphere."[199]

Second, the issue of anachronisms in the Book of Mormon (things that wouldn't have been known at the time the events occurred between 600 BC to AD 400) is a significant indicator that the truth-claims concerning the Book of Mormon cannot reasonably be true. Look at the following:

- Wheeled Chariots are mentioned although they had not been invented.
- The compass is mentioned even though it had not yet been invented.
- Silk is mentioned even though the silk worm was not in existence.
- Steel had not yet been developed in Nephi's time.
- Swords and scimitars are mentioned even though metallurgy was

---

[199] James A. Beverley, *Nelson's Illustrated Guide to Religions* (Nashville, TN: Thomas Nelson, 2009), 373.

not being practiced.[200]

In addition, archaeologists do not utilize the Book of Mormon as a historical source as they attempt to evaluate ancient artifacts. Not a single person, place, or event that is unique to the Book of Mormon has ever been proven to exist. Michael Coe, professor emeritus of anthropology at Yale, states in unequivocal terms:

> The bare facts of the matter are that nothing, absolutely nothing, has ever shown up in any New World excavation which would suggest to a dispassionate observer that the Book of Mormon, as claimed by Joseph Smith, is a historical document relating to the history of early migrants to our hemisphere.[201]

Beverley cites the following statements by the reputable Smithsonian Institution:

> The Smithsonian Institution has never used the Book of Mormon in any way as a scientific guide. Smithsonian archaeologists see no direct connection between the archaeology of the New World and the subject matter of the book. [202]

Third, the Book of Mormon is a figurative dictionary of 19th century Theological Debates. The significance of this observation is that these events could not have been understood at the time when the events of the Book of Mormon supposedly occurred. The following are clear examples of these unique 19th century theological debates:

- The Paedo vs. Credo Baptism debate was started in the 1500s.
- Predestination/Freewill debate was started by Augustine around AD 400 and continued through the 1500s. It is not mentioned in the Old Testament.

---

[200] Dr. Carl Moser, "The Book of Mormon" (seminar, Biola University, La Mirada, CA, 2013).
[201] Michael Coe, quoted in James A. Beverley, *Mormon Crisis: Anatomy of a Failing Religion* (Pickering, Ontario, Canada: Castle Quay Book, 2013), 72-73.
[202] James A. Beverley, *Mormon Crisis: Anatomy of a Failing Religion*, 70.

- The extent of the Atonement (Did Christ die for the elect or not?) was a distinct post-Reformation debate.
- The miraculous gifts of the Spirit were not an issue in the Old Testament or a debate from another continent.[203]

The presence of these theological debates is yet another piece of evidence that suggests the Book of Mormon is best defined as a story created and borrowed by Joseph Smith to address current issues facing the Christian church in the 1800s.

CONCLUSION

I believe that Mormonism is one of the single greatest internal threats facing the Christian church. Mormonism's attempt to masquerade its true beliefs behind Christian terms and pious platitudes cannot stand under the weight of evidence. In this chapter we have tried to answer the two most important questions of our day relating to Mormonism: 1) is Mormonism uniquely Christian? and 2) is Mormonism uniquely true?
The facts and evidence are in. Mormonism is not uniquely Christian because it fails the objective God, salvation, and Bible tests established by Dr. James Beverley earlier in this chapter. Mormonism is not uniquely true because both Joseph Smith and the Book of Mormon fail to stand up in the light of objective scrutiny.

Unfortunately, Mormonism has insulated Joseph Smith and the Book of Mormon with a façade of unquestioned allegiance. Loyalty to Joseph Smith as a prophet of God and to the holy book that God allegedly revealed to him has placed the Mormon faith on an unquestioned pedestal. In addition, Mormonism has been based upon a series of overly subjective tests of truth. All Mormons are taught a very simple truth from their earliest years. They are taught to pray and ask God if the Book of Mormon is true. The burning in the bosom that they experience is proof that their Mormon faith is indeed true. The following quote from the book of Moroni states the principle:

---

[203] Dr. Carl Moser, "The Book of Mormon" (seminar, Biola University, La Mirada, CA 2013).

Behold, I would exhort you that when ye shall read these things, if it be wisdom in God that ye should read them, that ye would remember how merciful the Lord hath been unto the children of men, from the creation of Adam even down unto the time that ye shall receive these things, and ponder it in your hearts. And when ye shall receive these things, I would exhort you that ye would ask God, the Eternal Father, in the name of Christ, if these things are not true; and if ye shall ask with a sincere heart, with real intent, having faith in Christ, he will manifest the truth of it unto you, by the power of the Holy Ghost. And by the power of the Holy Ghost ye may know the truth of all things.
Moroni 10:3-5

Unfortunately, this highly subjective defense of their religious system ignores the clear objective evidence against the authenticity of both the Book of Mormon and Joseph Smith. Dr. Beverley makes the following assessment of the shortcomings of Mormon theology:

The Church of Jesus Christ of Latter-day Saints is not the "only true Church." Many aspects of former and current LDS belief are not consistent with the true, authentic Christian faith and beliefs of the church founded by Jesus. These elements are so serious that Mormonism must be referred to as sub-Christian, anti-Christian or non-Christian at those points.[204]

As a result of the failure of Mormonism to adhere to the historic Christian beliefs, Mormons are left with a bankrupt founder and a bankrupt faith. This bankruptcy is eloquently expressed with these words:

Joseph Smith was largely a failure as a prophet of God. He did not restore the Gospel to the earth. Rather, Smith invented a gold Bible that is unhistorical. . . . LDS people are left with fables about the American natives, fraud about Egyptian documents, lies about

---

[204] James A. Beverley, *Mormon Crisis: Anatomy of a Failing Religion* (Pickering, Ontario, Canada: Castle Quay Book, 2013),156.

polygamy, confusion on the Godhead, a system of works righteousness and a minimizing of Jesus Christ.[205]

SUGGESTIONS FOR ADDITIONAL READING

Francis J. Beckwith, Carl Mosser, and Paul Owen, *The New Mormon Challenge: Responding to the Latest Defenses of a Fast-Growing Movement*
This book is a collection of eleven essays written by some of the leading evangelical scholars. Although this book is both deep and long (500 pages) it represents some of the sharpest and most penetrating evaluations of the modern Mormon movement.

James A. Beverley, *Mormon Crisis: Anatomy of a Failing Religion*
This book is written by one of the leading evangelical religion experts in America. It is short, accessible, and penetrating in its indictment of the sub-Christian views of Mormonism.

R. Philip Roberts with Tal Davis and Sandra Tanner, *Mormonism Unmasked: Confronting the Contradictions Between Mormon Beliefs and True Christianity*
This book is another good overview of the distinct difference between historic Christianity and the Mormon beliefs.

Richard Abanes, *One Nation Under Gods: A History of the Mormon Church*
This scholarly work contains an exhaustive collection of the unvarnished history of the early Mormon Church from the nineteenth century to the 2002 Olympics. This is a great resource for anyone interested in mastering the details of the early history of Mormonism.

---

[205] James A. Beverley, *Mormon Crisis*, 152-153.

Fawn Brodie, *No Man Knows My History*
This work in conjunction with *One Nation Under Gods* provides a compelling look at the life of Joseph Smith. It attempts to discern whether Joseph Smith actually transcribed a genuine revelation from God or simply invented a faith from his own imagination.

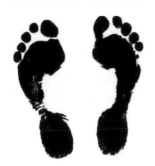

Mahatma Gandhi, who was one of the great symbols for non-violence, civil rights, and freedom across the world, expressed his views on the religions of the world with these words:

> I came to the conclusion long ago that all religions were true and that also that all had some error in them, and while I hold by my own religion, I should hold other religions as dear as Hinduism. So we can only pray, if we were Hindus, not that a Christian should become a Hindu; but our innermost prayer should be that a Hindu should become a better Hindu, a Muslim a better Muslim, and a Christian a better Christian.[206]

Famous stand-up comedian George Carlin once expressed the same idea in simpler terms, "Religion is like a pair of shoes, find one that fits for you, but don't make me wear your shoes."

We live in a culture where people are discouraged from answering the question, "Is Islam or Christianity true?" After all, our politically correct culture assumes that all religions are the same and that all paths eventually lead to God. Ultimately, it doesn't matter what you believe as long as you're happy.

In a world where all religions lead to God many people question why we even try asking which religion is true. Christianity is routinely considered divisive due to its exclusive truth claims. Christians are routinely dismissed as being narrow-minded and rigid.

---

[206] Mahatma Gandhi, *Young India*, 19 January 1928.

Rabbi Schumley Boteach expresses the sentiment and spirit of our day:

> I am absolutely against any religion that says that one faith is superior to another. I don't see how that is anything different than spiritual racism. It's a way of saying that we are closer to God than you, and that's what leads to hatred.[207]

Unfortunately, we've lost the ability to discuss the truthfulness of ideas. Religious discussion is limited, the pursuit of truth is limited, and the expression of opinion is limited.

Within the modern church there is a growing percentage of believers who are hesitant to express their opinions about other religions. They don't want to sound judgmental. They don't want to stir up trouble. They don't want to be antagonistic. For some Christians, and the vast majority of our secular friends, the content of this chapter is extremely uncomfortable. However, it's important to remember that both the founder of Christianity and the apostles made some very exclusive truth claims:

> Jesus answered, "I am the way and the truth and the life. No one comes to the Father except through me."
> John 14:6

> Salvation is found in no one else, for there is no other name under heaven given to men by which we must be saved.
> Acts 4:12

> [5] For there is one God and one mediator between God and men, the man Christ Jesus, [6] who gave himself as a ransom for all men—the testimony given in its proper time.
> 1 Timothy 2:5-6

---

[207] Schumley Boteach, quoted in Lee Strobel, *The Case for Faith: A Journalist Investigates the Toughest Objections to Christianity* (Grand Rapids: Zondervan, 1998),14

These truth claims demand that Christians learn how to defend our faith in a sensitive yet straightforward fashion.

Although the question of whether Islam or Christianity is true may be offensive to many and ludicrous to others, it is a question that must be asked. After all, the presence of Islam continues to grow. The Christian is increasingly likely to interact with a person who either came from an Islamic country, was raised Muslim, or is a committed believer to Islam. Think about its reach:

> Although the question of whether Islam or Christianity is true may be offensive to many and ludicrous to others, it is a question that must be asked.

- > Islam is the world's second largest religion behind Christianity.
- Over sixty-five nations in the world have substantial Islamic populations.
- There are more Muslims in the U.S. than Episcopalians.
- There are more Muslims in the U.S. than Methodists.
- Soon there will be more Muslims in the U.S. than Jews.

The issue facing us is not whether an evangelical Christian is in danger of accidently slipping into Islam without knowing it. The issue is that our culture has discouraged Christians from insisting that our faith is true. In addition, too many Christians see Muslims as an evil to be fought rather than a people to be loved in the name of Jesus. Christians must understand and graciously explain the difference between our faiths. We must work at building relationships with Muslims in an effort to share the message of Jesus.

BACKGROUND OF ISLAM

Any discussion about Islam must begin with an understanding of and appreciation for the background and core beliefs of this tremendously influential religion. All too often, people are tempted to embrace the talking points against a particular religion without first understanding that religion's view of the world.

This chapter will begin with a brief but helpful background of the Prophet Muhammad, the five pillars of Islam, and the six articles of faith.

THE PROPHET MUHAMMAD

Muhammad was born in Mecca in AD 570. When he was forty, Muhammad had a series of disturbing visions. He claimed that the angel Gabriel appeared to him in a cave and gave him revelations to recite. The key message he received from his revelations was that Allah was the one true God. Muhammad's message met tremendous resistance because the Arabs of his day were polytheistic. Mecca's main shrine, the Kaaba, was home to 360 idols.

Muslims believe that in AD 620 the angel Gabriel brought Muhammad to Jerusalem where he had the opportunity to converse with Jesus, Moses, and Abraham.

Two years later he was forced to flee from Mecca to Medina. For the following eight years the prophet engaged in repeated military battles with his enemies. By AD 630, Muhammad triumphed, took over Mecca, and destroyed the idols in the Kaaba. He returned for a final pilgrimage to Mecca where he died on June 8, 632.

> Every portion of his life is significant and revered—his family life, military career, political strategies, and economic views. This is one of the reasons why a Muslim's allegiance to Muhammad is so strong.

It's impossible to overestimate the importance of Muhammad to Islam. Every detail of the Prophet Muhammad's life has become an example for all Muslims. Every portion of his life is significant and revered—his family life, military career, political strategies, and economic views. This is one of the reasons why a Muslim's allegiance to Muhammad is so strong and why a Muslim's faith intersects with every single aspect of his or her life.

THE 5 PILLARS OF ISLAM

The five pillars or observances in Islam are the foundational practices or duties that every Muslim must observe. The pillars also serve as the key to understanding the worldview of the typical Muslim. Each of these pillars is non-negotiable. They define every single aspect of the life of the Muslim.

Pillar #1: The Creed

Muslims are expected to publicly recite the Shahadah, which is, "There is no god but Allah and Muhammad is the Prophet of Allah." One must state this aloud publicly in order to become a Muslim. It is repeated constantly by the faithful.

Pillar #2: Prayers

Muslims are expected to perform prayers five times a day: at dawn, noon, afternoon, evening, and night. These prayers involve a series of postures (standing, kneeling, and with hands and face on the ground) to be performed while facing Mecca, the holy city.

Pillar #3: Almsgiving

Muslims are expected to give alms to the Muslim community that amount to 1/40th (or 2.5%) of one's income. This offering is used for the benefit of widows, orphans, and the sick, or it can be used toward furthering Islam. Since the giving of alms helps the giver to salvation, recipients feel no sense of debt to the giver.

Pillar #4: Fasting

Muslims are expected to fast during the month of Ramadan. During this month Muslims abstain from food, drink, smoking, and sexual relations during the daylight hours. At sundown they are allowed to partake of these pleasures again until sunrise the next morning. The fast develops self-control, devotion to God, and identification with the destitute.

Pillar #5: Pilgrimage

Every Muslim is expected to make an official pilgrimage to Mecca at least once in his or her life. If one is unable to go due to health or financial resources a Muslim is permitted to have another person make the pilgrimage by proxy.

SIX ARTICLES OF FAITH

The six articles of faith are the fundamental doctrines of Islam. All Muslims are expected to believe in and submit to these tenets.

ARTICLE #1: GOD

There is no God but Allah. Allah is said to have seven primary characteristics: He has absolute unity and is all-seeing, all-hearing, all-speaking, all-knowing, all-willing, and all-powerful. In the language of the Qur'an God's relationship with man is described in terms of master and slave. God requires that man submit to Him.

ARTICLE #2: ANGELS

Gabriel, the leading angel, appeared to Muhammad and was instrumental in delivering the revelations of the Qur'an to the prophet. Each human being is said to have two recording angels who list all of his or her deeds, good or bad. These recorded deeds will be brought forth at the final judgment.

ARTICLE #3: HOLY BOOKS

There are four inspired books: the Torah of Moses, the Psalms of David, the Gospel of Jesus Christ, and the Qur'an. The Qur'an contains Allah's final message to mankind and supersedes all previous revelation. The Qur'an is the final arbiter of any conflicting truth claims. Only the Qur'an has been preserved in an uncorrupted state. Muslims believe that the former three books have been corrupted by Jews and Christians.

ARTICLE #4: PROPHETS

There are allegedly over 100,000 prophets who have been sent to human beings throughout history. The most important ones number less than thirty. Muhammad is the last and greatest of Allah's messengers. Some of the prominent prophets include Adam, Noah, Abraham, Moses, David, Solomon, Jonah, John the Baptist, and Jesus. Here are the messages that these prophets have given:

- Abraham received the Scrolls of Abraham, a message that Muslims believe has been lost.
- Moses and Aaron received the Torah or Taurat.
- David received the Psalms or Zabur.
- Jesus received the Gospels or Injil.
- Muhammad received the Qur'an.

ARTICLE #5: FUTURE JUDGMENT

There will be a day of judgment and a resurrection. Those who follow and obey Allah will go to the Islamic heaven called paradise, which is a place of pleasure. Those who oppose Allah will be tormented in hell, which is a place of unimaginable suffering. On the day of judgment Allah will weigh each man's deeds in the balances.

ARTICLE #6: BELIEF IN THE DECREES OF GOD

God has the ability to create good or evil whenever He wishes. Both good things and evil things are the result of God's decree. It is the duty of every Muslim to believe this.

CRUCIAL DIFFERENCES BETWEEN ISLAM AND CHRISTIANITY

Although there are some surface similarities between Islam and Christianity (belief in one God, creation, heaven, hell, angels, and a final judgment) there are huge and fundamental differences between the two major religions. In fact, the differences between Islam and Christianity are too great and profound to be ignored or explained away as insignificant. These differences demand a serious investigation to

> The differences between Islam and Christianity are simply too great and profound to be ignored or explained away as insignificant.

determine which faith best represents the reality about God. It is not my intent to demean Islam or to diminish the historic impact of Muhammad's life. In that spirit, I will attempt to use Islamic theologians and spokesmen when possible to ensure that I accurately reflect the Muslim views and differences from Christianity.

The simple reality is that Islam challenges five foundational doctrines of the Christian faith. As such, it is absolutely necessary for Christians to have the tools to graciously respond to claims from our Islamic friends who question the veracity of Christianity. This chapter summarizes the following essential doctrines of Christianity:

- Doctrine of God.
- Doctrine of Sin/Salvation.
- Doctrine of Christ's Death.
- Doctrine of Christ's Deity.
- Christian Scriptures.

DIFFERENCE #1: THE CHRISTIAN DOCTRINE OF GOD

Although both Christianity and Islam believe in one supreme God, it is important to understand why the Christian concept of a triune God results in such negative reactions by Muslims. In fact, the moment we begin to describe the Christian concept of God we run directly into a roadblock of misunderstanding and resistance.

MISUNDERSTANDING #1: THE CHRISTIAN CONCEPT OF THE TRINITY DENIES THE ONENESS OF GOD.

Islam was established within the polytheistic culture of tribal Arabia where people believed in many gods. Out of this climate came the Islamic belief that "there is no god but Allah." Listen to a description of their viewpoint by a respected Muslim theologian and from the Qur'an:

> The Unity of Allah is the distinguishing characteristic of Islam. This is the purest form of monotheism, i.e., the worship of Allah Who has neither begotten nor beget nor had any associates with Him in His Godhead. Islam teaches this in the most unequivocal terms. [208]

---

[208] Alhaj Ajijola, *The Essence of Faith in Islam,* quoted in Norman L. Geisler and Abdul Saleb, *Answering Islam: The Crescent in the Light of the Cross* (Grand Rapids: Baker Books, 1993), 261.

Because of this uncompromising emphasis on God's absolute unity, in Islam the greatest of all sins is the sin of shirk, or assigning partners to God. "God forgiveth not (the sin of) joining other gods with him, but He forgiveth Whom He pleaseth other sins than this one: one who joins Other gods with God, Hath strayed far, far away (from the Right)."
4:116

Unfortunately, our Muslim friends deeply misunderstand the concept of the triune nature of God. They are offended by a doctrine that sounds like polytheism. Yet, the doctrine of the Trinity does not teach that we believe in three gods. According to Christian monotheism, God is one in essence, but three in persons. The Bible clearly affirms that there is only one God (Deuteronomy 6:4; 1 Corinthians 8:6). However, Christianity teaches that there are personal distinctions within the fundamental unity of God's nature. In other words, within the nature of one God there are three co-eternal, co-equal persons: the Father, the Son, and the Holy Spirit. The three persons only share one essence—that of the one creator of the universe—Almighty God.

> The Bible clearly affirms that there is only one God (Deuteronomy 6:4; 1 Corinthians 8:6). However, the Bible also teaches that God's being is complex, that is, that there are personal distinctions within the fundamental unity of His nature.

Gifted Christian apologist Norman Geisler shares this insight:

For Muslims God not only has unity but he has singularity. But these are not the same. It is possible to have unity without singularity. For there could be plurality within the unity. Indeed, this is precisely what the Trinity is, namely, a plurality of persons within the unity of one essence. Human analogies help to illustrate the point. My mind, my thoughts, and my words have a unity, but they are not a singularity, since they are all different. Likewise, Christ can be an expression of the same nature as God without being the same person as the Father.[209]

MISUNDERSTANDING #2: THE CHRISTIAN CONCEPT OF THE TRINITY IS TOO COMPLEX.

Muslims often complain that the Christian concept of the Trinity is simply too complex. It's important to realize that the early Christian church did not invent the concept of the Trinity in order to dazzle the surrounding world with its intellect and understanding of complex concepts. Historically, the church was compelled to embrace the concept of the Trinity for a simple and powerful reason—the testimony of Scripture and the extraordinary claims of Jesus of Nazareth. Simply put, the concept of the Trinity is the best explanation for three unquestioned truths that are systematically revealed in Scripture. Each of these Scriptures reveals a different aspect of God's nature:

- Truth #1: There is only one God: Deuteronomy 6:4; 1 Timothy 2:5.
- Truth #2: Three persons are declared to be deity: 1 Corinthians 1:3; John 1:1; John 8:58; Acts 5:4, 5.
- Truth #3: All three persons are simultaneously mentioned as distinct individuals: John 14 and John 16.

Great Christian thinker C.S. Lewis expressed it this way:

If Christianity was something we were making up, of course we could make it easier. But it is not. We cannot compete, in simplicity, with people who are inventing religions. How could we? We are dealing with Fact. Of course anyone can be simple if he has not facts to bother about.[210]

---

[209] Norman L. Geisler and Abdul Saleb, *Answering Islam*, 263.
[210] C.S. Lewis, *Mere Christianity* (New York: Harper Collins, 2002), 145.

MISUNDERSTANDING #3: THE CHRISTIAN CONCEPT OF THE TRINITY IS A LOGICAL CONTRADICTION

Muslims also complain that the Christian concept of the Trinity is a deep logical contradiction. Muslim scholars point to the mathematical impossibility of the Trinity. How does 1 + 1 + 1 = 1? In addition, Muslims mistakenly believe Christianity teaches tritheism rather than monotheism.

The challenge for Christians is to explain the Trinity in a way that is both logically consistent and consistent with our historic Christian roots:

> Christians do not affirm God to be one and three at the same time and in the same sense (that would be a contradiction). What Christians claim is that in one sense God is one (he is one in essence or being) and in a very different sense there is a divine plurality (three eternal persons or distinctions or relationships or dimensions). Thus there can be no charge of logical contradiction against this doctrine.[211]

Simply put, the doctrine of the Trinity is not a contradiction. The law of non-contradiction maintains that something cannot be both true and false at the same time and in the same sense. The concept of the Trinity is not the belief that God is three persons and only one person at the same time and in the same sense. Instead, the concept of the Trinity is the belief that there are three persons in one nature. God is one in the sense of his essence but three in the sense of his persons.

Allow me to illustrate using the profession of my daughter, Janelle, who is a gifted television producer. Presently, she collaborates with one of the top reporters on the West Coast to prepare news stories for various programs. It is a logical contradiction for a person to claim that Janelle is a producer at her job and at the same time claim she is not a producer. In other words, something can't be true and false at the same time and

---

[211] Abdul Saleeb, "Islam," in *To Everyone an Answer: A Case for the Christian Worldview*, ed. Francis J. Beckwith, William Lane Craig, and J.P. Moreland (Downers Grove: InterVarsity Press, 2004), 357.

in the same sense. Of course, it is entirely possible for a person to claim that Janelle is a producer, wife, and mother. That is not a contradiction because it is describing three different roles that Janelle plays in her life, and all of them quite well.

> The concept of the Trinity is not the belief that God is three persons and only one person at the same time and in the same sense. Instead, the concept of the Trinity is the belief that there are three persons in one nature. God is one in the sense of his essence but three in the sense of his persons.

The doctrine of the Trinity does not teach that one being is three beings or that three persons are one person. The doctrine of the Trinity claims that there are three persons in one nature or being. Since the meanings of "being" and "persons" are different, the doctrine of the Trinity is not a contradiction, just a mystery. In other words, when Christians claim that God has one essence and three persons we mean he has one "What" and three "Whos."

DIFFERENCE #2: CHRISTIAN DOCTRINE OF SIN/SALVATION

Christianity teaches that all of humanity is sinful by virtue of birth and by virtue of choice (Rom. 3:23; Rom. 5:12). Islam doesn't believe in the inherent fallenness of humanity. They believe that every child is born pure and true. A person departs from the truth via imperfect education. Muslim teaching is in sharp contrast to that of Christianity. Islamic scholar Isma'il R. Al Faruqi expresses the Islamic view:

> In the Islamic view, human beings are no more 'fallen' than they are 'saved.' Because they are not 'fallen,' they have no need of a savior. But because they are not 'saved' either, they need to do good works—and do them ethically—which alone will earn them the desired 'salvation.'[212]

---

[212] Isma'il R. Al Faruqi, *Islam* in Norman L. Geisler and Abdul Saleb, *Answering Islam: The Crescent in the Light of the Cross*, 43.

Religion is like a giant set of Legos®—all the pieces are designed to connect together. This is especially true of Islam. If you consider the logical implications of certain Muslim doctrines you quickly realize that,

- If there is no inherent sinfulness of man there is no need for a Savior.
- If there is no need for a Savior then there is no need for the crucifixion of Jesus.
- If there was no need for the crucifixion then Christ died needlessly and if he died needlessly, his teachings regarding his death were false.

> God cannot arbitrarily forgive anyone for anything without there being a just basis for this forgiveness. Lacking the crucifixion, the Muslim system has no way to explain how Allah can be merciful when he is also just.

With no need for the sacrifice of Christ, Islam teaches that obedience to the will of Allah is the foundation of experiencing forgiveness. Badru D. Kateregga describes it this way:

> Islam does not identify with the Christian conviction that man needs to be redeemed. The Christian belief in the redemptive sacrificial death of Christ does not fit the Islamic view that man has always been fundamentally good, and that God loves and forgives those who obey his will.[213]

Islam teaches that Allah is absolutely just. One of the challenges facing Islam is how God's absolute justice is satisfied. In other words, how is man's injustice removed? God can't overlook evil. God can't simply close His eyes and ignore it.

Martin Luther, who was the great Protestant reformer in the 16th century, expressed it this way:

---

[213] Badru D. Kateregga and David W. Shenk, *Islam and Christianity: A Muslim and a Christian in Dialogue* (Grand Rapids: Eerdmans, 1997), 141.

Christ, the son of God stands in our place and has taken all our sins upon his shoulders . . . He is the eternal satisfaction for our sin and reconciles us with God the Father.[214]

Absolute justice demands that the absolute standard of God be met. If a judge unjustly acquits a criminal without payment of a fair penalty, the judge himself becomes implicated in the crime. In the same way, if God's holy justice demands that those who do not accept him be eternally punished for their sins, then it would seem to follow that God cannot arbitrarily forgive anyone for anything without there being a just basis for this forgiveness. Lacking the crucifixion, the Muslim system has no way to explain how Allah can be merciful when he is also just. Geisler explains it this way:

> In Muslim theology—with its rejection of the cross—there is forgiveness but no real basis for this forgiveness. . . . After all, a truly just God cannot simply close his eyes to sin; he cannot overlook evil. So unless someone capable of paying the debt of sin owed to God does so, God is obligated to express his wrath, not his mercy, upon them. Lacking the crucifixion, the Muslim system has no way to explain how Allah can be merciful when he is also just.[215]

Christianity states that God is obligated to express his wrath and his mercy. The crucifixion of the God/man Jesus Christ explains how God can be merciful when he is also just. The Apostle Paul described it this way:

> God presented him as a sacrifice of atonement, through faith in his blood. He did this to demonstrate his justice . . . at the present time, so as to be just and the one who justifies those who have faith in Jesus.
> Romans 3:25-26

---

[214] Martin Luther, *Sermons 1*, vol. 51, *Luther's Works*, ed. John W. Doberstein and Helmut T. Lehmann (Philadelphia, PA: Muhlenberg Press, 1959), 92.
[215] Norman L. Geisler and Abdul Saleb, *Answering Islam: The Crescent in the Light of the Cross*, 283.

Muslims should be urged to consider the uniqueness of Jesus Christ. Jesus gave people assurance of salvation and showed people how much God genuinely loved them:

> 25 I am the resurrection and the life. He who believes in me will live, even though he dies; 26 and whoever lives and believes in me will never die.
> John 11:25-26

> 11 And this is the testimony: God has given us eternal life, and this life is in his Son. 12 He who has the Son has life; he who does not have the Son of God does not have life.
> 1 John 5:11-12

It's important to remember the unique internal dilemma that an average Muslim feels when considering his or her chance of going to heaven. Imagine if you were told that there is no original sin and that you have the ability to be good if you follow the example of Muhammad. Imagine that you believe in a future judgment day when Allah will be absolutely just and righteous. You are told to be a good Muslim and follow Muhammad's standard. However, you're frustrated that you can't follow Muhammad's standard perfectly and that you have no certainty of your final destination. Just imagine the fear in a person's life when he or she doesn't know the exact standard that will allow that person into paradise.

The Christian should be sympathetic to the natural fear that Muslims may feel whenever they think of the future judgment. Contrast this with the grace that is offered the Christian in the person of Jesus Christ. What a difference! What an opportunity for us to gently describe our assurance that is offered through the uniqueness of Jesus Christ. This is a natural opening in our discussions with Muslim friends and neighbors.

DIFFERENCE #3: THE DEATH OF JESUS CHRIST

It's important to realize that the starkest difference between Islam and Christianity is the issue of whether or not Jesus of Nazareth was crucified. Muslims claim that the crucifixion of Jesus of Nazareth never happened. The Qur'an is emphatic that Jesus did not die on the cross. In fact, the Islamic religion teaches that there is no need for a Savior on the cross.

On the other hand, Christians believe that Jesus died on the cross for the sins of mankind. In fact, the holy book of the Christian faith, the Bible, distinctly teaches that Jesus died on the cross. His death is the linchpin of our entire faith.

It's important to understand that this difference is not a minor issue within the Muslim belief system. The following observations from an influential Muslim scholar clearly illustrate the importance of denying the crucifixion. Shaikh Ahmed Zaki Yamani states:

> Muslims claim that the crucifixion of Jesus of Nazareth never happened. The Qur'an is emphatic that Jesus did not die on the cross. In fact, the Islamic religion teaches that there is no need for a Savior to die on the cross.

In the great debate between Christians and Muslims . . . there are areas of fundamental principles where no amount of logical discourse can bring the two sides nearer to each other and where therefore the existence of an impasse must be recognized. . . . Issues like the Trinity, the Divinity of Christ and the Crucifixion, so central to Christian beliefs, have no place in the Islamic faith, having been categorically refuted by the Quran.[216]

This issue illustrates a very important point one must consider when having discussions with Muslims. Every debate in Muslim law is settled by what the Qur'an teaches. Furthermore, Muslims believe that the Qur'an is perfect and contains no errors. They don't pay attention to attacks upon the credibility of the Qur'an and don't question anything it teaches.

---

[216] Shaikh Ahmed Zaki Yamani in Norman L. Geisler and Abdul Saleb, *Answering Islam: The Crescent in the Light of the Cross*, 273.

Despite Islam's insistence that the Qur'an is infallible, the facts of history must be used to demonstrate the overwhelming evidence that Christ died on the cross. Some of the evidence for the crucifixion is cited in Footprint Eight of this book, but it bears repeating since this point is so essential in presenting the evidence for the death and resurrection of Jesus Christ. Remember, the following points are accepted by most secular and evangelical historians:

- Jesus announced many times during His ministry that He was going to die. In Matthew 17: 22-23, Jesus predicted the following, "The Son of Man is about to be betrayed into the hands of men and they will kill Him, and the third day He will be raised."

- The nature of Roman crucifixion assures death. The Roman soldiers, who were accustomed to crucifixion and death, pronounced Jesus dead (John 19:33).

- Modern medical authorities who have examined the circumstances and nature of His death have concluded that Jesus actually died on the cross. Observe the following conclusion:

Clearly, the weight of the historical and medical evidence indicates that Jesus was dead before the wound to his side was inflicted. Accordingly, interpretations based on the assumption that Jesus did not die on the cross appear to be at odds with modern medical knowledge.[217]

- It is a firmly established belief by modern New Testament authorities that the death and burial of Jesus Christ literally occurred. Resurrection expert Gary Habermas observes:

Although nineteenth-century liberals decimated each other's views individually, twentieth-century critical scholars have generally

---

[217] William D. Edwards, Wesley J. Gabel, and Floyd E. Hosmer, "On the Physical Death of Jesus Christ," Journal of the American Medical Association, 255. No.11 (1986): 1457 in Gary Habermas & Michael Licona, The Case for the Resurrection of Jesus, 101.

rejected naturalistic theories as a whole, judging that they are incapable of explaining the known data. . . . That even such critical scholars have rejected these naturalistic theories is a significant epitaph for the failure of these views.[218]

- Non-Christian historians and writers from the first and second centuries recorded the death of Christ.

Tacitus, the most important Roman historian of the first century wrote:

Nero fastened the guilt and inflicted the most exquisite tortures on a class hated for the abominations, called Christians by the populace. Christus, from whom the name had its origin, suffered the extreme penalty during the reign of Tiberius at the hands of one of our procurators, Pontius Pilatus.[219]

Lucian, the second century Greek writer wrote of Christ as "the man who was crucified in Palestine because he introduced a new cult into the world." Thallus, the first century historian (AD 52) spoke of the eclipse when he said that people were "discussing the darkness which fell upon the land during the crucifixion of Christ."

Muslims not only deny the historical evidence for the death and crucifixion of Jesus Christ, they also reject the implication of the cross—salvation by grace through Christ. Muslims believe that Allah, who has control over all things, would not allow a prophet like Jesus to suffer such a humiliating death at the hands of His enemies. They question whether the humiliation and murder of Jesus is consistent with God's mercy and wisdom and whether it is consistent with the dignified role of a prophet of God.

---

[218] Gary R. Habermas and Antony G. Flew, *Did Jesus Rise from the Dead? The Resurrection Debate* (San Francisco, CA: Harper & Row Publishers, 1987), 21.
[219] Cornelius Tacitus, *The Annals* 15.44 in Gary Habermas & Michael Licona, *The Case for the Resurrection of Jesus*, 49.

Geisler explains the reasoning of this viewpoint:

> Many Western scholars find Muhammad's reason for dismissing the Christian doctrine of salvation through the cross in the fact the major prophets in history have always been victorious against their enemies. If the Christ of God were killed on the cross by his adversaries, then what would have become of the constant Qur'anic theme that those who did not obey God's prophet did not triumph? Was not the admission of the cross an acknowledgment that the unrighteous had ultimately triumphed over the righteous?[220]

In light of the Christian view of sin and salvation, it is important to make a couple of observations about the weakness of the Islamic position on these issues. First, the Bible teaches that Jesus died for our sins (I Cor 15:3). Specifically, He was "made to be sin for us" (2 Cor 5:21). The Bible teaches that Jesus took our place. This concept of life for life is not foreign to Islam. It is the same principle behind their belief in capital punishment; when a murderer takes another's life, he must forfeit his own as a penalty.

Perhaps no concept in Christian terminology receives such a violent reaction from Muslims as Jesus as the "only begotten" Son of God. To the Islamic mind the expression "begetting" means creating, and God cannot create another God.

Second, Muslims have to recognize that human beings are sinful. Otherwise, why do they need God's mercy? If Muslims do not believe that people are inherently evil, why do they believe that so many Christians have committed the greatest of all sins, attributing partners to God? If unbelievers are sent to hell to suffer, it must imply great sinfulness to deserve such a severe penalty. The Qur'an expresses the irony this way, "If God were to punish Men for their wrong-doing, He would not leave, on the (earth), a single living creature" (16:61).

---

[220] Norman L. Geisler and Abdul Saleb, *Answering Islam: The Crescent in the Light of the Cross*, 272.

Third, it's also interesting that the Qur'an gives a compelling example of the concept of a substitutionary atonement in Abraham's sacrifice of his son on Mount Moriah. Listen to the word of the Qur'an:

He said: "O my son! I see in vision that I offer thee in sacrifice. . . . "So when they had both Submitted their wills (to God), And he laid him Prostrate on his forehead (For sacrifice), We [God] called out to him, "O Abraham! . . . And We ransomed him With a momentous sacrifice"
37:102-7

The Qur'an's use of the words sacrifice and ransom are identical to the Christian concepts used to refer to Christ's death on the cross.

DIFFERENCE #4: THE DEITY OF JESUS CHRIST

Perhaps no concept in Christian terminology receives such a violent reaction from Muslims as that of Jesus as the "only begotten" Son of God. To the Islamic mind the expression "begetting" means creating, and God cannot create another God. He cannot create another uncreated being. In the Islamic mindset this is particularly offensive because it would involve God in the fleshly process of physical procreation. The Qur'an says the following:

> The expression "Son of God" is a descriptive title given to Jesus Christ to indicate that He is unique in his relationship to God the Father and that He is one with Him in His very nature and being. The term does not imply that Jesus was produced by God having physical relations with Mary.

The Christian belief in the divinity of Christ amounts to committing the unpardonable sin of shirk and is condemned throughout the Qur'an. "They do blaspheme who say: 'God is Christ the son of Mary.' . . . Whoever joins other gods with God, God will forbid him the Garden, and the Fire will be his abode."
5:75

Unfortunately, too many Muslims jump to the false conclusion that Christianity teaches that Jesus was the offspring of physical, sexual relations between God and the Virgin Mary. Many times they believe this baseless idea without even listening to what Christians mean by the expression "Son of God."

Although it is probably not helpful to debate the various meanings for Arabic words with your Islamic friends it is helpful to make the following observation. There are two Arabic words for the expression "son." One word (walad) denotes a son born of sexual relations, whereas another word (ibn) can be used in a figurative or metaphorical sense. In fact, the Qur'an uses the word "son" in the same way as the Bible does. The terms "son of the path" and "son of Satan" are both used figuratively and obviously don't involve physical reproduction. The expression "Son of God" is a descriptive title given to Jesus Christ to indicate that He is unique in his relationship to God the Father and that He is one with Him in His very nature and being. The term does not imply that Jesus was produced by God having physical relations with Mary. The Son of God has always existed, and he came into the world by the virgin birth.

JESUS' CLAIMS OF DEITY

Although Islamic scholars state that Jesus never claimed to be God, there are a handful of Scriptures that clearly reveal Jesus' own claims of deity.

CLAIMS TO BE JEHOVAH: The word Jehovah or Yahweh was the name God gave Himself in the Old Testament. It was the name revealed to Moses (Exodus 3:14) and was to be used exclusively to refer to the Supreme Creator of the world. In fact, Isaiah 42:8 says, "I am Jehovah, that is my name; and my glory I will not give to another, neither my praise unto graven images."

> The biggest misunderstanding stems from the Biblical concept of Jesus as the "only begotten" Son of God (John 1:18; cf. 3:16). Unfortunately, Muslims misinterpret this expression to refer to a physical act as if God was creating another God—an unthinkable act of blasphemy in the Muslim faith.

In His public ministry, Jesus claimed to be Jehovah on many occasions. Although Jehovah in the Old Testament vowed not to share his glory with anyone, Jesus made this request of His father when He said,

"Father, glorify thou me in thy own presence with the glory which I had with thee before the world was made" (John 17:5). Yet, Jesus made His greatest claim when He stated, "Before Abraham was, I am" (John 8:58). This claim of "I am" is equivalent to the expression used in Exodus 3:14 and was understood by the surrounding Jewish leaders as a claim of divinity (John 10:31-33).

CLAIMS TO BE EQUAL WITH GOD: Jesus claimed certain prerogatives and powers that were held by God Himself. For example, Jesus claimed to forgive the sins of the lame man when he said, "My son, your sins are forgiven" (Mark 2:5f). When he was challenged by Jewish leaders, who asked, "Who can forgive sins but God alone?" Jesus immediately offered proof of his ability to forgive by healing the lame man.

CLAIMS TO BE HONORED AS GOD: Jesus also claimed that he should be honored as God. When Jesus said, "Honor the Son, even as they honor the Father. He who does not honor the Son does not honor the Father," everyone around Him clearly understood the implication of His words. The Jews knew He was making a claim of deity because they immediately reached for stones in an attempt to stone Him for blasphemy (John 5:18).

MUSLIM MISUNDERSTANDING OF JESUS' STATEMENTS

There are a handful of concepts and Scriptures that Muslims deeply misunderstand. As we mentioned earlier in this chapter, the biggest misunderstanding stems from the Biblical concept of Jesus as the "only begotten" Son of God (John 1:18; cf. 3:16). Unfortunately, Muslims misinterpret this expression to refer to a physical act as if God was creating another God—an unthinkable act of blasphemy in the Muslim faith. Orthodox Christians do not believe that this expression is the equivalent of "make" or "create." Rather, it refers to a special relationship that the Son has with the Father. Listen to how Geisler describes this relationship:

> The phrase "only begotten" does not refer to physical generation but to a special relationship with the Father. It could be translated, as the New International Version does, God's "One and Only" Son. It does not imply creation by the Father but unique relation to him. Just

as an earthly father and son have a special filial relationship, even so the eternal Father and his eternal Son are uniquely related.[221]

There are also a handful of Scriptures containing the words of Jesus of Nazareth that Muslims either misunderstand or distort:

Why do you call Me good? No one is good except God alone.
Mark 10:18

Typically, Muslims use this verse to claim that Jesus denied being God when he rebuked the rich young ruler, but Jesus never denied His deity. Not once did Jesus say "I am not God" or "I am not good." He simply rebuked a wealthy young man for making this careless statement without thinking through its implications. He was turning the man's words against him in an attempt to force him to consider the unique nature of Jesus as God.

My Father is greater than I.
John 14:28

This is another of Jesus's statements that Muslims take out of context. Clearly, there are many verses that express the uniqueness of the person of Jesus and His claims to deity (John 5:23; John 8:58; John 10:30, 33). Jesus regularly claimed to be equal in nature with God, but His comments here are designed to emphasize that the Father is greater in office, and not greater in nature.

That they all may be one, as You, Father are in me, and I in You; that they also may be one in Us.
John 17:21

> Muslims believe that the text of Scripture has been changed or forged. They believe that doctrinal mistakes have crept into Christian teaching.

Muslims argue that if Jesus is God because He is in God, why are the

---

[221] Norman L. Geisler and Abdul Saleb, *Answering Islam: The Crescent in the Light of the Cross*, 257.

disciples not God, as they are also in God? They miss a simple point. Jesus was specifically talking to His disciples in that instance and was speaking in relational terms. In other words, we can have an intimate relationship with God but we cannot be of the same essence as God.

DIFFERENCE #5: THE CHRISTIAN SCRIPTURES

In order to support the claim that the Qur'an is the inspired word of God that supersedes all previous revelations, Muslims attack its chief rival, the Bible. Muslims believe that the text of Scripture has been changed or forged. They question how our Scriptures can be true. They question our right to make exclusive truth claims when our many denominations extol their doctrine as "the right one." Ultimately, they believe that doctrinal mistakes have crept into Christian teaching:

> The Injil spoken of by the Qur'an is not the New Testament. It is not the four Gospels now received as canonical. It is the single Gospel which, Islam teaches, was revealed to Jesus, and which he taught. Fragments of it survive.[222]

Over the years Muslim critics have adopted the viewpoint of secular liberals who question the historic accuracy of Christianity. In his book, *What Did Jesus Really Say?* Misha'al ibn Abdullah confidently concludes:

> With every passing day, the most learned among the Christian community are slowly recognizing the truth and drawing closer to Islam. These are not Muslims who issued this statement. These are not liberal Christians. These are the most learned and most highly esteemed men of the Anglican Church. These men have dedicated their whole lives to the study of the religion of Jesus, and their study has driven them to the truth which God had already revealed to

---

[222] A. Yusuf Ali, *The Holy Qur'an*, quoted in Norman L. Geisler and Abdul Saleb, *Answering Islam: The Crescent in the Light of the Cross,* 210.

them in the Qur'an 1400 years ago: That Jesus was not God. That God is not a Trinity. And that the stories of the ministry of Jesus in the Bible have been extensively tampered with by the hands of mankind.[223]

The Islamic views about the Bible are critically flawed. The Qur'an urged Muhammad and/or doubting Christians to look to the Bible of their day (the seventh century) to resolve their doubts. Listen to the words from the Qur'an:

> Most Muslims are totally unaware that the New Testament is the most accurately copied ancient book in the world.

> If thou wert in doubt as to what we have revealed unto thee, then ask those who have been reading the Book (the Bible) from before thee; The truth hath indeed come to thee from thy Lord; so be in no wise of those who doubt.
> 10:94

If Muslims are told to resolve their religious doubts by turning to the Bible of Muhammad's day, logically, they shouldn't have any problems trusting the Bible of today because the New Testament text of Muhammad's day has been confirmed to be the exact same as the manuscripts we use today. By their own admission, Muslims should have confidence in looking to the Bible we use today. Unfortunately, most Muslims are totally unaware that the New Testament is the most accurately copied ancient book in the world.

Furthermore, Islamic scholars recognize the textual scholar Sir Frederic Kenyon as an authority on ancient manuscripts. Kenyon is unequivocal in his support for the reliability of the New Testament Scriptures:

> The number of manuscripts of the New Testament, of early translations from it, and of quotations from it in the oldest writers of

---

[223] Misha'al ibn Abdullah, quoted in Abdul Saleeb, "Islam," in *To Everyone An Answer: The Case for the Christian Worldview*, ed. Francis J. Beckwith, William Lane Craig, and J.P. Moreland (Downers Grove: InterVarsity Press, 2004), 355.

the Church, is so large that it is practically certain that the true reading of every doubtful passage is preserved in one or other of these ancient authorities. This can be said of no other ancient book in the world.[224]

The interval, then, between the dates of original composition and the earliest extant evidence becomes so small as to be in fact, negligible, and the last foundation for any doubt that the Scriptures have come down to us substantially as they were written has now been removed. Both the authenticity and the general integrity of the books of the New Testament may be regarded as finally established.[225]

The topic of the reliability of the New Testament Scriptures is dealt with extensively in Footprint Seven, which is titled, "Can You Trust the Bible?" Readers who want more tools to discuss the reliability of the Bible should read this chapter.

APPROACHING MUSLIMS

One of the tragedies of Christian ministry to Muslims is that it has been negatively influenced by the horrific actions of Muslim extremists. As a result, many Christians are hesitant to approach Muslims like they would other non-Christians whom they are hoping to impact for Christ. With this in mind please consider the following reminders:

- Muslims are just like everyone else. Build friendships and relationships first. Don't feel pressured or rushed into talking about theology or doing evangelism.

- Don't be afraid to have discussions about your faith and spiritual things. Muslims, especially from other countries, often see American

---

[224] Sir Frederic G. Kenyon, *The Bible and Archaeology: A Survey of the Results of Archaeological Discoveries During The Past Hundred Years* (New York: Harper & Brothers Publishing, 1940), 10-11.
[225] Sir Frederic G. Kenyon, quoted in F.F. Bruce, *The New Testament Documents: Are They Reliable?* (Downers Grove: InterVarsity Press, 1981), 20.

Christians as cold, secular, and undisciplined. Seeing a Christian who is openly captivated by Jesus can be a big eye-opener.

- If the opportunity presents itself and spiritual things are being discussed, don't be afraid to ask, "How can I pray for you today?" or "What would you like God to do for you in your life?" This is a great question to ask and shows your Muslim friend that you care about them.

- If talking about spiritual things, by all means read the Scriptures to your Muslim friend. Show that you hold the Word of God in the greatest regard and that your theology stems from it. Many Muslims believe that we don't read our Scriptures and get most of our theology from Roman and Greek philosophers, as well as from the Roman Catholic Church.

- Books of the Bible that are most helpful for Muslims to read are those from the OT Law, the Psalms, or the Gospels. Even though Muslims believe that these books are not as complete as the Qur'an, they still see them as messages from God and will listen to them. Getting a Muslim to read the Scriptures is something for which we can be quite thankful.

- The ideal Gospel for a Muslim to read is Luke because it presents Jesus as a man who ends up being much more than a man. A less than ideal Gospel is Mark, since it immediately introduces the concept of Jesus as the Son of God, which is a concept that must be explained in detail in order to not offend Muslims.

- If you are asking Muslims about their faith, avoid talking about the concept of Jihad. Muslims are tired of non-Muslims only wanting to talk about the concept of Jihad with them when they discuss Islam. Imagine if the only thing your non-Christian friends ever wanted to discuss with you was the Crusades. That's how Muslims feel.

- Pray for your Muslim friends. Muslims are very responsive to the supernatural. Pray that the Lord would speak to your Muslim friend through the Holy Spirit. There are many modern-day examples of Muslims who came to Christ through dreams and visions.

- If your Muslim friend or family comes over to your house and one of their prayer times approaches, they might want a place to pray. Provide a space in your house for them to do so. Then let them know that in a different space in your house, you and your family will be praying in the name of Jesus.

Conclusion

This chapter has focused on five striking differences between Christianity and Islam—differences that continue to point out the reality that one view is correct and one view is false. Because these differences not only place a clear divide between over fifty percent of the world's population but also represent two entirely different viewpoints of God, Jesus, and the afterlife, it is crucial that everyone genuinely consider the evidence behind Islam and Christianity.

Christianity and Islam can't both be true due primarily to their fundamentally different viewpoints on the death and crucifixion of Jesus Christ and the essence of mankind's salvation. The observation by a Muslim convert to Christianity is crucial:

> All men agree that man, as his name indicates, is a bundle of forgetfulness, disobedience, and transgressions. His life never remains so pure as to be absolutely free from the stain of sin. Sin has become man's second nature. It is a true saying that 'to err is human.' The question is how can one escape accountability and punishment? How is one to be saved? What does Islam have to say about it? And what is the message of Christianity? It is my duty to investigate this important matter honestly and without prejudice.[226]

This investigation includes the remarkable claims of and evidence for the unique miracles that surrounded the life and ministry of Jesus of Nazareth. Jesus offered unique supernatural confirmation of His claims, which was the very quality Muhammad recognized as the mark of a true

---

[226] Sultan Muhammad P. Khan, *Why I Became a Christian,* quoted in Mark Hanna, *The True Path: Seven Muslims Make Their Greatest Discovery* (Colorado Springs, CO: International Doorways Publishers, 1975), n.p.

prophet in biblical times (2:92, 210, 248). No other religious leader, including Muhammad, has been confirmed by miracles similar to the miracles which surrounded the life and ministry of Jesus.

Geisler summarizes the logical argument that points to the truthfulness of Christianity:

1. Only Christianity has unique miracles confirmed by sufficient testimony.
2. What has unique miraculous confirmation of its claims is true (as opposed to contrary views).
3. Therefore, Christianity is true.[227]

---

[227] Norman L. Geisler and Ronald M. Brooks, *When Skeptics Ask: A Handbook on Christian Evidences* (Grand Rapids: Baker Books, 1990), 97.

SUGGESTIONS FOR ADDITIONAL READING

Norman L. Geisler and Abdul Saleeb, *Answering Islam: The Crescent in the Light of the Cross*
This book represents a very thorough presentation of the core differences between Christianity and Islam. It is a more academic work but faithfully presents the issues.

James A. Beverley, *Understanding Islam*
This book is a helpful overview of the Islamic religion. James Beverley does an excellent job of presenting the beliefs of Islam in a compassionate and artful fashion. This book is extremely short and easy to read.

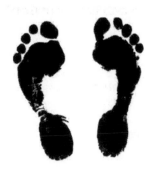

APPENDIX A:
IS JESUS THE ONLY WAY
TO GOD?

At some point most everyone has wrestled with the question, "Is Jesus the only way to God?" It's pretty hard to avoid this question in our culture. After all, we live in a pluralistic culture where people have come to believe that all religious beliefs have equal value and are equally true. Our secular culture is increasingly intolerant of those within the Christian faith who believe we possess the only true path to God. People are more comfortable saying, "All religions are the same," or "All religions lead to God." We should consider the following observations when formulating a response to those who question the exclusive truth claims of Christianity:

1. **The claim that all religions are the same is simply not accurate.** Think for a moment about the two major religions of the world, Christianity and Islam. The Christian and Islamic faiths represent over fifty percent of the world's population. Christians claim that Jesus died on the cross for the sins of mankind. His death is the linchpin of the Christian faith. Muslims claim that the event never happened. In fact, the Islamic religion teaches that there is no need for a savior to die on the cross. These claims represent the core of their religion. Both of these religions can't be right. At least one of them is mistaken.

2. **If all religions eventually lead to God imagine the disappointment when two religions teach two different views of heaven.** Imagine that one religion teaches that heaven is a morally perfect place while another religion teaches that it is a place where one's greatest fantasies can be indulged. By this reasoning, if all religions lead to heaven, some people will hate the very place that they've been looking forward to all of their lives.

3. **If all religions eventually lead to God imagine the shock when two religions teach totally different concepts of God.** Some religions believe God is a perfected man. Others believe He is equivalent to all of creation. Still others believe He is a benevolent and loving God. Others believe God demands obedience to a specific code of behavior. Think of the shock these people will experience when they get to heaven and find out that the God they've been worshipping is not their God after all. Imagine the horror of getting to heaven and discovering that your version of God does not exist. Of course, the bigger problem is resolving how God can be consistent with Himself when so many paths to Him clearly contradict each other. Think about it for a moment. Christianity believes that a person's sins must be removed solely by the sacrifice of Christ on the cross. The Qu'ran teaches that Allah is free to pardon sin at his discretion and there is no need for someone's substitutionary death. The goal of Buddhism, rather than to lead people into a personal relationship with God, is to attain the state of Nirvana. These different paths of salvation contradict the very nature of God.

4. **The belief that all religions lead to God is a religious claim.** If a person insists that the way to heaven is paved only with sincerity, goodness, and belief in God that person is making a religious claim. That person is claiming that this is how one can appease God. How much sincerity and goodness are required? Where is the line drawn? Ultimately, if God is the one who draws the line, shouldn't we seek to know where He has drawn it? Since none of us can fulfill the requirements for acceptance by God, we must entrust our eternal destiny to Jesus. We must believe in Jesus' deity, atoning death, and resurrection.

5. **The exclusive truth claims of Christianity have their origin in Jesus Himself. Jesus claimed and proved to be the only way to God (John 14:6; John 8:24).** Jesus' earliest followers taught the same exact thing as Jesus Himself (Acts 4:12; Rom 10:1-2; 1 Tim 2:5). Jesus' claims were so extraordinary we would expect that He would provide supernatural proof (resurrection from the dead). This proof is unique from all other religions and is consistent with a religion that makes an exclusive truth claim. No other religious

founder claimed to be God in the flesh and claimed that He would be resurrected from the dead as proof of His deity—no one! Such a proof does not depend on one's personal taste or opinion. He either rose from the dead, which confirmed his personal claims, or he didn't, which revealed him to be just another false teacher.

6. **Skeptics often claim that Christians are intolerant of other religions. However, the claim of pluralism is equally intolerant and offensive.** The only difference is that pluralism's intolerance is expressed toward Christians. The pluralist is no different than the Christian who believes the exclusive truth claims of Christianity, except in what the pluralist believes is absolutely true. Pluralists are clearly inconsistent when they expect tolerance of others yet don't demand it of themselves.

7. **The deepest human problem is human moral failure. Christianity proposes a unique solution to this problem—moral forgiveness through the death of Jesus.** Most religions agree with Christianity on some issues, but they all contradict Christianity on the core issues. Our assertion that Christianity is the exclusive truth claim does not mean that we are right about everything or that all other religions are wrong about everything. It just means that only one religion is deeply true as it relates to the core human moral failure.

8. **Holding a view that your religion is exclusively true does not necessarily lead to arrogance and intolerance.** Everyone holds some convictions in life that require denial of other viewpoints. However, we can hold those viewpoints without embracing arrogance and intolerance. Christians should care not only about the pursuit of objective truth but also about our interactions with people of other religious beliefs. Christians can engage in dialogue without exploding in aggression. In fact, 1 Peter 3:15 tell us, "Always be prepared to give an answer to everyone who asks you to give the reason for the hope that you have. But do this with gentleness and respect." In other words, we are supposed to engage in dialogue with a gentle spirit and an understanding of where people are coming from.

9. **Some complain that the exclusive truth claims of Christianity are unfair to anyone who happens to miss or not hear about the message of Jesus. What about those who lived before Jesus? What about those who live where Jesus is unknown? What about those who can't understand the Christian message?** Ultimately our explanation to this question must be based upon the justice of God (opposition to evil) and grace of God (persistent love for people). It is possible that God will ultimately give all people who genuinely seek Him the opportunity to receive salvation. It is also possible that God will bring the gospel within reach of those who seek Him. Although we clearly don't know all of God's ways He will be consistent with His own character. [Note: some additional answers are provided in Appendix B: What About Those Who Have Never Heard the Gospel?]

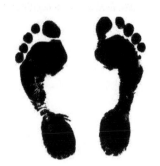

APPENDIX B:
WHAT ABOUT THOSE WHO
HAVE NEVER HEARD THE
GOSPEL?

One of the most foundational claims of Christianity is that salvation only comes through personal faith in the crucifixion of Jesus Christ, who died for the sins of humanity (John 14:6; Acts 4:12; 1 Timothy 2:5). However, if knowledge and belief in Christ are necessary for salvation, how can a person be held responsible if he or she has never heard the gospel? If billions of people throughout the history of humanity never heard about Jesus, how is that fair? How can God judge people who have never been told about Jesus? In response to this question of fairness we should consider the following observations:

1. **God will make sure that those who desire to repent will have the opportunity.** Acts 17:26 states that God "determined the times set for them and the exact places where they should live. God did this so that men would seek him and perhaps reach out for him and find him, though he is not far from each one of us." Furthermore, God is committed to reaching people in unusual ways. This truth is revealed in the story of God instructing Philip to go to a desert road that led from Jerusalem to Gaza. An Ethiopian eunuch was reading in Isaiah but did not know the significance of the passage (Acts 8:26-31). God sent Philip as a direct answer to the eunuch's need for answers as he searched for God.

2. **God will be righteous and fair in all His dealings.** We don't have access to all the facts about the situation of every person who has ever lived. We can't look into the hearts of individual people. However, we do know that God is righteous and fair in all His dealings. When Abraham appealed to God on behalf of Sodom and Gomorrah he acknowledged that God is incapable of mistreating the righteous as He judges the wicked. Genesis 18:25 says, "Will not the Judge of all the earth do right?" This means that God will do what is right according to His infinite standard of justice and morality.

It is impossible for a holy and perfect God to do anything less than what is absolutely perfect. God will dispense both justice and righteousness in a perfect fashion.

3. **Middle knowledge is God's knowledge of what His free creatures would do under any circumstance. This knowledge includes what an individual might have done if he or she had access to the news of the gospel.** This means that if God knew that a person would of his or her own free will respond to the news of the gospel, He would find a way to extend the reach of the gospel to that location.

4. **God doesn't judge people on the basis of information they don't possess. He judges them on the information that is already in their possession.** We don't believe that people are judged by information they don't have (death and resurrection of Jesus)—that's not fair. God judges them because they reject the information He has already given them. Scripture teaches that every person knows at least three things about God apart from any special revelation from Him. In other words, everyone has access to this knowledge—everyone! First, humanity is aware that God is powerful by virtue of creation (Romans 1:18-20). Second, humanity is aware that God is moral by virtue of conscience (Romans 2:14). Third, humanity is aware that God is good by virtue of providence (Acts 14:16-17). Instead of responding positively to these clear truths, Romans 1 tells us that people intentionally hold down the truth much like a person holds down a spring so that it doesn't pop up. A person's lack of responsiveness to general revelation precludes a person from receiving further revelation. Gifted Christian theologian John Feinberg expresses this concept with the following observation, "Those who don't get that information don't fail to get it because it was impossible to attain it; rather they fail to get it because they reject even the truth they have, and don't seek further truth about God."[228]

---

[228] John S. Feinberg, *The Many Faces of Evil: Theological Systems and the Problems of Evil* (Wheaton: Crossway Books, 2004), 437.

APPENDIX C:
IS ETERNAL
PUNISHMENT (HELL) FAIR?

Hell is one of the most clearly taught doctrines within the pages of Scripture. However, it is also one of the doctrines that most disturbs both Christians and non-Christians. The concept of eternally punishing a person for the sins of one lifetime seems extreme. Visions of torture, fire, punishment, and excruciating pain don't seem to be consistent with the God of love. We must attempt to answer the many troubling issues that surround the concept of hell. We should consider the following observations in response to this question of fairness:

1. **Christians should be careful about making eternal judgments about the salvation of other people.** Christians should never be flippant about the eternal destiny of people. Although we can testify to the Christian message regarding Christ, we aren't in a position to evaluate the internal soul of an individual. Many issues in the spiritual life are messy. We simply can't figure it all out. We must trust that God will do right and will be eternally fair. Genesis 18:25 says, "Shall not the Judge of everything do right?"

2. **God will leave no stone unturned when reaching out to save everyone so that they can spend eternity with Him. His eternal love will extend to every corner of the earth and will reach out to embrace everyone.** Christian thinker and philosopher William Lane Craig makes this observation, "The Bible makes it very clear that God desires every person to be saved, and by His Spirit He seeks to draw every person to Himself. The only obstacle to universal salvation is therefore human free will."[229]

---

[229] William Lane Craig and Ray Bradley, "The Craig-Bradley Debate: Can a Loving God Send People to Hell?," *LeadershipU,* accessed March 25, 2015, http://www.leaderu.com/offices/billcraig/docs/craig-bradley0.html.

3. **Heaven is a place where people must choose to be in the presence of God. God has granted people the dignity of free will. It is logically impossible for God to make someone freely do something against their will.** In creating the world, God chose not to interfere with mankind's free choice. Ultimately, God will make the same decision for eternity. Only those who wish to be with Him in heaven will indeed be there. Craig makes this observation, "It's logically impossible to make someone freely do something. God's being all-powerful doesn't mean that He can do the logically impossible. Thus, even though He is all-powerful, God cannot make everyone freely be saved. Given human freedom and human stubbornness, some people may go to hell despite God's desire and efforts to save them."[230]

4. **Heaven is a destination where people must choose to be a certain kind of person. If God has given people free will there's no guarantee that everybody's going to choose to cooperate with Him.** Richard Swinburne, a great Christian intellectual and a philosopher at Oxford University in England, put it this way: "Heaven is the type of place where people with wrong beliefs and a bad will would not fit, and heaven must be freely and not coercively chosen. . . . People with a bad will or people with a good will, but with false beliefs about what God, heaven, and the good really are, will not be suited for life in heaven. Can God force the bad to become good? NO . . . not if he respects our freedom. God can't make people's character for them." [231]

5. **Hell is a fitting punishment for the eternally unrepentant. The Bible teaches that the impenitence of the wicked will continue forever (Rev 16:9).** One of the most common descriptions of hell includes the expression "weeping and gnashing of teeth." This expression is almost always associated with anger—not with anguish. Christian philosopher Dallas Willard observes that the idea

[230] William Lane Craig and Ray Bradley, "The Craig-Bradley Debate," accessed March 25, 2015.
[231] Richard Swinburne, quoted in Gary Habermas and J.P. Moreland, *Beyond Death: Exploring the Evidence for Immortality* (Eugene: Wipf & Stock Publishers, 1998), 294.

seems to be that the eternally unrepentant "have become the kind of people so locked in their own self-worship and denial of God that they cannot want God."[232]

6. **Some people suggest that instead of hell God should give people a second chance once this life is over. In reality, God has designed this life to be a series of second, third, fourth, and one hundredth chances to say, "God I want you to rule in my life."** God wants to give people extra chances, but He has to do it in a way that will honor our freedom of choice. If God were to bring us into His presence or give us a glimpse of death and hell, His presence would be so powerful and so commanding that people would be coerced into believing. G.K. Chesterton put it this way, "Hell is God's great compliment to the reality of human freedom and the dignity of human choice." [233]

7. **Hell is not simply a place for good folks who make honest mistakes or who fall short by the smallest degrees.** When we offend God—who is an infinite, holy being—the debt that is incurred becomes eternal. How do you pay an infinite debt? The world religions answer that a person must do good, but think of how absurd this would be in a court of law. Imagine attempting to avoid any penalties for running a red light by promising to only go through green lights in the future. This would never pay the debt incurred the one time you were caught breaking the law by going through a red light, would it? Since we have broken the law, God justly judges us. A substitute is needed since we cannot pay an infinite debt. Only an infinite person, who is both God and man, can pay an infinite debt.

---

[232] Dallas Willard, *Renovation of the Heart: Putting On the Character of Christ* (Colorado Springs: NavPress, 2012), 57.
[233] G.K. Chesterton, quoted in Lee Strobel, *The Case for Faith: A Journalist Investigates the Toughest Objections to Christianity* (Grand Rapids: Zondervan, 1998),169.

8. **God cannot bring about a good and just world where everyone will freely choose to follow Him. God cannot also bring about a just world where no one goes to hell without sending the wrong message to free beings.** Part of the function of the eternal message of hell is to remind all of heaven and its inhabitants that sin is utterly wicked and that obedience to God is a forever virtue. C.S. Lewis stated it this way, "In the long run the answer to all those who object to the doctrine of hell, is itself a question: 'What are you asking God to do?' To wipe out their past sins and, at all costs, to give them a fresh start, smoothing every difficulty and offering every miraculous help? But he has done so, on Calvary. To forgive them? They will not be forgiven. To leave them alone? Alas, I am afraid this is what he does."[234]

9. **Hell is not a place of torture; hell is separation or banishment from God.** Many Christians and non-Christians think of hell as a place of divine torture where God causes people horrific physical pain in a literal lake of fire. Terms like the "lake of fire," "brimstone," and the "worm that never dies" are viewed as examples of eternal torture. Obviously, this notion of hell as a literal torture chamber is not only hard for Christians to understand and process; it is also extremely difficult to explain to our unbelieving friends. Here are a handful of reasons why I believe that some of the images used to describe hell might be better explained as figurative expressions:

- **Some descriptions of hell can't be taken literally because they are logically inconsistent**. In other words, literal descriptions would be mutually exclusive—they can't both be true at the same time. For example, Jude calls hell the "blackest darkness" (Jude 13) yet flames in a lake of fire would bring light.
- **Eternal fire was intended for spirit beings, not physical beings**. The Gospel According to Matthew clearly teaches that the lake of fire was created for spirit beings like the devil and his angels. However, physical fire impacts physical bodies with physical nerve endings, and not spirit beings.

---

[234] C.S. Lewis, *The Problem of Pain* (New York: Macmillian Publishing Co., 1940), 116.

- **Descriptions of hell and heaven are symbolic pictures designed for a first century audience.** What better way to describe the judgment of the future life than to compare it to the smoldering valley of Gehenna? The valley of Gehenna is the place where Ammonites used to burn children in sacrifice to their god, Molech. Ultimately, people began to burn garbage and refuse using sulfur, which is the flammable substance we now use in matches and gunpowder. In addition, Scripture describes hell as a place where "their worm does not die, and the fire is not quenched" (Mark 9:48). In Jesus' day thousands of animals were sacrificed and the remaining blood and fat was gathered in a pool of waste. Worms fed constantly on the waste. It was a disgusting place, and likening hell to this place was designed to remind people of the awfulness of hell.
- **Words are frequently used symbolically as expressions of hyperbole.** Revelation 19:15 describes Jesus with these words, "Coming out of his mouth is a sharp sword with which to strike down the nations." Jesus will not have a literal sword coming out of his mouth—it is symbolic of him bringing judgment at his Second Coming.
- **Fire is often used in a non-literal sense within Scripture.** In the New Testament, John says of the exalted Christ, "his eyes were like blazing fire" (Rev.1:14). Fire is also used figuratively for discord (Luke 12:49), judgment (I Cor. 3:15), sexual desire (1 Cor. 7:9), and unruly words (James 3:5-6).

I don't doubt the presence of hell. It is the worst possible situation where people experience utter heartbreak, loneliness, and the loss of everything good. However, hell is not a torture chamber. Not every description of hell must be taken literally—some descriptions must be taken figuratively. If we don't we are in danger of creating a picture of hell that only serves to alienate the skeptic from considering the claims of Christ because they view God as barbaric and inhumane. We should avoid trying to explain the physical chemistry of hell and focus on the spiritual chasm between God and man and how the gospel is the only solution to this problem.

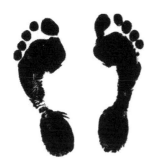

APPENDIX D:
HOW CAN ORIGINAL
SIN BE FAIR?

Many people complain about the unfairness of "original sin." After all, how can a person be judged and/or held responsible for the sin of Adam—a sin that he or she personally never committed? For many people in the 21st century, the concept of "original sin" conjures up images of the Dark Ages and is an assault on reason and fairness. Here's why it's important for Christians to believe in the doctrine of original sin:

1. **The doctrine of original sin is the best explanation for the presence of human evil.** Without original sin, what could possibly explain the pervasive reality of evil in every different culture and era? G.K. Chesterton once said, "Certain new theologians dispute original sin, which is the only part of Christian theology which can really be proved." [235] Even non-Christian Darwinist Michael Ruse makes the following observation, "I think Christianity is spot on about original sin—how could one think otherwise, when the world's most civilized and advanced people (the people of Beethoven, Goethe, Kant) embraced that slime-ball Hitler and participated in the Holocaust? I think Saint Paul and the great Christian philosophers had real insights into sin and freedom and responsibility, and I want to build on this rather than turn from it." [236]

2. **The transmission of a fallen sin nature is consistent with how we inherit other aspects of our human nature.** For example, people clearly inherit genetic dispositions, personality traits, and

---

[235] G. K. Chesterton, quoted in Paul Copan, *Loving Wisdom: Christian Philosophy of Religion* (Danvers: Chalice Press, 2007), 142.
[236] G. K. Chesterton, quoted in Paul Copan, *Loving Wisdom: Christian Philosophy of Religion*, 142.

physical characteristics. Doesn't it make sense that people inherit a fallen sinful nature if it appears that all of humanity exhibits the same basic moral failure?

3. **The doctrine of original sin serves as the basis for important Christian doctrines.** For example, why is Jesus described as the last Adam if there was no first Adam who was an actual man who sinned? Why does Scripture portray all of humanity as sinful and deserving of punishment? Remember, if humanity is universally flawed due to the presence of sin it justifies God's judgment, demonstrates God's patience, and magnifies the significance of Christ's sacrifice.

4. **Finally, the doctrine of original sin (that we inherited from the original Adam) is clearly taught throughout the Bible.** Romans 5:12 says, "Therefore, just as sin came into the world through one man, and death through sin, and so death spread to all men because all sinned." Romans 5:18 states, "One trespass led to condemnation for all men." Even David writes in Psalm 51:5, "Behold, I was brought forth in iniquity, and in sin did my mother conceive me".

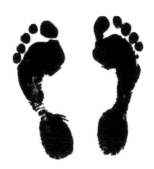

In the Old Testament the Lord commanded the nation of Israel to exterminate the entire Canaanite civilization including the children. Many people question the morality of God to judge children who were morally innocent. In addition, many people wonder how God's actions in the Old Testament differ from modern-day genocide. We should consider the following observations in response to this question of fairness:

1. **God's actions were morally permissible because it was not genocide. God's actions were the moral equivalent of capital punishment for someone who has committed a heinous crime.** This action was morally permissible because God, as the ultimate moral lawgiver, saw actions that were morally indefensible, morally unredeemable, and worthy of death. The Canaanite civilization was unlike anything we have ever witnessed. Archaeological evidence shows that the Canaanites fully embraced incest as part of everyday life. However, the abomination didn't stop there. The people not only participated in molestation and rape, they offered children to their god, Molech. Think about the horror of people who witnessed these abominations. What was it like to live within a culture of rampant sexual molestation and child sacrifice? What was it like to witness children, siblings, and neighbors being burned to death? God was compelled to bring this civilization to an end—it was simply too heinous and unable to be redeemed.

2. **Modern society clearly sees a difference between genocide (which is immoral) and capital punishment (which is justified).** For example, over sixty civilized nations of the world justify the total eradication of ISIS because of their morally indefensible actions. This coalition of nations is not guilty of genocide. These nations are condemning the totally indefensible and immoral actions of a group

of people. This is the moral equivalent of what happened in the Old Testament.

3. **This was the only way for God to totally and absolutely remove the cancerous Canaanite civilization.** The Canaanite emphases on child sacrifice, bestiality, and other heinous activities had totally saturated their culture. God deemed that their culture had reached a point of immorality at which the people's moral conscience had become seared and beyond repair. At this point, God could no longer tolerate the negative impact of this morally repugnant culture.

4. **God was able to see all of the possible free acts of people. He was also able to see the future acts of those Canaanite children.** Christians believe that God has completely infallible knowledge. The concept of middle knowledge affirms that God knows all of the potential worlds that could or might exist and consequently all of the potential actions that free individuals would embrace. By virtue of God's middle knowledge, He would have foreseen the possible worlds in which future generations of Canaanites would have continued to perpetrate odious acts upon the world.

5. **A skeptic in the mid-20th century would find himself or herself endorsing a decision very similar to God's decision in regard to the Canaanites.** For example, an overwhelming majority of people today would not object to God taking Hitler's life in 1889 when he was born because we have knowledge of how his future turned out. However, those living in 1889 would not have possessed the same knowledge we have today and would likely object to God taking the life of an innocent child. This is essentially the position that God takes because, due to middle knowledge, He knows every possible action that free individuals might make in every potential world.

6. **It is important to remember that an all-knowing God would have clearly understood the practical implications of allowing the Canaanite children to live.** If the Canaanite children had grown up and discovered what happened to their parents they most

likely would have developed a deep-seated desire to take revenge upon the Israelites. In addition, we also know that everywhere the Canaanites traveled, their vile religion (including child sacrifices) polluted other nations. God knew that if another generation was allowed to live, they would continue to embrace their immoral practices.

7. **I think it is important to remember that God instituted a theocracy during the Old Testament period of time.** It was God's desire to exhibit His standard of morality and justice within one specific nation. It was clear throughout Israel's history that they were susceptible to embracing the false religions and immorality of surrounding nations. In order to protect His divine purpose for the nation of Israel it was imperative that He stop this particularly odious culture from continuing to negatively influence His people.

APPENDIX F:
WHY DOESN'T GOD PREVENT CHILDREN FROM SUFFERING, DISEASE, OR DEATH?

Of all the expressions of suffering and evil it seems that both Christians and unbelievers struggle with the reality that children suffer and die from disease or illness. Our hearts break when we see children devastated by disease at such an early age. For many people, it's too much for us to process emotionally. It's very important that we carefully evaluate whether or not children should be insulated from suffering:

1. **Although any question regarding children tends to be more emotional and seemingly unanswerable, we answer this question in the same way that we would answer the question, "Why does God allow suffering and sickness in the lives of people?"** In a fallen world where human beings have free will, God cannot intervene in every single instance of disease and/or suffering. In order to do so, God would have to stop the biological processes in human beings. God would have to change the genetic makeup or the genetic flaw that is latent within each person in humanity. God would have to supernaturally reach in and stop the spread of disease, whether that would require Him to stop people drinking water, touching other people, and engaging in other forms of human contact. In his book entitled *The Many Faces of Evil*, Dr. John Feinberg makes this observation, "Because of the fall there are negative consequences for the natural order. . . . In a fallen world people die as God said they would, and if they are going to die, they must die of something. One of the causes of death is disease. Some of these diseases may be contracted early in life and others may arise only later. Some diseases may kill slowly

while others kill quickly. Some diseases are genetically based, while others result from germs in our world." [237]

2. **When people ask why God doesn't prevent children from suffering or having diseases, ultimately a person has to ask, "To what age should children be indestructible?"** Would God be obligated to totally insulate and protect children from suffering or disease until they are one year old? Six years old? Fifteen or twenty-one years old? Furthermore, what would it be like to live with or parent children who are indestructible? Theoretically, children could do anything they wanted and be insulated from the effects of their actions. Children could jump in front of moving trains or drink poison to impress their friends or defy their parents. Parents would no longer need to exercise good parental control because it would be unnecessary. Remember, natural laws have to work with regularity for actions to mean anything at all.

3. **Ultimately, every single person is going to face death. Every single person will die as a result of murder, accident, disease, or old age. There are no exceptions.** Although we think that God should deal with the death of children in a fundamentally different manner, there really is no philosophical distinction between how God should handle adults and how He handles children. Ultimately, God will refuse to step in and prevent the physical death of people. We want to control the timing of this and/or choose the exact method of our death, but this would require God to regularly suspend the laws of nature, which would render life on earth absurd. Although God refuses to stop the process of death in this life, He has provided a way for all of humanity to live forever with Him in heaven.

---

[237] John S. Feinberg, *The Many Faces of Evil: Theological Systems and the Problems of Evil* (Wheaton: Crossway Books, 2004), 195.

APPENDIX G:
HOW DOES HEAVEN
CHANGE OUR PERSPECTIVE
ON SUFFERING?

The Christian view of suffering is unique. We believe that God is preparing an eternal home in heaven for believers. Although we may face immense suffering in our seventy or more years on earth, God has promised that He will allow us to live forever with Him in heaven. This perspective is designed by God to be a lens through which we evaluate everything. Here are some of the ways that eternity should impact our perspective as we face suffering:

1. **God asks us to compare our suffering in this life with the incomparable bliss we will experience in the presence of a perfect and loving God.** This may be one of the implications of James 1:12 which says, "Blessed is the man who perseveres under trial, because when he has stood the test, he will receive the crown of life that God has promised to those who love him." Eternity dwarfs our suffering. C.S. Lewis, who was no stranger to pain, put it this way, "Scripture and tradition habitually put the joys of heaven into the scale against the sufferings of earth, and no solution of the problem of pain that does not do so can be called a Christian one."[238]

2. **God rewards our actions and our virtue in this life.** At the final judgment of Jesus Christ (2 Corinthians 5:10) we will be rewarded for our lives here as Christians. The positive impact of our lives as ambassadors for Christ will be clearly seen as gold, silver, and precious stones, or wood, hay, and stubble.

---

[238] C.S. Lewis, *The Problem of Pain* (New York: Macmillan Publishing Co., 1976), 144.

3. **God has promised to praise our faith when Jesus Christ returns.** 1 Peter 1:6-7 says, "Faith—of greater worth than gold, which perished even though refined by fire—may be proved genuine and may result in praise, glory and honor when Jesus is revealed." Clearly there is an eternal payoff for hanging onto our faith during trials.

4. **God will grant us a place of honor for times when we have suffered for Him.** Philippians 1:29 says, "For it has been granted to you on behalf of Christ not only to believe on him, but also to suffer for him." We've been given the blessing of suffering for His sake. Although suffering is never easy it has the potential to be a tremendous honor in God's heavenly kingdom.

5. **Our personal love of and closeness to Christ will be experienced in heaven at a depth and richness which we have no scale to measure.** Our joy in Him, our love for Him, our feeling for Him, our faith in Him, and our worship of Him will transcend anything that we might have experienced in this life. The very thought of our future reality with Christ will cultivate strength through suffering. He is worth it all. So many times of close praise and worship to the Lord Jesus will be magnified beyond all present understanding.

ABOUT THE AUTHOR
DR. BRENT STRAWSBURG
PRESIDENT OF BRENT STRAWSBURG APOLOGETICS

INTRODUCTION

Dr. Strawsburg has served in ministry for over thirty years, pastoring two different churches. During this time he utilized apologetics in every aspect of ministry—on college campuses, when equipping others, during outreach efforts, and when preaching on apologetic topics from the pulpit. Dr. Brent has studied with some of the sharpest minds in the United States and can teach apologetics in a way that is accessible to everyone in the church. Dr. Brent is a highly sought after speaker for churches and conferences. He has a unique ability to make every apologetic topic accessible and practical for every single person in attendance. He received a Master of Divinity from Talbot School of Theology, a Master of Arts in Christian Apologetics from Biola University, and a Doctor of Ministry from Dallas Theological Seminary.

NON-PROFIT STATUS

Dr. Brent Strawsburg is Founder and President of Brent Strawsburg Apologetics (BSA), which specializes in making apologetics relevant for the church. BSA is a registered 501(c)(3) non-profit whose mission is "Using Christian Apologetics to Shape Culture, Strengthen Faith & Empower Witness."

SPEAKING TOPICS

The following are some of the topics that Dr. Strawsburg is able to address:

- HOW TO DISARM YOUR DOUBTS
- HOW TO TALK TO SKEPTICS
- WHY DOES GOD ALLOW EVIL & SUFFERING?
- WHERE IS GOD WHEN IT HURTS?
- HOW CAN FAITH SURVIVE A RELATIVISTIC CULTURE?
- IS BELIEF IN GOD REASONABLE?

- CAN YOU TRUST THE BIBLE?
- THE RESURRECTION: MYTH OR MIRACLE?
- IS ETERNAL PUNISHMENT (HELL) FAIR?
- IS JESUS THE ONLY WAY TO GOD?
- FACING END OF LIFE ISSUES WITH A LOVED ONE
- IS MORMONISM CHRISTIAN?
- IS ISLAM OR CHRISTIANITY TRUE?
- HOMOSEXUALITY & SAME-SEX MARRIAGE

AVAILABLE RESOURCES

If Dr. Brent Strawsburg comes to your church he will provide the following resources:

- Publicity for all messages/seminars
- Message notes or syllabus
- PowerPoint® presentations
- Insight/Advice on strategies for incorporating apologetics within the church
- Apologetic Resources

All of Dr. Brent's materials provide the highest quality graphics and technology to engage the listener throughout the presentation. Brent has assembled a team of gifted professionals to put together a syllabus & PowerPoint® presentation that accompanies every seminar/message. His website www.brentstrawsburg.com contains examples (PDF, PPT, MP3 Sound, and MP4 Video) of practical and engaging seminars and messages.

MINISTRY OPTIONS

Dr. Brent has been quite successful in offering a range of ministry options that effectively help churches to strengthen faith and empower witness. Here are some of the options:

Defending the Faith Conference: This format effectively rallies the entire church in order to focus on select apologetic topics. Dr. Brent offers two or three seminars over the weekend of the conference, culminating in a Sunday morning message. This effectively touches everyone within the church. The seminars provide in depth and practical insight for those interested while also providing access to everyone on Sunday morning.

Weekend Seminars: This format features two or three seminars that address specific topics of interest to a church. These seminars can be offered on Friday night/Saturday morning, Saturday as a half-day event, or Saturday night.

Mid-week Seminars: This format uses a couple of evenings featuring one or two seminars per evening along with Q & A sessions.

Sunday Morning Messages: Churches sometimes place all the emphasis on addressing apologetic topics on Sunday morning. They commit to a single Sunday, back-to-back Sundays, or a regular schedule during which Dr. Brent returns to address key topics necessary to defend the Christian faith.

Church Conferences: Groups like Mission ConneXion (Pacific Northwest) utilize BSA in addressing apologetic topics in their apologetic track seminars during their two-day conference. This approach can work for denominational, mission, or equipping/evangelism conferences.

COST

Dr. Strawsburg will come to your church for a very reasonable cost (transportation, housing, and honorarium). Upon request he can supply your church with a document detailing his speaking fees.

CONTACT

Dr. Strawsburg can be contacted in the following ways:

Brent Strawsburg Apologetics
11462 Martha Ann Drive
Rossmoor, CA 90720
714-393-1823
www.brentstrawsburg.com
Brent.strawsburg@gmail.com

Made in the USA
San Bernardino, CA
09 September 2015